THE
ULTIMATE AUDITION BOOK
VOLUME IV

222 Comedy Monologues
2 Minutes and Under

Smith and Kraus Monologue Books

The Ultimate Audition Book V.1: 222 Monologues, 2 Minutes & Under
The Ultimate Audition Book V.2: 222 Monologues, 2 Minutes & Under from Literature
The Ultimate Audition Book V.3: 222 Movie Monologues, 2 Minutes & Under
Monologues From Classic Plays 468 B.C. to 1960 A.D.
Monologues From Contemporary Literature Vol. I
Kiss and Tell RESTORATION Comedy of Manners: Scenes, Monologues and Historical Context
100 Great Monologues From The RENAISSANCE **Theatre**
100 Great Monologues From The NEO-CLASSICAL **Theatre**
100 Great Monologues From The 19TH CENTURY ROMANTIC & REALISTIC **Theatres**
A Brave and Violent Theatre Monologues, Scenes and Historical Context for 20TH
    CENTURY IRISH DRAMA
100 Women's Stage Monologues From The 1980's
100 Men's Stage Monologues From The 1980's
The Great Monologues From The EST Marathon
The Great Monologues From The Humana Festival
The Great Monologues From The Mark Taper Forum
The Great Monologues From The Women's Project
Ice Babies in Oz: Character Monologues For Actors
Street Talk: Character Monologues For Actors
2 Minutes & Under: Character Monologues For Actors
Uptown: Character Monologues For Actors
The Best Women's Stage Monologues of 2004
The Best Women's Stage Monologues of 2003
The Best Women's Stage Monologues of 2002
The Best Women's Stage Monologues of 2001
The Best Women's Stage Monologues of 2000
The Best Women's Stage Monologues of 1999
The Best Women's Stage Monologues of 1998
The Best Women's Stage Monologues of 1997
The Best Women's Stage Monologues of 1996
The Best Women's Stage Monologues of 1995
The Best Women's Stage Monologues of 1994
The Best Women's Stage Monologues of 1993
The Best Men's Stage Monologues of 2004
The Best Men's Stage Monologues of 2003
The Best Men's Stage Monologues of 2002
The Best Men's Stage Monologues of 2001
The Best Men's Stage Monologues of 2000
The Best Men's Stage Monologues of 1999
The Best Men's Stage Monologues of 1998
The Best Men's Stage Monologues of 1997
The Best Men's Stage Monologues of 1996
The Best Men's Stage Monologues of 1995
The Best Men's Stage Monologues of 1994
The Best Men's Stage Monologues of 1993

If you require prepublication information about upcoming Smith and Kraus books, you may receive our annual catalogue, free of charge, by sending your name and address to Smith and Kraus Catalogue, PO Box 127, Lyme, NH 03768. Or call us toll-free at (888) 282-2881, fax (603) 643-1831 or find us on the web www.smithandkraus.com

THE
ULTIMATE AUDITION BOOK VOLUME IV

222
Comedy
Monologues
2 Minutes & Under

EDITED BY IRENE ZIEGLER ASTON
AND JOHN CAPECCI

MONOLOGUE AUDITION SERIES

A Smith and Kraus Book

A Smith and Kraus Book
Published by Smith and Kraus, Inc.
177 Lyme Road, Hanover, NH 03755
www.smithandkraus.com

First Edition: July 2005
10 9 8 7 6 5 4 3 2 1

Manufactured in the United States of America
Cover and Text Design by Julia Gignoux, Freedom Hill Design

The Library of Congress Cataloging-In-Publication Data
The ultimate audition book: two hundred and twenty-two comedy monologues, two minutes and under / edited by Irene Ziegler Aston and John Capecci, Laurie Walker.
— 1st ed.
p. cm. — (Monologue audition series)
Includes bibliographical references.
ISBN-10 1-57525-420-4 vol.4 ISBN-13: 978-1-57525-420-3
1. Monologues. 2. Acting — Auditions. 3. Drama. I. Beard, Jocelyn. II. Series.
PN2080.U48 1997
808.82'45 — dc21 97-10471
CIP

Contents

FEMALE SERIOCOMIC MONOLOGUES

MALE COMIC MONOLOGUES

MALE SERIOCOMIC MONOLOGUES

FEMALE/MALE MONOLOGUES

INDICES

INTRODUCTION

If you've ever searched for a good comic monologue — whether for a professional audition, a class, or a competition — you know how frustrating the hunt can be. To rephrase the old theater adage (attributed to actor Edmund Kean): Dying is easy; finding comic monologues is hard.

You can stop rifling through those other monologue collections, looking for the rare selection that doesn't begin with a phrase like "I have two weeks to live," "There's something you should know," or "You ungrateful bastard." We've combed over some of the world's best comic writing — and sacrificed a good year of our lives — to bring you *222 Comic and Seriocomic Monologues: Two Minutes and Under*. It's all funny stuff here: 222 classic and contemporary works; roles for men and women ages seven to 100; entertaining voices from writers as varied as Christopher Durang and Langston Hughes, Dorothy Parker and Steve Martin, Margaret Cho and Molière.

In our continuing effort to offer you new sources of monologues, we've drawn from plays, novels, short stories, poems, television scripts, comedy sketches, essays, comic strips, lyrics, and memoirs. You'll find shades of comedy from light to dark: situational humor, word play, absurdity, surrealism. These monologues are alternately romantic, silly, militant, downright zany — first-rate character work by both new and established comic writers.

What Is a Comic Monologue?

In The Ultimate Audition Series, we define a *monologue* simply as "a short, self-contained work or excerpt that features a central speaker and contains some change in thought, emotion, or action." Comic monologues are the ones that fit that description and also are funny.

You may not feel that all the monologues here are funny; that's fine. Humor is personal. And that's about as far into The Examination of Comedy as we'll go, bypassing the psycho-sociopolitical analysis. Sometimes a banana peel is just a banana peel.

But we will say this: Not every bit of humorous writing makes a good performance monologue. In a good comic monologue, the words arise from, or hint at the character who is speaking. Without some sense of the character's world (someone saying something funny, somewhere), the performer isn't given much to sink his or her oversized wax teeth into. So, the selections we've included in this collection all contain a good dose of character and attitude, either explicitly (as in a play) or implicitly (as in many poems or essays). In either case, it's the performer's challenge to fill in the gaps and put flesh on the funny bones. We probably don't need to mention this, but we'll mention it anyway: In order to fully understand and ultimately embody the characters in this book, you are strongly advised to read the play, novel, poem, etc. the monologue comes from. These characters exist beyond these page, and the greater context must be fully explored in order to answer these all important questions: who, what, when where, why?

So, What's a Seriocomic Monologue?

In this collection we make a distinction between "comic" and "seriocomic" monologues. Put simply: Comic monologues "go for the gut"; seriocomic monologues aim a little higher and to the right.

We identify seriocomic monologues — those that are partly serious, partly comic — primarily through their use of humor. A comic monologue is, first and foremost, intentionally funny. But a seriocomic monologue uses humor to express, or sometimes mask, a more serious intent. The seriocomic monologue shows characters laughing through their tears ("Storage"), employing humor to address important issues ("America: It's Gotta be the Cheese"), or, like a Cyrano de Bergerac, metaphorically slicing enemies with saber wit (*Lysistrata*).

The seriocomic monologue offers the performer the opportunity to strike that delicate balance between comedy and drama. And like most good monologues, seriocomics have, at some point, a "turn" in thought, emotion, or action. Often that turn is found in the shift from the comedic to the dramatic — the monologue's equivalent of "but, seriously, folks..."

What You Won't Find Here

Traditional Stand-Up Routines. Traditional stand-up is usually based in observational humor ("Hey, what's up with the whole "metric system thing?" Who invented THAT?"). Observational humor relies upon a comic's distance from the rest of the world, and while this form of comedy may provide hilarious insight into humanity, when it is set down on the page, observational humor doesn't offer much character or action for the performer to embody. The speakers of good comic monologues are not distanced. They are funny-in-the-world.

Unproduced writing. While many of the authors represented here appear in print for the first time, their works have been produced at least once.

Bathroom Humor. Flatulence and clumsy sex acts just don't crack us up like they used to.

A Lot of Original Monologues. We think that writing a monologue expressly for an audition is cheating, kind of. But not entirely, because we did include a few.

How to Use This Book

At the back of this volume, you'll find all 222 monologues neatly arranged and cleverly indexed according to gender, age, comic/seriocomic, classic/contemporary, and voice, to help identify those most suited to your comic needs.

Age is noted exactly only when specified by the author. More often, we've indicated an age range (20s, 20s-30s). In some instances, we've used a plus sign to show the character could be older than indicated, as in 40+.

Classic/Contemporary refers to when the monologue was written, not necessarily when the character is speaking. "Classic" texts are those that were written prior to the early 1920s.

Voice refers to indications of class, geography, ethnicity, nationality, sexual identity, or physicality that may help performers gain entry into an individual character, or closely "match" themselves to a monologue. The language of any text will reveal a certain level of education, class, or knowledge. Sometimes, however, a monologue arises out of specific cultural experience, demonstrated either through content or language. Those are the selections you'll find listed in the "Voice" index.

Whenever possible, we've attempted to excerpt monologues with a minimum of editing. Where editing was necessary, omissions are indicated by parenthetical ellipses (. . .). All other ellipses were part of the original text.

Many of the contexts for the monologues are delightfully obvious. In those cases, we offer no "set up." However we do offer occasional pithy remarks to help performers situate the monologues, give useful background or textual information, or simply say what we thought was so damn funny.

Why Is It Difficult To Find a Good, Brief, Comic Monologue?

Partly because comic performance is more often based in the act; Dramatic performance is more often based in the telling. In other words: if you take away a character's funny walk, stage business, double-takes, pratfalls, and props, you have precious few words left. So, it's tough to find a good comic character speech that sustains for a full two minutes. But we suspect it all boils down to a kean observation: Comedy is hard.

Comic Monologues

Absence of Gray Matter

Josh Weckesser

Play
Comic
F
Teen
Contemporary

Every high school has a Kim Kutledge. Her attitude is, "Attention must be paid!" But for heaven's sake, Kim, just sit down.

My name is Kim Kutledge and I am broken. I'm not really broken in the way that a tree becomes broken in a tropical storm or the way an egg becomes broken when it is dropped to the kitchen floor before it can be put in the omelet. I am broken like a bone, painfully and somewhat grotesque to look at, but under the right conditions and proper care I will heal. *(Beat.)* What I mean to say is that I am a poet. Really, I am. Listen to this. It's a love poem.

(Clears throat.)
Excuse me, but if you would
Give me the chance, I think I could
Do what I need to make you feel good

(Long pause.) What? No applause? Now you see what I'm talking about, broken. I wasn't even blessed with being tortured. Poe and Dante were tortured, I am simply ineffectual and unloved. I know what you're thinking, "Surely you jest, who would not love you?" The answer is the source of my pain and the reason I cannot heal. I do not love me. (…) On the plus side nothing is ever my fault, I can always point the finger at someone else. On the downside I talk to myself a lot. Like now for example. None of you are real. I bet you didn't know that, and I kinda hate to break it to you because I'm sure you think you're real, but I just made every one of you up. (…) But you wanna know the worst part? Would Keanu Reeves please stand up? *(Pause.)* See? He's not here! He's never here! I'm so broken that I can't even control my own hallucinations even after I've accepted that fact that they're hallucinations. (…) *(Beat.)*

Maybe I should go see a psychiatrist about this. I'm pretty sure it's not normal. (…) I'm sure he'd ask me, "Do you occasionally feel like you're onstage?" and I'd say no but he'd see through it because he'd be a good psychiatrist, and I'd never go see a bad one. So I'd admit to sometimes feeling like I'm onstage and he'd ask me if I'd like to see Keanu Reeves appear and I'd deny that too, but he'd see through it again. (…) Then I'd ask him how he knew and he'd tell me that it's a pretty common thing, he used to go through something similar. It's hero worship gone horribly awry, something about not having the confidence to want to see some- one actually interesting. All I'd have to do to avoid these things was to believe in myself, have some confidence. *(Epiphany.)* Yes, I think that's it! Of course that's it. I can do that. I can love myself, I can. And I will. *(Pause.)* Right?

All Mistaken, or The Mad Couple

James Howard

Play
Comic
F
18
Classic

Mirida, an eighteenth-century tease, enjoys toying with her suitors.

I'll lay my head, ne'er a girl in Christendom
Of my age can say what I can: I'm now
But five years in th' teens, and I have fool'd
Five several men. My humor
Is to love no man, but to have as many
Love me as they please, come cut or long tail.
'Tis a rare diversion, to see what several
Ways my flock of lovers have in being
Ridiculous. Some of them sigh so damnably
That 'tis as troublesome as a windy day.
There's two of them that make their love together,
By languishing eye-casts; one of them has
One eye bigger than the other, and looks like a tumbler;
And that eye's like a musket
Bullet, and I expect every minute when he
Will hit me with it, he aims so right at me.
My other lover looks asquint, and to
See him cast languishing eyes would make a
Woman with child miscarry. There is also
A very fat man, Master Pinguister, and
A very lean man that loves me. I tell the
Fat man I cannot marry him till he's
Leaner, and the lean man I cannot marry
Him till he's fat. So one of them purges
And runs heats every morning, to pull down
His sides, and th'other makes his tailor stuff
His clothes to make him show fatter. O, what
Pleasure do I take in fooling of mankind!

All Mistaken, or The Mad Couple

James Howard

Play
Comic
F
18
Classic

*Mirida, an eighteenth-century tease, tells her suitor she
would prefer hanging to marriage.*

Hold, sir, I forbid the banns. I'd
Rather hear a long sermon than
Hear a parson ask me: Mirida,
Will you have this man your
Wedded husband, to have and to hold,
From this day forward, for better for worse
In sickness or in health and so forth,
Ay, and perhaps after we have been
Married half a year, one's
Husband falls into a deep consumption,
And will not do one the favor to
Die neither, then we must be
Ever feeding him with caudles.
Oh, from a husband with consumption
Deliver me. And think how weary I should be
Of thee, Philidor, when once we were
Chain'd together: the very name of
Wife would be a vomit to me; then
Nothing but "Where's my wife? Call
My wife to dinner, call my wife to supper;"
And then at night, "Come wife, will you
Go to bed?" That would be so troublesome,
To be call'd by one's husband every night
To go to bed. Oh, that dull, dull,
Name of husband. If you please, sir, never propose
Marrying to us, till both of us have
Committed such faults as are death
By the law; then, instead of

Hanging us, marry us.
And then you shall hear how
Earnestly we shall petition
Your highness to be hang'd rather than
Married.

The Altruists

Nicky Silver

Play
Comic
F
20s-30s
Contemporary

Sydney, a rather shallow, anorexic soap opera actress, is talk-
ing to her boyfriend Ethan.

Ethan, I have had it! I can take it no more. Do you hear me? You can
pretend to be asleep, I don't care. (…) I AM NOT HAPPY! How could
I be? Am I supposed to enjoy your condescension? Should I love your
humiliating me in front of your friends? (…) How do you think I feel when
I'm introduced as "just" an actress? As if what I did for a living didn't bring
joy into the world! As if what I do for a living didn't make this life more
bearable for the disenfranchised you pretend to care about! There is dignity, profound dignity in my life, in my work! But you choose to sneer
at it. People LOVE SOAP OPERAS! I get mail by the bushel, letters by
the trillion! I have fans! I have followers! All over this country people are
worried about Montana Beach! Will she leave Brock for Brick? Will she
kick her ugly habit? Will she find her mother, true love, or the meaning
of life!? People care about me! Who cares about you?! I ask you. Who
cares about you! Not I! Not I, Ethan!

The Altruists

Nicky Silver

Play
Comic
F
20s-30s
Contemporary

Sydney, a rather shallow, anorexic soap opera actress, has had it with her boyfriend Ethan.

I HAVE BEEN HEROIC! Only a heroine, only a mythic figure, could overcome the scolds and the scandals — when you told everyone we knew, my friends, my family, my THERAPIST, whom you had no business talking to in the first place — when you told everyone in New York City that I gave you syphilis, when we both know, we know without a doubt that Maria Potney gave you syphilis during that demonstration — and you in turn gave it to me! THAT WAS NOT FUNNY! I made allowances because every now and then, once a week, once a month, once in a blue moon, you made love to me and I saw fireworks, I heard orchestras! You made love to me and I remembered the beginning, when we made love nonstop, like Olympians! I put up with everything, I entered your world of East Village, Alphabet City, anti-trend-trendies, of sit-ins and marches and protests, because it felt good to have you inside of me! But no more! NO MORE, ETHAN! I'M A PERSON! I HAVE FEELINGS! I HAVE A BREAKING POINT AND I HAVE REACHED IT!

Always Ridiculous

Jose Echegaray

Play
Comic
F
20s
Classic

Remedios discovers her captive audience has found a way to escape.

You may say what you like, Don Cosme, I can't agree that Teresina is quite as complex as you think she is, and I'm certainly not subject to illusions. I know the World; I'm not an ingenuous child; I say I'm not because, good Lord! no widow has any business to be one. Although I must admit that as far as years go, and in looks and manner, I am still something of a child. But that's because of certain characteristics. Don't you think so? Why don't you speak? You understand my character? *(Turning toward DON COSME and looking carefully at him.)* Good Lord! the man's asleep again! Up at ten this morning, it's now eleven. And he sleeps! No, sir! I must have somebody to talk to. Teresina is in the garden flirting with the two of them — spinning like a planet between her two poles, Juan and Eugenio. Don Pablo has gone on his usual walk. Don Hilarion? No one knows where he is! Here I am left alone with Don Cosme, and he sleeps, leaving me in full monologue. I won't stand it! I came to this house on the express condition that I should not be bored, and the condition is not being fulfilled. The place is beautiful — *Art*, Oh! plenty of Art — pictures, tapestry, statues, bronzes, porcelains; and *Nature*, Oh! a great deal of Nature, woods and flowers and lakes and water-falls and sunsets! But all that's not enough. There is no Life! No warmth! As they say nowadays, the warmth of humanity. And he goes on sleeping! This life is giving that man softening of the brain. Don Cosme! Oh, Don Cosme! *(Striking him with her fan.)* Open your eyes!

The Arkansas Tornado

Kathleen A. Rogers

Play
Comic
F
17
Contemporary

Howdy speaks into a video camera. She has issues.

The Secret History of My Body, Part Thirty. The perfection of my flesh. This episode is dedicated to Mrs. Becker.

I don't know why you think I don't have any ambition, just because I don't feel like going to college next year. I won't be working in the drive-through at Dunkin Donuts forever. I do have a career goal, Mrs. Becker. I'm going to join the World Wrestling Federation and become BOOGER WOMAN. The Fattest, The Ugliest, The Most Disgusting. I'll wear a real tight costume — shiny material, slimy green — gold cape — silver boots. I'll slime all over the ring. Ooze all over the place. Booger Woman will have it all: fan clubs, videos, T-shirts, trading cards, action figures, sports drinks. She's the hero for all the fat girls. I'll build a booger empire, a chain of restaurants, the Boogerterias, and all the food will be slimy and gross, like the school cafeteria. I'll have my own theme park: Snot World. I will be fabulous. I will be world-class! I will be everywhere! And you, Mrs. Becker, you will be where you've always been: NOWHERE!

As You Like It

William Shakespeare

Play
Comic
F
20s
Classic

Phebe weighs her conflicting feelings for a "peevish boy."

Think not I love him, though I ask for him;
'Tis but a peevish boy; yet he talks well.
But what care I for words? Yet words do well
When he that speaks them pleases those that hear.
It is a pretty youth; not very pretty;
But sure he's proud; and yet his pride becomes him.
He'll make a proper man. The best thing in him
Is his complexion; and faster than his tongue
Did make offense, his eye did heal it up.
He is not very tall; yet for his years he's tall.
His leg is but so so; and yet 'tis well.
There was a pretty redness in his lip,
A little riper and more lusty red
Than that mixed in his cheek; 'twas just the difference
Betwixt the constant red and mingled damask.
There be some women, Silvius, had they marked him
In parcels as I did, would have gone near
To fall in love with him; but, for my part,
I love him not nor hate him not; and yet
I have more cause to hate him than to love him;
For what had he to do to chide at me?
He said mine eyes were black and my hair black;
And, now I am rememb'red, scorned at me.
I marvel why I answered not again.
But that's all one; omittance is no quittance.
I'll write to him a very taunting letter,
And thou shalt bear it. Wilt thou, Silvius?

Bad Dates

Theresa Rebeck

Play
Comic
F
30s-40s
Contemporary

Haley's decided to re-enter the dating scene, but she is having one bad experience after another.

So I'm like, OK, this is just a date that's not going to work out. (…) And then, there's actually a point in the evening where having completely given up on this guy I sort of perversely got interested in his story. He starts talking about his ex-girlfriend. And the more he talks about her, the clearer it becomes that he's still, really, kind of in love with her. And the more I listen to him, the more I realize that this is more or less a first date for him, too, he's recently broken up with this woman he really loved, and now he's trying to get back on the horse. And this thought honestly makes me feel a little warmly toward him, I sense that we are fellow-travelers. And so I say to him, as a fellow-traveler, well, why did you break up? And he tells me this story about how — that your relationship with a person is like a movie. That when you're in a relationship, you see the movie, in your head, and that you need to see how the rest of the movie is going to go. And he realized that he couldn't see where the movie was going. He didn't know the end of the movie, with this woman. So he had to break up with her. And he looked so sad. Meanwhile, I'm listening to this, and trying to understand, so I say, What do you mean, a movie? And he goes through the whole thing again, about looking for the end of the movie, and your life with someone, and the relationship, and the end of the movie, so I say, you mean like death? Looking for the end of the movie, you're thinking about dying? And he says, No no no, it's not about death. It's about the End of the Movie. And we go around in circles like that for a while, and finally I say to him, I don't know, is it possible that you broke up with the woman you loved because of some insane metaphor?

Battle of the Sexes

Cynthia Heimel

Essay
Comic
F
20s-30s
Contemporary

Everyone who thinks the speaker's boyfriend is married, raise your hand.

I am involved in a long-distance relationship. He lives in Boston, I live in New York. I fly up there one weekend a month, he flies down to New York whenever he feels like it.

No, that's not fair. He usually flies down for a few days every month, too, it's just that I'm so annoyed with him. Here's why:

I could move up there. I've been offered a job, a good job. Not that I'm crazy about Boston, everybody's very snooty and every time you have to drive around the corner to get milk you get hopelessly lost and end up in Marblehead or somewhere and people have to send out search parties, and then the search parties get lost, and anyway there aren't even any good clothing stores or nightclubs.

But I love him, and if we could live together I could get used to ending up in Marblehead incessantly and getting all my outfits from catalogs.

Guess what? (I bet you already have.) He doesn't want me to move. It's so sickening I actually puked a few times last night.

He doesn't say, "I don't want you up here, Clarice." No. He says his place is too small. We'll move, I say. It's not a good time, he says, the real estate market is so bad, he would take a bath if he sold his place. But, I point out, if the market's bad, it's bad for everyone, not just you, you moron, and since everybody's taking a bath, you could get a place real cheap and that would cancel out the bath you think you'll take.

"You just don't understand anything," he says.

I understand everything. "How about if I got my own apartment near you?" I ask.

"That would be interesting," he says.

"But do you want me to?" I ask.

"It might be kinda nice."

"Look, could you just say 'I want you to' or 'I don't want you to'?"

"I'll call you later, the doorbell's ringing."

"Wait!"

But he's already hung up the phone. The doorbell has rung really opportunely in the past few weeks.

So look, this man loves me, I know he does. So what is he doing? I can't believe it. I thought he'd be so thrilled. He hates me.

The Beaux' Stratagem

George Farquhar

> Play
> Comic
> F
> 30+
> Classic

Mrs. Sullen warns her sister-in-law against marrying the strong, silent type.

…[Y]onder I see my Corydon, and a sweet swain it is, Heaven knows! Come, Dorinda, don't be angry; he's my husband, and your brother, and, between both, is he not a sad brute? O, sister, sister! If ever you marry, beware of a sullen, silent sot, one that's always musing, but never thinks. There's some diversion in a talking blockhead; and since a woman must wear chains, I would have the pleasure of hearing 'em rattle a little. Now you shall see, but take this by the way. He came home this morning at his usual hour of four, wakened me out of a sweet dream of something else, by tumbling over the tea-table, which he broke all to pieces; after his man and he had rolled about the room, like sick passengers I a storm, he comes flounce into bed, dead as a salmon into a fishmonger's basket; his feet cold as ice, his breath hot as a furnace, and his hands and his face as greasy as his flannel night-cap. O matrimony! He tosses up the clothes with a barbarous swing over his shoulders, disorders the whole economy of my bed, leaves me half-naked, and my whole night's comfort is the tunable serenade of that wakeful nightingale, his nose! Oh, the pleasure of counting the melancholy clock by a snoring husband!

Bebe's by Golly Wow

Yolanda Joe

Novel
Comic
F
40s
Contemporary

Bebe, a single woman, analyzes modern romance.

See, there are two kinds of expectations. To the left, y'all, is what you think is due you. To the right, y'all, is what you think will happen to you. My expectations of love relationships are about as high up as the street curb. And that's bad to say but I'm being Girl Scout honest, cross-my-heart-hope-ta-choke-on-some-thin-mints.

Hey, ask me to cluck and strut and call me chicken but I hate a struggle. But, sister-girl me ain't no wimp. I can work through a struggle but I hate every gosh darn minute of it. Some people get off on a struggle, rise to the occasion — it brings out the best in them. Brings out the nasty in me because I'm mad as a stung bear that I've got to struggle. I want good times, all the time. Now I'm no "Cinderella looking for a shoehorn." I know that life doesn't work out magically like that, particularly in ways of love. But I know I'm due better. And this Isaac? This Isaac could be what's due me, could be my "Betcha By Golly Wow" but I don't wanna organize a parade for him just yet. No, not yet.

I think I'll wait.

Between the Lines

Lee Smith

Short story
Comic
F
35+
Contemporary

Joline B. Newhouse, a small-town newspaper columnist, knows what she knows and reveals more than she intends.

"Peace be with you from Mrs. Joline B. Newhouse" is how I sign my columns. Now I gave some thought to that. In the first place, I like a line that has a ring to it. In the second place, what I have always tried to do with my column is to uplift my readers if at all possible, which sometimes it is not. After careful thought, I threw out "Yours in Christ." I am a religious person and all my readers know it. If I put "Yours in Christ," it seems to me that they will think I am theirs because I am in Christ, or even that they and I are in Christ *together*, which is not always the case. I am in Christ but I know for a fact that lot of them are not. There's no use acting like they are, but there's no use rubbing their face in it, either. "Peace be with you," as I see it, is sufficiently religious without laying all the cards right out on the table in plain view. I like to keep an ace or two up my sleeve. I like to write between the lines.

This is what I call my column, in fact: "Between the Lines, by Mrs. Joline B. Newhouse." Nobody knows why. Many people have come right out and asked me, including my best friend Sally Peck and my husband Glenn. "Come on, now, Joline," they say. "What's this 'Between the Lines' all about? What's this 'Between the Lines' supposed to mean?" But I just smile a sweet mysterious smile and change the subject. I know what I know.

And my column means everything to folks around here. Salt Lick community is where we live, unincorporated. I guess there is not much that you would notice, passing through — the Post Office (real little), the American oil station, my husband Glenn's Cash 'N' Carry Beverage Store. He sells more than beverages in there, though, believe me. He sells everything you can think of, from thermometers and rubbing alcohol to nails to frozen pizza. Anything else you want, you have to go out of the holler and get on the interstate and go to Greenville to get it. That's where my column appears, in the *Greenville Herald*, fortnightly. Now there's word with a ring to it: fortnightly.

Black Thang

Ato Essandoh

Play
Comic
F
20s-30s
Contemporary

Keisha is recounting her experience with trying to rent a horse-drawn carriage for her wedding. She's talking to her friend and roommate, Mattie, who is white.

So I met the horses last night. Champ and Lucky Lady. You know, to pull my bridal carriage. So now is the time I find out that Omar's grandmother is deadly afraid of horses. Some childhood trauma she had when she was like two when her pet rabbits got trampled to death by a wild stallion …

(…) But you would think that after what, seventy-eight years she would have gotten over something like that. Right? I mean come on, she was raised on a farm. She eats fried chicken for Christ sakes (…) So they bring out Champ and Lucky Lady, you know, the horses? And my grandmother-in-law-to-be totally freaks out. I mean freaks out. (…) I mean she starts banging her head screaming "Bunny!" "Bunny!" "Bunny!" which totally freaks out Lucky Lady who proceeds to take the biggest grossest shit I've ever seen right in front of us. I mean ten pounds of shit just drops out of this horse's ass. Just like that. And I'm like: "Is this normal?" And apparently it is? (…) So to hell with the horses I'm renting a limo.

But the One on the Right

Dorothy Parker

Short story
Comic
F
30+
Contemporary

The torment of being stuck with a socially challenged dinner partner.

I knew it. I knew if I came to this dinner, I'd draw something like this baby on my left. They've been saving him up for me for weeks. Now, we've simply got to have him — his sister was so sweet to us in London; we can stick him next to Mrs. Parker — she talks enough for two. Oh, I should never have come, never. I'm here against my better judgement, to a decision. That would be a good thing for them to cut on my tombstone: Wherever she went, including here, it was against her better judgement. This is a fine time of the evening to be thinking about tombstones. That's the effect he's had on me, already, and the soup hardly cold yet. I should have stayed at home for dinner. I could have had something on a tray. The head of John the Baptist, or something. Oh, I should not have come.

Well, the soup's over, anyway. I'm that much nearer to my Eternal Home. Now the soup belongs to the ages, and I have said precisely four words to the gentleman on my left. I said, "Isn't this soup delicious?"; that's four words. And he said, "Yes, isn't it?"; that's three. He's one up on me.

At any rate, we're in perfect accord. We agree like lambs. We've been all through the soup together, and never a cross word between us. It seems rather a pity to let the subject drop, now we've found something on which we harmonize so admirably. I believe I'll bring it up again; I'll ask him if that wasn't delicious soup. He says, "Yes, wasn't it?" Look at that, will you; perfect command of his tenses.

Here comes the fish. Goody, goody, goody, we got fish.

Butterflies Are Free

Leonard Gershe

Play
Comic
F
20s
Contemporary

Jill, a child of the sixties, explains the circumstances of her first marriage.

I can't talk about him. No, I will talk about him. Every once in a while it's good to do something you don't want to do, it cleanses the insides. He was terribly sweet, and groovy looking, but kind of adolescent, ya know what I mean? Girls mature faster than boys, boys are neater, but girls mature faster. When we met, it was like fireworks! It was a marvelous kind of passion that made every day seem like the Fourth of July! Anyways … the next thing I know, there we are, standing in front of the Justice of the Peace, getting married!? It's only been like 2 or 3 months and we're getting married?! I'm not even out of high school! I've got two big exams tomorrow and they were on my mind too, and then I hear the words, "Do you Jack, take Jill, to be your lawful wedded wife?" UGH!!! Can you imagine going through life as "Jack and Jill"?! Then I hear, "Until death do us part." And all of the sudden, its not even a wedding anymore, more like a funeral service! And there I am being buried alive! … UNDER JACK BENSON! I wanted to scream, go running out into the night! But I couldn't. It was 10 o'clock in the morning and well, you can't go running out into 10 o'clock in the morning. So instead, I passed out. If only I'd fainted, before I said, "I do."

By Faith Alone

Marjorie Benton Cooke

Play
Comic
F
40+
Classic

It's the early 1900s, and Mrs. Frederick Belmont-Towers has found a marvelous new key to enlightenment.

Is that you, Helen? Come in. You must excuse me for seeing you up here, but this is my day for treatment and I don't get up till afternoon. Oh, didn't you know? I'm taking a course with Omarkanandi, this famous Hindu priest. You haven't heard of him? Oh, my dear, he is too wonderful. You know what an invalid I've been for years? I've had no sympathy in my suffering — Fred thinks it's all nonsense, says I'm a hypochondriac, and all that, but Omarkanandi says my condition has been simply pitiful! He's so sympathetic, Helen. He wears a long red robe, and a turban and the queerest rings, and his eyes are the most soulful things. Well, it's hard to tell you just what he does. He sits beside me, and holds my hands and looks into my eyes and talks to me, in his soft Oriental voice. He says he is the medium of infinite strength and power, and that he transmits it to me. Well, he thinks in time that I can draw on this power myself, without him. He says that I'm so highly strung that the winds of evil play on me. He says my chronic indigestion is simply a wind of evil, and that I must harden myself against it. I told him I didn't care so much about the indigestion itself, but it was ruining my complexion. He said when I got myself into harmony with the Infinite my skin would be like a rose leaf — so you can see for yourself the thing is worthwhile. (…) Helen, you ought to have him come see you; he'd do wonders for you. Only five hundred for the course, and it's nothing when you think what he does for you. *(Listens to Helen's sarcasms in surprise.)* Why, Helen! I'm afraid you're like Fred, too worldly and suspicious to grasp these truths. As Omarkanandi says, you must be saved "by faith alone!" *(Turns her head, as if at interruption.)* Who is it, Maria? Omarkanandi? Ask him to come up. Good-bye, Helen, do run in again. *(Watches her go out, and sighs.)* Poor, trivial thing, she hasn't the capacity for great thoughts and spiritual experiences, as I have.

The Casket Comedy

Titus Maccius Plautus

Play
Comic
F
35+
Classic

Halisca begs her audience's help in finding a lost box, trusted to her by her mistress, Casina.

If heaven doesn't rescue me, I'm dead and done for, with not a soul to look to for aid! Oh, how miserable my own heedlessness makes me! Oh! how I dread what will happen to my back, if my mistress finds out I've been so negligent! *(Thinking.)* Surely I had that little casket in my hands and received it from her here in front of the house — and where it is now I don't know, unless I dropped it somewhere about here, as I suspect. *(To audience.)* Dear gentlemen, dear spectators, do tell me if anyone of you saw him, the man who carried it off or who picked it up. Did he go *(Pointing.)* this way, or that? *(Pauses, then indignantly.)* I'm none the wiser for asking or pestering them — the creatures always enjoy seeing a woman in trouble! Now I'll *(Scans the ground.)* examine the footprints here, in case I can find any. For if no one passed by after I went inside, the casket would be lying here. *(Looking about again, then hopelessly.)* What am I to do? I'm done for, I fancy! It's all over, my day has come, unlucky, fated wretch that I am! (…) But I'm delaying myself by not setting to work. To work, Halisca! Eyes on the ground, eyes down! Track it — sharp now — like an augur! *(Looks for footprints, her nose close to the ground.)* He went this way … here's the mark of a shoe in the dust … I'll follow it up this way! Now here's where he stopped with someone else … Here's the scene of some sort of fracas … No, he didn't go on this way … he stood here … from here he went over there … A consultation was held here … There are two people concerned, that's clear as day … Aha! Just one person's tracks! … He went this way … I'll investigate … From here he went over here … from here he went — *(After an energetic and futile search.)* nowhere! *(With wry resignation.)* It's no use. What's lost is lost — the casket and my cuticle together. I'm going back inside.

Catholic Schoolgirls

Casey Kurtti

> **Play**
> **Comic**
> **F**
> **7**
> **Contemporary**

Elizabeth has been elected to give a tour of the church to a group of kindergarten students, the poor bastards.

OK everybody. This … is church. This is God's house. If you ever want to talk to Him, you just come in here and sit in one of those long chairs and start talking. But not too loud. Or else you might wake up one of those statues. And they are praying to Jesus. *(Bows head.)* Oh! I forgot to tell you. Whenever you hear the name Jesus *(Bows head.)* you have to bow your head or else you have a sin on your soul. Now, over there is the statue of Jesus' *(Bows head.)* mother. Her name is the Blessed Virgin Mary. She is not as important as Jesus *(Bows head.)* so you don't have to bow your head when you hear her name. Over there is the statue of Jesus' *(Bows head.)* father. Hey, *(Points at small child.)* you didn't bow your head. Don't do that cause you'll get a black spot on your soul and you go straight to hell. Now, in hell it is really hot and you sweat a lot. And these little devils come and they bite you all over the place. But if you're really good, you get to go to heaven. Now, in heaven they have this big refrigerator full of lots of stuff to eat! Like ice cream, and chocolate and donuts and it never runs out. But the best part about heaven would have to be that you can talk to anybody you want to. Let's just say that I wanted to talk to … *(Thinks real hard.)* Cleopatra! Well, then I would go up to one of the Saints and I would get a permission slip and I would fill it out. Then I would hand it to Jesus *(Bows head.)*. Hey! *(Looks at small child again.)* You didn't bow your head! OK, I warned you. And then, I would fly across heaven, cause when you get in they gives you wings, and I would have a nice chat with Cleopatra. I just hope everyone I like get accepted into heaven, or else I won't ever see them again. One more thing, if you ever ask Jesus *(Bows head.)* a question and He answers you, make sure you write down the answer really quick, so you don't mess it up. Because, if you mess up an answer from Him, it could get you in real trouble.

Check, Please

Dave Tucker

Play
Comic
F
20s-30s
Contemporary

Could there be a relationship between Tina's name, the size of her brain, and the scope of her small talk?

You're from Phoenix? That's in the desert, isn't it? I've never been to a desert. Though it might be nice. Just dry, I think. (…) Arid? Oh, well that's good. I would think you'd want a lot of air in the desert. To cool you off. And all that sand. It would be like living at the beach. Except that there's no ocean. Which means it wouldn't be very crowded on the weekends.

Oh. Well that's nice. I saw a movie once about a cowboy that got lost in the desert — I think it was Glenn Ford — and he was captured by Indians, Comanches, I think. And they tied him to the ground with stakes and put a rawhide thingy around his head. Maybe it was Apaches. Then they wet the rawhide with water, and as it dried in the sun, it got tighter and tighter and split his head open. No, I think it was Apaches.

You would have liked it. It would remind you of Phoenix, I think. It was over the border, in Mexico. A place called Chihuahua. But it didn't have anything to do with those little dogs. So do they do that in Phoenix? The trick with the rawhide around your head. Like the Comanches. Or Apaches.

No? Oh, well that's probably a good thing.

The Coal Diamond

Shirley Lauro

Play
Comic
F
20s-30s
Contemporary

Lena disses one of her penny-pinching coworkers at the Research Department of Southeastern Missouri Farm Insurance Co., Valley Center, Missouri, circa 1955.

Tight? Girl, I mean to tell you she puts Jack Benny to shame! Why she lives in a rented room over Ramsey's Auto Parts Store. Hasn't even got a hot plate to her name! She makes a complete diet outa soda crackers and skim milk, and she won't even chip in on the baby showers or birthday cards for the rest of the force! (…) Isn't that the limit though? Why, when she first came in here to work and I knew she was a stranger in town, yah know? I tried to find her a place to live. I told her about my apartment … the Glenview Arms? Them real swell apartments over by the river? (…) So, anyhow, she says, how much do they cost, and I says I pay $60 a month, and … (…) That was three years ago. Anyhow. You should seen ole Wanda's face when I told her. Flabbergasted is the only word to name the state of that girl's face. I figured her out then and there. (…) She is too tight! … Among other things …

The Coal Diamond

Shirley Lauro

Play
Comic
F
20s-30s
Contemporary

Inez shows newcomer Pearl around her new work space, the Research Department of Southeastern Missouri Farm Insurance Co., Valley Center, Missouri, circa 1955.

Jist never you mind, Pearl, honey. It's OK. Why, we're all so tickled to git us a fourth, we're about to die! Now jist let me name you around. Everyone: This here's my friend, Pearl Brewster, like I said. Jist started to work here Monday. They stuck her in Underwriting. (…)

This here's Betty Jean McGaffee. (…) her husband works out to the Firestone Plant. First Shift! (…) this little gold-haired honey jist graduated high school a year ago June, and already got herself this good job in Research, a husband on First Shift, and a kid almost due! (…)

And finally … this is Lena Travis, Boss of the Research Section! Lena is terrible smart at insurance and bridge. Only thing is — she can't get her a man! (…) Heck! I was only teasin', Lena! Truth is, Pearl, honey, Lena is jist too dang good for any old man! Why, Betty Jean and me, we never had such a wonderful girl to work for ever in our lives as Lena Travis. And that's a fact! (…) Well, it's the Lord's truth, Lena, and you know it is. Why, we're jist crazy about workin' for you!

Confessions of a Shopaholic

Sophie Kinsella

Novel
Comic
F
20s-30s
Contemporary

Rebecca Bloomwood, shopaholic, is being hounded by her bank for unpaid credit card bills. When an unattractive millionaire takes a fancy to her, she sees a way out of her financial woes.

I'm going to be a millionairess. A multimillionairess. I knew it. Didn't I know it? I knew it. Tarquin's going to fall in love with me and ask me to marry him and we'll get married in a gorgeous Scottish castle just like in Four Weddings (except with nobody dying on us).

Of course, I'll love him, too. By then.

I know I haven't exactly been attracted to him in the past ... but it's all a matter of willpower, isn't it? I bet that's what most long-term successful couples would say counts in a relationship. Willpower and a desire to make it work. Both of which I absolutely have. You know what? I actually fancy him more already. Well, not exactly *fancy* ... but just the thought of him makes me feel all excited, which must mean something, mustn't it?

(...) I can do this [I tell myself firmly]. I can be attracted to him. It's just a matter of self-control and possibly also getting very drunk. (...) Alcohol is obviously going to be the key to our marital happiness.

The Country Wife

William Wycherly

Play
Comic
F
20s
Classic

Mrs. Pinchwife devises a clever way to send to her would-be lover the letter her husband would have her write, and the letter she wants to write.

For Mr. Horner — So, I am glad he has told me his name; Dear Mr. Horner, but why should I send thee such a letter, that will vex thee, and make thee angry with me? — well, I will not send it — Ay, but then my husband will kill me — for I see plainly, he won't let me love Mr. Horner — but what care I for my husband — I won't, so I won't send poor Mr. Horner such a letter — but then my husband — But oh — what if I writ at bottom, my husband made me write it — Ay, but then my husband would see't. Can one have no shift? Ah, a London woman would have had a hundred presently; stay — what if I should write a letter, and wrap it up like this, and write upon't too. Ay, but then my husband would see't. I don't know what to do — But yet ye gads, I'll try, so I will — for I will not send this letter to poor Mr. Horner, come what will on't.

Dear, Sweet, Mr. Horner — So — *(She writes, and repeats what she hath writ.)* my husband would have me send you a base, rude unmannerly letter — but I won't — so — and would have me forbid you loving me — but I won't — so — and would have me say to you, I hate you poor Mr. Horner — but I won't tell a lie for him — there — for I'm sure if you and I were in the country at cards together — so — I could not help treading on your toe under the table — so — or rubbing knees with you, and staring in your face, 'till you saw me — very well — and then looking down, and blushing for an hour together — so — but I must make haste before my husband come; and now he has taught me to write letters; you shall have longer ones from, who am
Dear, dear, poor dear Mr. Horner, your most
Humble Friend and Servant to command
'til death, Margery Pinchwife.

Stay, I must give him a hint at bottom — so — wrap it up just like t'other — so — now write, For Mr. Horner. But oh now what shall I do with it? for here comes my husband.

Cuthbert's Last Stand

Andrew Biss

Play
Comic
F
45+
Contemporary

The deliciously twisted Mrs. Pennnington-South grapples with her son's sexuality.

You see, it suddenly struck me — you were…oh, I don't know…three, I think — and I'd just been watching one of those gritty documentary programmes on BBC 2; the ones where, rather than feeling enlightened, I just end up feeling guilty for being me. Anyway, this particular one happened to be about homosexuality and how it could all be a result of your genes or molecules, or some such thing. And that's when it hit me. That's when I saw a little chink of light in all of that darkness. It occurred to me that perhaps…perhaps there *was* a way out for you, after all. Perhaps you weren't fated to replay this moribund existence that we'd all been embalmed in.

(Placing her hands to her face.) Oh…how I wracked my brains, searching, praying for some beacon of hope within the bosom of our bloodline. There was your aunt Millicent, of course, who'd run off to Tangiers with her housekeeper and precious little else. But that had been generally ascribed by most as a matter of pure domestic necessity — especially in an underdeveloped country. And then, in a moment of inspired joy, I recalled your cousin Vivian, with his penchant for strolling in the park after dark, and his overall lack of interest in the feminine gender. Oh, how I clutched to that image. I prayed, with *all* the religious fervour I could muster — which, admittedly, wasn't much — that that would be *your* destiny, too. I *wanted* that for you. I wanted that *so* badly.

(Tenderly.) But, Darling, you haven't disappointed me.

(Beat.) Well, you've disappointed me, yes, of course you have – how could you not? I mean, after all, Cuthbert, I'd tried so hard; I'd hoped so deeply, so passionately. But it's not as if I'd have tried to force you into accepting something that you didn't want. Of course, I blame your father entirely. He would insist on buying you some hideous … oh, I don't

know what it was — some sort of action combat doll — for your seventh birthday. I *begged* him not to. I pleaded with him, I wept openly. But he was immovable. I tried to console myself. I imagined — clung to the possibility — that once you'd gotten around to removing his camouflage fatigues to see the exquisite perfection of the naked male form before your eyes, you might … something might be … awakened within you.

(Beat.) But I never saw it. All I ever saw were those ghastly little war games you'd create, with bombs exploding and guns firing and tanks looming on the horizon. And I think, even then, I might have had my suspicions of you. But I was your mother: I saw what I wanted to see.

Cuthbert's Last Stand

Andrew Biss

Play
Comic
F
45+
Contemporary

Mrs. Pennington-South, not exactly Mother of the Year, vows to protect her son from a life of happiness and companionship.

Thirty years of my life I've squandered on that anonymous hotel guest legally defined as my husband and your father. And I'll never get them back, Cuthbert — they're gone.

(To herself, incredulously.) Three decades! Three decades of "Christ, is that the time!" first thing in the morning, and "This should only take a minute, dear," last thing at night: (…) And as the years went by I began to feel as though my entire insides were completely hollow, as if…as if I could just as easily have been his car…or his golf bag.

(Beat.) Until you came along, that is. Then I felt real again. Suddenly I felt as if I mattered — as if it all meant something. I'd hold you in my arms and look down at your…well, your…your strange-looking head, and —

(Beat.) Oh, darling, don't look like that. Of course, you've grown up to be devilishly handsome, but I'm afraid when you popped out of me you had a *very* peculiar look to you. Your eyes were unusually small and beady-looking, you had no hair, and your lips just sort of jutted out. It was quite disconcerting to some of our friends at the time, I'm afraid. The general consensus had you likened to a duck-billed platypus, which, naturally, I strenuously denied. Until I actually saw one, that is, and then I felt rather silly and foolish, because, of course, you looked *exactly* like a duck-billed platypus. But the point is I loved you — no matter what you looked like, and no matter how disturbing your appearance was to others. And I wanted the best for you, and I didn't want to see you dragged down into that same mindless morass and drudgery that was suffocating me. I vowed that I would do *everything* in my power to spare you from that.

'dentity Crisis

Christopher Durang

Play
Comic
F
30+
Contemporary

Jane tells her therapist she no longer believes in fairies.

When I was eight years old, someone brought me to this ... theater. Full of lots of other children. We were supposed to be watching a production of *Peter Pan.* And I remember that something seemed terribly wrong with the whole production. Odd things kept happening. For instance, when the children would fly, the ropes they were on would just keep breaking ... and the actors would come thumping to the ground and they had to be carried off by stagehands. And there seemed to be an unlimited supply of understudies, to take their places, and then they'd just fall to the ground. And then the crocodile that chases Captain Hook, seemed to be a real crocodile, it wasn't an actor. And at one point it fell off the stage and crushed a couple of kids in the front row. And then some of the understudies came and took their places in the audience. And from scene to scene, Wendy just seemed to get fatter and fatter until finally by the end of act one she was completely immobile and they had to move her offstage with a cart.

You remember how in the second act Tinkerbell drinks some poison that Peter is about to drink in order to save him? And then Peter turns to the audience and he says that, "Tinkerbell is going to die because not enough people believe in fairies. But if all of you clap your hands real hard to show that you do believe in fairies, maybe she won't die." So, we all started to clap. I clapped so long and so hard that my palms hurt and they even started to bleed I clapped so hard. Then suddenly the actress playing Peter Pan turned to the audience and she said, "That wasn't enough. You did not clap hard enough. Tinkerbell is dead." And then we all started to cry. The actress stomped off stage and refused to continue with the production. They finally had to lower the curtain. The ushers had to come help us out of the aisles and into the street. I don't think that any of us were ever the same after that experience. It certainly turned me against theater. And even more damagingly, I think it's warped my total sense of life. I mean nothing seems worth trying if Tinkerbell is just going to die.

The Double-Dealer

William Congreve

Play
Comic
F
20s
Classic

Lady Plyant vacillates from outrage to being flattered upon learning Mellefont wants to marry her stepdaughter in order to procure her, the stepmother.

[H]ow can you talk of heaven, and have so much wickedness in your heart? Maybe you don't think it a sin — they say some of you gentlemen don't think it a sin — maybe it is no sin to them that don't think it so — indeed, if I did not think it a sin — but still my honor, if it were no sin — but then, to marry my [husband's] daughter, for the conveniency of frequent opportunities [to procure me, her stepmother] — I'll never consent to that, as sure as can be, I'll break the match. Nay, nay, rise up, come, you shall see my good nature. I know love is powerful, and nobody can help his passion: I know 'tis not your fault nor I swear it is not mine. How can I help it if I have charms? And how can you help it, if you made a captive? I swear it's a pity is should be a fault — but my honor — well, but your honor, too — but the sin! — Well, but the necessity — oh, Lord, here's somebody coming, I dare not stay. Well, you must consider of your crime, and strive as much as can be against it — strive be sure — but don't be melancholy, don't despair — but never think that I'll grant you anything; oh, Lord, no; — but be sure you lay aside all thoughts of marriage, for though I know you don't love Cynthia, only as a blind for your passion to me: yet it will make me jealous — oh, Lord, what did I say? Jealous? No, no, I can't be jealous, for I must not love you — therefore, don't hope — but don't despair neither, oh, they're coming, I must fly!

driver's ed

Steven Schutzman

Play
Seriocomic
F
16
Contemporary

Patricia's stream of consciousness moves from comic to creepy, and back.

I have the highest-grade point average in my class. I make my own clothes and could play the flute professionally. It's something to fall back on, my mother says. I also sing and dance. Last year I was the star of the school musical. I have never failed at anything. All the boys are idiots. When I sleep down in the basement, I can hear my mother and her boyfriend Donny through the air conditioner ducts. Donny has a silver Jaguar. He let me drive it once in the parking lot of the old fairgrounds. My mother waited only seven months before she'd let Donny sleep over. Do you think that's enough time? I don't. After my father died, I used to see his ghost sitting on my windowsill and his ghost seemed happy and that made me happy. Ghosts can't talk and they can't hear you talk. It's not like Hamlet at all. Ghosts just want to be in the room with you. They just want you to see them. I filled a whole composition book the night I first saw Dad again. My hand couldn't stop. Whenever I read it over it makes me cry. I will be reading it over my whole life. "Let me introduce you to who I was and let who I am now express the terrible surprise of what has happened to me." How could a twelve-year-old girl write that? I'm a virgin. I have my father's eyes. For more than a year afterward, every night at six o'clock the dog would sit by the door and wait for Dad. My brother who's in college now thought it was the sequence of cars coming home to the neighborhood, every car but Dad's, so it fooled the dog. The dog has lived in that house all his life and so have I. He will be famous one day, my brother not the dog. I started sleeping in the basement when my mother started letting Donny stay over, for privacy, but when their lovemaking noises come through the ducts I can't help but listen. If I asked, would you kiss me just once?

The Dutch Courtesan

John Marston

Play
Comic
F
20s
Classic

Crispinella gives her treatise on the loathsome act of kissing.

Pish, sister Beatrice! prithee read no more; my stomach o' late stands against kissing extremely. (…) By the faith and trust I bear to my face, 'tis grown one of the most unsavory ceremonies. Body o' beauty, 'tis one of the most unpleasing, injurious customs to ladies. Any fellow that has but one nose on his face, and standing collar and skirts also lined with taffety silk, must salute us on the lips as familiarly — Soft skins save us! there was a stub bearded John-a Stile with ployden's face saluted me last day and stuck his bristle through my lips; I ha' spent ten shilling in pomatum since to skin them again. Marry, if a nobleman or a knight with one lock visit us, though his unclean goose-turd-green teeth ha' the palsy, his nostrils smell worse than a putrified maribone, and his loose beard drops into our bosom, yet must kiss him with a curtsy. A curse! for my part, I had as lief they would break wind in my lips.

The Dutch Courtesan

John Marston

Play
Comic
F
20s
Classic

Crispinella grants her friend's husband immunity from the otherwise tainted pool of married men.

Marry? No, faith; husbands are like lots in the lottery: You may draw forty blanks before you find one that any prize in him. A husband generally is a careless, domineering thing that grows like coral, which as long as it is under water is soft and tender, but as soon as it has got his branch above the waves is presently hard, stiff, not to be bowed but burst; so when your husband is a suitor and under your choice, Lord, how supple his is, how obsequious, how at your service, sweet lady! Once married, got up his head above, a stiff, crooked, knobby, inflexible, tyrannous creature he grows; then they turn like water: More you would embrace, the less you hold. I'll live my own woman, and if the worst come to the worst, I had rather price a wag than a fool. (…)

Virtuous marriage? There is no more affinity betwixt virtue and marriage than betwixt a man and his horse. Indeed, virtue gets up upon marriage sometimes and manageth it in the right way, but marriage is of another piece; for as a horse may be without a man, and a man without a horse, so marriage, you know, is often without virtue, and virtue, I am sure, more oft without marriage. But thy match, sister, by my troth, I think 'twill do well. He's a well-shaped, clean-lipped gentleman, of a handsome but not affected fineness, a good faithful eye, and a well-humored cheek. Would he did not stoop in the shoulders, for thy sake.

The Ecclesiazus

Aristophanes

Play
Comic
F
20s-30s
Classic

Praxagora, disguised as a man, makes a case for women.

[H]earken to me, you will be saved. I assert that the direction of affairs must be handed over to the women, for 'tis they who have charge and look after our households. They are worth more than you are, as I shall prove. First of all they wash all their wool in warm water, according to the ancient practice; you will never see them changing their method. Ah! if Athens only acted thus, if it did not take delight in ceaseless innovations, would not its happiness be assured? Then the women sit down to cook, as they always did; they carry things on their head as was their wont; they keep the Thesmophoria, as they have ever done; they knead their cakes just as they used to; they make their husbands angry as they have always done; they receive their lovers in their houses as was their constant custom; they buy dainties as they always did; they love unmixed wine as well as ever; they delight in being loved just as much as they always have. Let us therefore hand Athens over to them without endless discussions, without bothering ourselves about what they will do; let us simply hand them over the power, remembering that they are mothers and will therefore spare the blood of our soldiers; besides, who will know better than a mother how to forward provisions to the front? Woman is adept at getting money for herself and will not easily let herself be deceived; she understands deceit too well herself. I omit a thousand other advantages. Take my advice and you will live in perfect happiness.

Flesh and Bones

Kathy Coudle King

Play
Comic
F
20s
Contemporary

Billi, an aspiring blues singer, has been rejected by a booking agent because she is overweight. Her friend suggests she give up chocolate.

Give up chocolate? Don't you see what you're asking me? You're asking me to give up the one constant in my life. The one dependable support system in this damned, unpredictable world. You act like this is some small modification, like closing the toilet seat. This is a colossal alteration of the very fiber of my being. Why not just take me out and shoot me? That would be humane. That — would be merciful. (…) And don't you start talking health food, 'cause in an emotional crunch, carob just don't cut it! Look, what you don't understand is the rich history chocolate and I have. It isn't just so much cocoa and sugar. It's spiritual sustenance, too. Chocolate and I go way back. It was over hot fudge sundaes that Debbie Pulaski comforted me after my first break up with Larry Sullivan. It was with double fudge cake that you relayed the news that Debbie was dating Larry. And it was during a fudge-making party that you, Debbie, and I celebrated the triumph of sisterhood and the dumping of Larry. I could tell you stories of pot brownies and hot August nights with melted Hershey's kisses, but why get into it? Suffice it to say, if you take away my chocolate — I will die. Or at least suffer severe DT's. I guarantee, it won't be pretty.

Folé! Olé!

William Allen

Play
Comic
F
40s-50s
Contemporary

Nanette Folé prefaces her monologue with a modern dance as only she could dream up. Once she starts speaking, dance serves as punctuation.

Nanette Folé, rhymes with olé, from gay Paris. I am an actress born to the theater with a genetic death grip upon l'etape français. I emote, I resound, I emerge from the Rue de Rouge Ensemble — a small, intimate, Parisian, basement theater (…) dripping with angst and greasepaint. It was there that I, like a violently wrung sponge, soaked up the art of being; and it was there that I learned to regard life as a series of opportunities that could be seized, if one were alert, or ignored, if one were feeling rather emotionally tepid. And it was there that I would later meet … Eugene.

(…) Eugene was an icon, yet so human — a symbol of strength, yet so vulnerable! He taught me the meaning of life — his life and my life and our lives intertwined. It is to be. It is to find the truth. It is to seek beauty in all we do, no matter how mundane it appears to the others. (…) All of them out there living lives like ants in the bottom of a Coke bottle. (…) Nanette Folé! I center; I fathom; I write! And what do I write? I write poetry and I write checks (…); and for each of you artisans who accomplishes his or her task, a bonus check will be hand delivered par moi à vous, along with a haiku to commemorate the occasion. Phillipe — music — fade, but not too quickly. Let it glide gently to a whisper of its former self as I … melt … to a mere drip, drip, drip … of … artistic lust.

F-Stop

Olga Humphrey

Play
Comic
F
20s
Contemporary

Susanne, an actor from hell, takes on the audition from hell. Hellishly.

Juilliard. That's where I'm studying now. The best roles. Miss Julie. Blanche. Every one of the Three Sisters. Some student films for NYU so I have experience being under the lights. I like the lights.

Would you like me to do a monologue? I have all types: comic, tragic, naturalism, black comedy, Neil Simon, Beckett, lyrical realism, realistic lyricalism, Tide Ultra ... You name it, I got it, and I do it good, real good, better than just about anyone. But before I start, I want to ask you about the physicality you said you were looking for. I do just happen to be versed in tae kwan do and I also have a black belt in Uechiryu *[Pronounced Way-chee-ru.]* Karate, that's the Okinawan school. My older brother went into a state of Nirvana when Kung Fu premiered on American TV. Grasshopper this, Grasshopper that. Personally, I wanted to throttle Grasshopper. But my attitude was adjusted after I was jumped one afternoon by some acne-encrusted boys, who fondled me and then ran off. So I became a disciple as well. I have good flexibility from ballet, so I can certainly make foot-to-head contact — though not real contact. As we all know, it's the illusion we're after. I understand you're looking for someone to play Tiffany Jones, a voluptuous, kick-boxing, platinum-haired CEO, twenty-one years of age, who single-handedly takes on the Singapore Mafia when they try to launder money and run drugs through the Fortune 500 company she started from the ground up. You know, seldom have I connected with a role as I am connecting with this one. I know this woman. I feel her pain. Tiffany is every woman. Every woman is Tiffany. Gentlemen, I believe you need look no further. I'm ready to read for you, but first...

... may I ask that you make this light a little brighter?

Galaxy Video

Marc Morales

Play
Comic
F
20s-30s
Contemporary

An angry employee is asking the manager of a video store to have her job back.

I met you for a short time five days ago when I came into work. It was my first day. I was in the Folk Song Musical section fixing tapes when I noticed four tapes that were in the wrong place. Fort Apache, the Bronx, Empire Records, War Games, and The Way We Were. Are any of those films folk song musicals? I don't think so. Then this woman comes over to me and asks if we had that movie that had that guy in it who was in that movie with the girl who was in that movie with that guy. *(Pause.)* At that moment I decided that I hated people. So I turned myself inward to search for an answer for what to do. I can do stuff like that: I take yoga. Quit. That was the answer. Quit. So I quit. To myself, and I walked out. I went to my therapist Doctor Kubrick, and I asked him why? Why do I hate people? He replied, "Because you hate yourself." Wow. I do hate myself. But why? Why do I hate myself? I turned myself inward once again to find the answer. *(Pause.)* My art, I have been neglecting my art. I am an artist. I draw little stick people. I draw them well. But I've been neglecting them lately because of my yoga, and work. I love drawing my little stick people. You should always make time for those things that you love to do. *(Pause.)* I am better now. May I have my job back?

Goodnight Desdemona (Good Morning Juliet)

Ann-Marie MacDonald

Play
Comic
F
30s
Contemporary

Through a series of theatrical circumstances, Constance, an assistant professor of English, finds herself inside the play Othello where she discovers Desdemona is not the tragic victim that Shakespeare would have us believe, and gains the courage to fight her own battles in the world of academe.

I wish I were more like Desdemona.
Next to her I'm just a little wimp.
A rodent. Road-kill. Furry tragedy
All squashed and steaming on the 401
With "Michelin" stamped all over me. It's true:
People've always made a fool of me
Without my even knowing. Gullible.
That's me. Old Connie. Good sport. Big joke. Ha.
Just like that time at recess in grade five:
A gang of bully girls comes up to me.
Their arms are linked, they're chanting as they march,
"Hey. Hey. Get outta my way!
I just got back from the I.G.A.!"
I'm terrified. They pin me down,
And force me to eat a dog-tongue sandwich.
Now I know it was only ham …
O, what would Desdemona do to Claude,
Had she the motive and the cue for passion
that I have? She would drown all Queen's with blood,
and cleave Claude Night's two typing fingers from
his guilty hands. She'd wrap them in a box

of choc'lates and present them to Ramona.
She'd kill him in cold blood and in blank verse,
then smear the ivied walls in scarlet letters spelling "thief"!
to think, I helped him use me: a gull, a stooge,
a swine adorned with mine own pearls,
a sous-chef, nay! A scull'ry maid that slaved
to heat hell's kitchen with the baking stench
of forty-thousand scalding humble-pies,
O Vengeance!!!

Half Asleep in Frog Pajamas

Tom Robbins

Novel
Comic
F
40s
Contemporary

Q-Jo, a psychic, reacts to a stockbroker who has asked for a little help with the big board.

Now *you* listen, honey, and listen good. Do you really believe that if I could pick stocks that are gonna double — or winning lottery numbers or racehorses — that I'd be living in this one-bedroom apartment smoking rot-lung tobacco and wearing last year's turban? Come on! I'd be styling and smiling in a nice little villa in the Himalayan foothills; fountains, peacocks, Ram Dass in the guest suite, both a French chef and a weight-loss doctor on duty around the clock, so forth and so on. You get the picture. And another thing: I cannot accurately predict your future. We need to get that straight, too. I can't, no psychic can, and any that claim they can are swindlers.

A crystal ball, this is not, and you damn well ought to be glad about it. It isn't tea leaves or goat entrails, neither. What it is is a highly refined, highly efficient system of symbolic knowledge. The symbols that were carefully chose over the centuries speak directly to the deeper levels of the mind. The western mind. In the East, the *I Ching* cuts the very same mustard, but with a more, shall we say, intricate turn of the knife. Never mind that. The images here in the tarot will serve to open up and free certain aspects of your subconscious. Once the symbols have unlocked your subconscious, I can use my own psychic vision to read what the hell's going on in the recesses of your pumpkin. I read your subconscious thoughts — they're damn near as legible to me as *The Seattle Times* — but I don't read the future. *Comprende?*

He Said, Then I Said

Gus Edwards

Original monologue
Comic
F
20s
Contemporary

So, how does a girl go about getting a husband?

The man say to me, "You don't know nothing 'bout music." I say to him, "You don't know nothing 'bout womens." He say to me, "You don't know nothing 'bout life." So I says to him, "You don't know nothing 'bout nothing." So he say to me, "You wanna bet?" And I say, "Sure." Then he say, "What if I take you up to my room, lay you down on my bed, take all your clothes off a you, and then lay myself down on top of you, would you say that I know a little something about life then?" And I said, "I don't know, I'd have to see."

So that's what he did. He took me up to his room and all that other stuff. After it was over, he look at me and said, "Now will you admit I know a little something?" I told him that I thought he knowed a lot. He smiled and we started going out together regular. Now we is husband and wife with a baby on the way. So I guess it prove that he really did know something abut life.

You asked me and now I told you. The truth is I really don't know how a girl should go about getting a husband. I only know how I got mine.

Heading West

Philip Goulding

Play
Comic
F
20s
Contemporary

George, Edward, and Lizzie, emigrants from England, are passengers onboard a canal boat bound for Albany, N.Y. As they sit cramped in a storage room, they are suddenly interrupted by the entrance of Eliza, an ambitious, young would-be actress from the South.

(Eliza enters, theatrically.) You won't mind if I join you, I suppose? The sun is so low out there I declare a sensitive person might find themselves quite blinded. The glare! *(Introducing herself.)* Miss Dumbarton. Eliza. Shortened from Elizabeth by the grace of my dear mother. Well you've all found yourself a proper little hidie-hole here, though the air is somewhat stale if you'll forgive the observation. (…) No matter though, I say. (…) The world will forgive the route you traveled — if you dazzle with your entrance. (…) I'm an actress dears, though of course I'd be quite prepared to dance should the part properly require it. (…) let us draw on what talents we possess to entertain each other. That will at least perhaps make our trip seem shorter. Who'll go first? *(Silence.)* Then perhaps it had best be me. Now I ascertain you folks are all from England. So you'll be familiar with the works of Mr. Shakespeare? So, I shall perform one of his speeches — much edited and indeed improved by my fair hand. It is from a play no doubt you know, called *Cymbeline.* I shall need one of you to take a part. *(To George.)* If you wouldn't mind? You shall play the headless corpse of Cloten. The part simply requires of you that you remain supine.

(Performing.)
Yes, sir, to Milford-Haven; which is the way? —
I thank you. By yond bush? Pray, how far thither?
'Ods pittikins! can it be six mile yet? —
I have gone all night. 'Faith, I'll lie down and sleep.

But, soft! no bedfellow! O gods and goddesses!
(As if seeing the body [George] for the first time.)
Good faith,
I tremble stiff with fear: but if there be
Yet left in heaven as small a drop of pity
As a wren's eye, fear'd gods, a part of it!
A headless man! The garments of Posthumus!
(Eliza starts to manhandle George.)
I know the shape of's leg: this is his hand;
His foot Mercurial; his Martial thigh;
The brawns of Hercules: but his Jovial face
Murder in heaven? — How! — 'Tis gone.
O! Give colour to my pale cheek with thy blood,
That we the horrider may seem to those
Which chance to find us: O, my lord, my lord!

(She falls across George and is still for a moment. Then she stands, bows, takes the handkerchief from George's face and holds it to her nose.) Thank you, thank you, you really are most kind. And now if you'll excuse me, I feel I must take the air. Oh … I have further deduced by the way, that you are farmers. You are wondering how? Observation, my dear fellow travelers, is nine tenths of my craft. An artist must develop heightened senses if she is truly to convince. There also lingers in this compartment a powerful aroma, not unlike a beast of the field which has sadly passed away. *(She exits.)*

Hold Please

Annie Weisman

Play
Comic
F
20s
Contemporary

Jessica, a young office worker, has just been let go.

I thought her severance speech was a real cop out. Totally derivative. I can't believe I was so into Diana. She's not such hot shit as I thought. Actually, I'm psyched to be fired because now I can pursue my true interest. Hip-hop music. Listen to this.

> *(A rap.)*
> Think you can fuck with a bitch like me?
> Nigga PLEASE
> I'm the typa woman who could bring ya to yo knees
> I put you on hold
> Call you cold
> Open your mail
> And not break a nail
> Duplicate triplicate
> Bring it on
> I'm hip with it
> I'll staple you shut like Carni Wilson's belly
> Stop your attempt at talkin' like a militant Israeli
> I'll turn you over face down and fax you to Japan
> Then Scan your ass digitally and do it all again.

(She takes off her headphones.) I made it up. It's called Secretary Rap. I want to be the first rap artist with an exclusively clerical content. My name is gonna be White Out.

Hold Please

Annie Weisman

Play
Comic
F
20s
Contemporary

Erika is a receptionist in an office. She sits at a cubicle, has on a headset, and is visibly pregnant.

SolomonSanbornSachs can I help you? Hello Diana. How was jail? Yes everything's fine. Yes, I did. I was able to do that. Yes. Will do. Uh, Diana? I just had a question, I know we went over this at seminar but I just wanted to ask you about the new break policy. I wanted to ask when we can take breaks, you know, some of the Tier 2 people were wondering … *(Beat.)*

Oh good, cuz, you know, it's kind of hard, what with the baby and all, I mean my fiancé, Jai Sun, that's his whole name, Jai Sun, he's Korean, he wants me to stop working, but I don't think I need to stop until I have her. But I do need my breaks. *(Beat.)*

No, no, I'm sorry. Yes of course. I understand. Of course. *(Beat.)*

What? Oh, I said Korean. He's Korean. Koreans don't always dominate genetically. She could look like anyone in my family. We have strong strong genes. So … *(Beat.)*

No, they haven't told me that it's a girl. I just sort of know. You just do. Trust me. You just do. *(Beat.)*

Oh, no no I'm sorry. Of course I'll order your lunch for you.

An Ideal Husband

Oscar Wilde

Play
Comic
F
20s
Contemporary

Mabel Chiltern wishes Tommy would get it right.

Well, Tommy has proposed to me again. Tommy really does nothing but propose to me. He proposed to me last night in the music-room, when I was quite unprotected, as there was an elaborate trio going on. I didn't dare to make the smallest repartee, I need hardly tell you. If I had, it would have stopped the music at once. Musical people are so absurdly unreasonable. They always want one to be perfectly dumb at the very moment when one is longing to be absolutely deaf. Then he proposed to me in broad daylight this morning, in front of that dreadful statue of Achilles. Really, the things that go on in front of that work of art are quite appalling. The police should interfere. At luncheon I saw by the glare in his eye that he was going to propose again, and I just managed to check him in time by assuring him that I was a bimetallist. Fortunately I don't know what bimetallism means. And I don't believe anybody else does either. But the observation crushed Tommy for ten minutes. He looked quite shocked. And then Tommy is so annoying in the way he proposes. If he proposed at the top of his voice, I should not mind so much. That might produce some effect on the public. But he does it in a horrid confidential way. When Tommy wants to be romantic he talks to one just like a doctor. I am very fond of Tommy, but his methods of proposing are quite out of date. I wish, Gertrude, you would speak to him, and tell him that once a week is quite often enough to propose to any one, and that it should always be done in a manner that attracts some attention.

I'm the One that I Want

Margaret Cho

Essay
Comic
F
30+
Contemporary

Young Margaret discovers her love of the stage.

We had a Christmas pageant, and all the kids in the school were involved in a grand-finale number, singing a song for the Virgin Mary. The nuns kept saying during rehearsal, "When you see your parents out in the audience, don't wave. Do you hear me? Don't wave. If you wave, Jesus will be mad you messed up His song. Don't wave. If you wave, you will go to Hell. Don't wave. Don't wave."

When I went out on the stage, I saw my mom and my aunt in the crowd and they started to wave wildly! What could I do? I was having a moral dilemma. I kept seeing the nun's face in my mind's eye (Don't wave … don't wave …), but here was my mom and my aunt doing just that! I couldn't leave them hanging! In slow motion, my hand went up. It was like it wasn't even attached to me. I couldn't control it. It just started to move back and forth, and before I knew it, I was waving. My partner-in-crime, the boy of five, saw what I was doing and was not about to let me lead the revolution all by myself. He started to wave at his parents in the front row, who of course waved back, setting off another little kid and his parents and another and another. Pretty soon, the entire audience and all the kids on stage were waving at each other like we were on a float! Unfortunately, this was no parade. It was total Christmas-pageant anarchy and no one was even sure what to sing anymore and the nuns rushed us off the stage.

I thought I would be in trouble, but then when the pageant was over, we were let off for winter break, and by the time we got back, nobody remembered what happened or who waved first or anything. I was a bit disappointed that is was forgotten so easily, but I learned something very important that day: When you are on a stage and you wave, people wave back. This information would become very important for me later on.

The Importance of Being Earnest

Oscar Wilde

Play
Comic
F
45+
Contemporary

Lady Bracknell implores Algernon to dispense with petty annoyances in preparation for her upcoming fete.

Well, I must say, Algernon, that I think it is high time that Mr. Bunbury made up his mind whether he was going to live or die. This shilly-shallying with the question is absurd. Nor do I in any way approve of the modern sympathy with invalids. I consider it morbid. Illness of any kind is hardly a thing to be encouraged in others. Health is the primary duty of life. I am always telling that to your poor uncle, but he never seems to take much notice … as far as any improvement in his ailment goes. Well, Algernon, of course if you are obliged to be beside the bedside of Mr. Bunbury, I have nothing more to say. But I would be much obliged if you would ask Mr. Bunbury, from me, to be kind enough not to have a relapse on Saturday, for I rely on you to arrange my music for me. It is my last reception, and one wants something that will encourage conversation, particularly at the end of the season when every one has practically said whatever they had to say, which, in most cases, was probably not much.

Jesus Loves Good Christians

Adrienne Dawes

Play
Comic
F
20s
Contemporary

Marcy, seated on a bar stool in a pool of bright light, expounds on cigarettes, spirituality, and the meaning of life.

Oh my God, do you know how expensive vitamins are these days? According to Yellow, aka Mom, in the good ole sixties, you could buy your B12 and your acid for less than what my long distance costs me! Now, it's like fucking $10.50 for a bottle of Echinacea! It's soooo ridiculous!

(Marcy takes a long drag from her cigarette.) Aaah. God that's great. I love cigarettes. Whoever invented them has my undying respect and love. *(Pause.)* I know I know. I'm smoking the nails in my coffin or some shit. But I'm an adult and this is my fucking choice. I know the 'truth' about big tobacco and all that. Whatever. (…)I mean, people die. It's like a part of life or whatever. At least I'm aware you know? (…) *(Marcy's cell phone rings.)* Ooh. That'll be my cellie. Excuse me. It'll be just one second. *(Into the phone)* Yeah? Hey. *(Pause.)* So like what is up with Atticus? Is he like, even alive? He took what?!! Doesn't he know that citrus juice is like toxic after a fast? (…) You can't starve yourself for weeks and then go out for a steak. No. I know he's vegan. It was a joke! You're obviously still pissed about the meditation circle. *(Marcy makes an annoyed face at the audience.)* Well Maggie Moo Moo or whatever the fuck her name was is a total cunt. Like I know when I am in touch with my chi, man. Whatever. I've got to go. Bye.*(Marcy rolls her eyes as she puts away her phone. She lights another cigarette and stares into the audience.)*

Serendipity. She can be such a bitch sometimes. Ever since we started taking tarot class together she like choked on some nasty cosmic vibe or something. I'm sorry, what was the question again?

Oh, right … my thoughts on spirituality. OK well I used to be like totally up in the air. I could go either way, insanely religious or like totally atheist, and it would change on the hour! But the whole atheism thing wasn't working for me because I really feel like I need to have something to believe in, you know.

So I've been like seeking enlightenment everywhere! I took yoga classes, tai chi classes, a thousand meditation courses, but then I realized that that is not my path either. I mean like I grew up a pagan — and the whole nudity thing and being in touch with nature was OK, like when you're four, but I just grew out of it you know. And like I thought that the whole foreign, exotic religious experience was the way to go until recently, I began looking in some weird places and you know what I found?

Christianity. Yup. Good old Jesus, Mary, and Joseph. I found this cute little church down the street from my apartment. And I just started going. It's hard to understand what the hell the priest is saying, because the entire sermon is in Vietnamese, but I totally love the feeling I get sitting in the glow of sunlight filtered through stained glass. It just feels right.

Juno Agonistes

Dave DeChristopher

Play
Comic
F
50
Contemporary

Lotht in a book, the reader dreamth.

(Dreaming, perhaps with her eyes closed.) I am on an island — Bimini, probably — some exotic place whose name ends in a vowe l ... I am on a beach, sitting in a tower made all out of bamboo and thatch ... and I am watching all the natives frolic ... gambol; *la* la *la* la *la* ... on the beach, which is uniformly white like a blank piece of paper ... just like a blank piece of paper. I am the only tourist remaining on the island, the rest having been killed in a freak fire-baton accident at the Tiki Lounge, and so I am something of a goddess to the natives, with my alabaster skin and naturally orange hair. The natives are dark. The men wear Speedos that shrink to reveal ribbons of paler flesh on their legs and lower backs. I am supplied with the complete works of Anne Rice and Rita Mae and Helen Gurley Brown ... up there in the tower with me. And the natives lob up coconuts, so I seldom have recourse to venture down, except at night ... when I rendezvous with my native paramour, *(She lisps his name.)* Jose Luis. He is a bullfighter on sabbatical.

He is from a poor — no, a very wealthy Andalusian family that made its fortune from a line of tapestries to which it lent its name. The Tropic — no, the Troca ... lahara family, the Trocalahar family of Bar-thelona. Jo-thay Lu-eeth Trocalahara of Bar-thelona... Thpain. Sometimes he likes to surprise me, of an afternoon, in my tower. *(She gestures right.)* I can see him slinking this way. He is wearing his Speedo, and a bright yellow shirt. He has intuited that yellow is my favorite color, the dear. In answer to his laserlike stare, I throw down the rope ladder which will allow him to climb up. Does he control me? I fold back the corner of page 93 of *The Queen of the Damned* and wait for his ascent.

Kitchen Sink Drama

Andrew Biss

Play
Comic
F
40s-50s
Contemporary

Joy, a self-possessed, independent thinker, well kept in her late forties, is brutally forthright with her friend, Elaine.

Look, let me just say right now that I am not about to lecture you about things that you, as an informed adult, should already be patently aware of — i.e., that in this day and age you simply cannot go around having unprotected sex with anyone, anywhere, whenever you feel like it; not just because of the risk of HIV infection, which is, of course, by far the most serious, but for a whole host of other unsavory social calling cards, such as hepatitis, gonorrhea, herpes, and crabs, to name but a few; but also because, even at your age, Elaine, you cannot rule out the possibility of pregnancy, because I remember reading some story recently where this French woman conceived at the age of 97, or something hideous like that, and even though it was all done with test tubes and lasers and things, the fact is you're not 97 and stranger things have happened; but more to the point, I desperately hope that you're not one of those troglodytes that still likes to believe that HIV and AIDS are the sole realm of homosexuals and sub-Saharan Africans, because if you are, you're not only an idiot, you're one of those lamentable and all-too-common by-products of the so-called "information age" that only ever reads the "informative headline," never the full story. So ... rather than lecture you, I will simply say this: What are you doing about it?

L.A.

Cynthia Heimel

Essay
Comic
F
40+
Contemporary

If only this narrator could do something impulsive and irrevocable, she'd have a really good time — if she didn't die.

How can I regain my youth?

I'm not talking about looks. I think the most middle-aged thing you can do is worry about wrinkles and sags and whether you look your goddamned age or not. I mean I go to parties where the chief topic is face-lifts-or-not and it's boring, boring.

I'm talking about attitude. I am now a small-minded, frightened person. I worry about the future. I worry about my bank account. I worry about taxes and mortgages and my health and am plagued by my own morbid attention to the stultifying details of my mundane little life. My mind doesn't sweep, or soar, or do anything more interesting than fret at three A.M.

I can't blame my job, or my lover, or my children. I'm living in the small bare prison cell of middle age.

I went to Woodstock, for chrissakes! I slept in a field with cows! I peed in bushes cavalierly! I tried heroin! I went to Who concerts and pushed through the crowds to the front! I hitchhiked across this goddamned country! Twice! I was stranded in Indiana both times and I didn't care! I've had crabs!

Now sometimes I go to the movies. If I'm sure there won't be a big line. I am pathetic.

But every once in a while, usually when I'm driving along an unfamiliar road and a good song comes on the radio, I become drenched with the same feelings I had twenty years ago. I remember who I used to be. And my heart almost bursts and I believe that anything in the whole world is possible and I roll down all the windows of my car, turn the radio up, and sing at the top of my lungs.

I really am pathetic.

So is there any way to regain those feelings on a regular basis? Feelings of freedom, feelings that anything could happen? Or does my aging condemn me to becoming more narrow, more doddering, and more trivial with every passing day?

Lady Windermere's Fan

Oscar Wilde

Play
Comic
F
45+
Contemporary

Amid a crazy quilt of gossip, the Duchess of Berwick implores her sister-in-law to get Windermere out of town — for his own good, of course.

Ah, what indeed, dear? That is the point. He goes to see her continually, and stops for hours at a time, and while he is there she is not at home to any one. Not that many ladies call on her, dear, but she has a great many disreputable men friends — my own brother particularly, as I told you — and that is what makes it so dreadful about Windermere. We looked upon *him* as being such a model husband, but I am afraid there is no doubt about it. My dear nieces — you know the Saville girls, don't you? — such nice domestic creatures — plain, dreadfully plain, — but so good — well, they're always at the window doing fancy work, and making ugly things for the poor, which I think so useful of them in these dreadful socialistic days, and this terrible woman has taken a house in Curzon Street, right opposite them — such a respectable street, too! I don't know what we're coming to! And they tell me that Windermere goes there four and five times a week — they *see* him. They can't help it — and although they never talk scandal, they — well, of course — they remark on it to every-one. And the worst of it all is that I have been told that this woman has got a great deal of money out of somebody, for it seems that she came to London six months ago without anything at all to speak of, and now she has this charming house in Mayfair, drives her ponies in the Park every afternoon and all — well, all — since she has known poor dear Windermere. It's quite true, my dear. The whole of London knows about it. That is why I felt it was better to come and talk to you, and advise you to take Windermere away at once to Homburg or to Aix, where he'll have something to amuse him, and where you can watch him all day long. I assure you, my dear, that on several occasions after I was first married, I had to pretend to be very ill, and was obliged to drink the most unpleasant mineral waters, merely to get Berwick out of town. He was so extremely susceptible. Though I am bound to say he never gave away any large sums of money to anybody. He is far too high-principled for that!

Love Allways

Renee Taylor and Joseph Bologna

Play
Comic
F
45
Contemporary

Just before her daughter's Sweet Sixteen party, Mother offers the excited young woman some advice she could have gone her entire life without hearing.

I love it. And I love your enthusiasm. Stay that way. Always remember, it's no sin to be a woman. You were born that way; it wasn't your fault. This is embarrassing for me to talk about ... I don't know whether you've noticed or not, Gina, but your body's starting to change. When I was your age, I didn't notice because my mother wasn't as modern as I am; and I thought it was dirty to look at my body. Then when I was twenty-five, I was married and had two children already, so I was too busy to look. Now I'm 45 and it's too depressing to look. Why should I make myself sick? Now that you're sixteen, you have a big decision to make — what kind of woman are you going to be? There are only two kinds — good and not-so-good. Let me tell you the difference. A not-so-good woman is only interested in pleasure and hot times and living only for the moment, and a good woman isn't interested in anything. It's live and let live. You don't bother me — I don't bother you. I left your father alone during the day and he left me alone at night. That was the joy of womanhood for me. My life had meaning. I was a good homemaker, a vivacious hostess, and a shrewd shopper. And in return, your father tried to be decent. Of course, things aren't always just peaches and cream, but he never humiliated me in a large crowd. He never made me cry on my birthday. And he never ran off with a fan dancer behind my back. But when I had you, I was happy for one reason. I knew you would be part of a new generation of women, and these are my hopes for you. You can have what I didn't have. All the things girls of my generation could never hope to have — drive, ambition, talent, and self-respect. Today you can hold out for a man with all those qualities. Today you don't have to rush into marriage, because a woman can play football; she could lead a safari; she could climb a mountain. They're letting women in all the unions. So take advantage of it. You could be a bullfighter, a boxing referee, a stunt woman. Live dangerously! Try different things. Then after college, you'll become a teacher and get married. That's why you have children, so they'll have a little better life than you have. Oh, how I wish I had this talk with my mother when I was your age, today I might have a real identity. I might have been Mrs. Somebody. *(Mother opens the door, revealing a foggily lit limbo area; crying.)* Now, go downstairs to your party and grit your teeth and be a woman. It's all you have. Try to make it enough.

Madame Fickle

Thomas Durfey

Play
Comic
F
20s
Classic

Madame Fickle? Gee, wonder what her motivation is ...

Ha, ha, ha, ha —
That heaven should give man so proud a heart,
And yet so little knowledge — silly creature,
That talks, and laughs, and kisses oft that hand
That steals away its reason as if nature
Had played the traitor and seduced the sex,
Without the aid of destiny, or women.
Ah, with what pleasant ease
The bird may be ensnared — Set but a wanton look,
You catch whole coveys; nay there is magic
Pertaining to our sex, that draws 'em in,
Though in the long vacation — and by heaven,
I am resolved to work my sly deceits
Till my revenge is perfect — thus far I've done well,
And I'll persevere in the mystery,
Wheedle 'em to the snare with cunning plots;
Then bring it off with quick designing wit,
And quirks of dubious meaning. Turn and wind
Like fox, in a storm, to prey on all,
And yet be thought a saint — thus queen I'll sit,
And hell shall laugh to see a woman's wit.

Make Me Laugh, Clown

Laurie Notaro

Essay
Comic
F
20+
Contemporary

I'm afraid of clowns, I'm not ashamed of it.

(…) As an adult, I feel capable of defending myself against a mime with a jolt from a pretend stun gun or a very real sucker punch, and then running away very fast. Clowns, however, are a different story. They carry forces of the dark side with them, impenetrable by any act of retaliation. Pop a clown's balloon, and he'll only mutilate a bigger, nastier one. Lock him in the trunk of a car and he'll multiply himself into six more clowns. Spit on a clown and he'll only want to give you a hug. I hate clowns so much that I become immobile and hypnotized with fear as soon as I see one. I think all clowns should go to clown prison for all of the very real damage they've done to America's youth. They already like wearing stripes, so that's not a problem, and instead of ostrich meat, Sheriff Joe could just toss a pack of balloons and some cans of Silly String into the cell and say, "Here you go, creepy clowns. Make your own damn lunch!"

I'd rather take on a band of collection agents armed with copies of my credit history than mess with a clown. I'm convinced that there's a Clown Underground Network, and if you mess with one, you're messing with the whole hive. Word gets out. You're flagged, and if you're within a five-mile radius of a rainbow fright wig, it will seek you out and trail you relentlessly, trying to give you an imaginary flower. If you take it, you've succumbed to the Dark Clown Power. Before you know it, you'll find yourself trying to stuff seventeen of your friends into a Volkswagen Jetta that you've just slapped a multicolored clown pride bumper sticker on.

I don't understand what kind of person would want to be a clown, I really don't.

Martian Gothic

Don Nigro

Play
Comic
F
20s-30s
Contemporary

Sonia is a spokesperson for the nuclear power industry. She is talking to Nofsinger, her boss.

Sometimes I perform cute experiments with static electricity, make little Susie's hair stand on end, that sort of thing. I'm a graduate of Mr. Wizard. I also do a number about how plutonium is so safe you can hold it in the palm of your hand. It's true, you can, really, if you don't mind having a hole in your hand the size of a half dollar. That way you can cry into your hands and still see the men coming to take you away. *(She demonstrates briefly.)* I'm joking. (…). Trust me. Would you be paying me all this money if I didn't know what I was doing? (…) And let me assure you how perfectly safe you will be, living in the shadow of this wonderful nuclear power facility we've built in your area whether you liked it or not. You have no doubt heard from certain members of the lunatic fringe wild charges about the dangers of such plants. Now, I don't want to be tacky here — I'm not sure I could be tacky if I wanted to — but most of these people have even less functioning brain matter than my sister, and they're not nearly as good looking. (…)

Mimiamboi

Herodas

Play
Comic
F
50+
Classic

Older, wiser Gyllis councils Metriche to get off her duff, get over her man Madris, and go get her some lovin'. In this version, the translator uses southern and southwestern regional American accents to capture the Ionic Greek dialect.

Well, now, dearie, how long's it going to be?
This solitary life, this single blessedness,
this makin' the bed creak all by yourself ... how long?
Mandris, that man of yours, it's been ten months
since he set out for Egypt, and nary a letter,
not even an alpha, from Mandris' fine white hand.
He has for-got-ten you; he drinks to forget,
he gulps his wine these days from a fine new goblet
(not like some weaker vessels I could mention) ...
and nacherly so:
Why, he's in the Land where Love lives —
Egypt the Gorgeous! Birthplace and homeland of, oh,
jest everythin there is in this world! You name it:
Riches, an' Physical fitness, an' Power, an' Peace,
an' Pee-rades, an' Pageants, an' Terribly Serious Thinkers,
an' Spring All Year, an' Glory, an' Fine Young Studs,
and the Holy Holy Home of the Sacred Siblings,
an' a king who's top-drawer, first-class, A-double-plus,
an' the Great State University, home of the Muses,
an' Wine, an' evry blessin you could want,
an' WIMMIN!
             Yes, wimmin!
                    So many, the sky's ashamed
to boast about her double handful of stars ...
And lookers?

Not mentionin' any names, but all
them goddesses that trotted over to Ida to enter
that beauty contest, well, they better look out.
(An' I better look out, too. No offense, up there!)
Anyway, what do you mean by spendin' these
best years of your life jist keeping your chair warm? Huh?
You stick with that, and before you know it, you're *old*
yes, OLD, and your bloomtime's swallowed up in ashes!

You need new vistas. Set yourself some bran-new goals …
jist for two-three days: Like Joy,
                              Or Love …
Might take a look-see at somebody new. Male.
You know what they say:
                              A ship that's hitched
to only one single anchor goes down with all hands.

New York Water

Sam Bobrick

Play
Comic
F
20s-30s
Contemporary

Linda tells an ardent suitor named Albert why any relation-ship with him could not possibly work out.

You see, Albert, I am an ultra, altruistic, dedicated Liberal, and you, it seems, you are a lowlife, scum-sucking, piece-of-vomit Conservative. Oh, Albert, had we only been of different races or religions, I know it would have been semi-smooth sailing for us all the way. But there are too many issues to overcome. Fair housing, the homeless, equal opportunity employment, taxing the piss out of the rich … Slowly, our lives will become entangled with these unsolvable problems, and whatever love and passion there was between us will go right down the crapper.

It will never work, Albert. We are who we are. I've learned long ago that it isn't us that molds the city. It's the city that molds us. The necessity to be it, to breathe it. The necessity to eat at this year's restaurant, to see this year's musical … to permit ourselves to live in vermin-infested, high-rent dumps, fearing constantly for our lives. The degradation of having to journey day in and day out, in the stinking, reeking, over-crowded public transportation, filled with distraught, miserable, short-tempered, Gothamites, frightened to death to make eye contact with one another, each trying to justify this horrendous existence just for the priv-ilege of being able to walk into the intimidating Metropolitan Museum two or three days a year and laud the fact that they don't have museums like this in Peoria. It doesn't make sense anymore, Albert. That I know. But it is our heritage and duty to pass it on.

Once Upon a Mattress

Jay Thompson, Marshall Barer, Dean Fuller

Play
Comic
F
40+
Contemporary

Queen Aggriavain bombards the young prince with a barrage of motherspeak.

Well then how can you say such a thing, I want you to get married, how many times have I said to you I want you to get married. Only this morning I was saying to your father: I said Sextimus, I want that boy to get married, it just isn't normal for a boy that age to stay single I said after all he is a prince, don't forget that, and he is next in line for the throne. I mean we're not exactly the oldest people in the world but on the other hand we're not going to live forever and I would just feel much better, much easier, and much more relaxed in my mind if I knew that that boy were married, settled and set and that's absolutely verbatim, exactly what I said to your father this morning. Of course he didn't say anything, he never does, but you know him just as well as I do and I don't have to tell you how impossible he is. If he makes me miserable and makes me suffer then I'll just have to put up with it, but I will not allow it to effect my son's attitude toward him or me. He may be a mean, stupid, dreadful, selfish, rotten man, but he is your father and I want you to respect him. After all there is only one person who really cares about you and really worries about your health, your happiness and your future and that's exactly what I'm talking about right now, your future and I want to make myself absolutely clear that I want you to get married, but I don't want you to marry just anyone. Marriage is a lifetime partnership and I wouldn't want my little boy to make the same mistake I did and wind up miserable the way I did. You are a prince, and you must marry someone suitable, someone who's good enough, smart enough, and fine enough for my good, nice, sweet, beautiful baby boy. And of course she has to be a princess, I mean a real princess. A genuine bonafide princess, just as I was. And that is what you want, isn't it? Someone like me? Of course you do. Oh God if I were only twenty years younger. Just remember this, you must trust me.

Picasso at the Lapin Agile

Steve Martin

Play
Comic
F
19
Contemporary

Suzanne explains her penchant for artists — in this case, Picasso.

I … it was about two weeks ago. I was walking down the street one afternoon and I turned up the stairs into my flat and I looked back and he was there, framed in the doorway, looking up at me. I couldn't see his face, because the light came in from behind him and he was in shadow, and he said "I am Picasso." And I said, "Well, so what?" And then he said he wasn't sure yet, but he thinks that it means something in the future to be Picasso. He said that occasionally there is a Picasso, and he happens to be him. He said the twentieth century has to start somewhere and why not now. Then he said, "May I approach you," and I said, "OK." He walked upstairs and picked up my wrist and turned it over and took his fingernail and scratched deeply on the back of my hand. In a second, in red, the image of a dove appeared. Then I thought, "Why is it that someone who wants me can hang around for months, and I even like him, but I'm not going to sleep with him; but someone else says the right thing and I'm on my back, not knowing what hit me?" (…)

So the next thing I know, he's inside the apartment and I said, "What do you want?" and he said he wanted my hair, he wanted my neck, my knees, my feet. He wanted his eyes on my eyes, his chest on my chest. He wanted the chairs in the room, the notepaper on the table; he wanted the paint from the walls. He wanted to consume me until there was nothing left. He said he wanted deliverance, and that I would be his savior. And he was speaking Spanish, which didn't hurt, I'll tell you. Well, at that point, the word *no* became like a Polish village; *(They look at her, waiting, then.)* unpronounceable. *(Proudly.)* I held out for seconds! Frankly, I didn't enjoy it that much 'cause it was kinda quick. (…)

So, then, as I was sitting there half dressed, he picked up a drinking glass, of which I have two, and looked at me through the bottom. He kept point it at me and turning it in his hand like a kaleidoscope. And he said, "Even though you're refracted, you're still you." I didn't ask. Then he said he had to be somewhere, and I thought, "Sure," and he left.

Pius and Me

Joe Byers

Play
Comic
F
32
Contemporary

Kitty Flynn Devanney tells a story that may or may not have taken place in the mid-1950s in a monastery in Portugal.

And guess what happens next: Who do you think we run into, right there in the courtyard of the monastery, wearing white pajamas and a white bathrobe and little white bedroom slippers? The Pope! His Holiness! The Holy Father of the whole Holy Catholic and Apostolic Church! Right there in front of me! Just like that, just coming out of the bathroom — because guess what? The Pope has body functions, too. Just like everyone else. Anyway, I start bawling, the minute I see him. You cry when you see the Pope, you know. At least Catholics do. And I pee myself a little, too. Just a drop. Meeting the Pope's like taking a shower in ice-cold holy water: I was as drunk as a skid row skunk — but suddenly I'm completely sober. So's everybody. Every single monk. Except some ass with an accordion, who's so bombed by this point he couldn't tell the Pope from Mamie Eisenhower. He's singing this idiotic drinking song that's got about a hundred choruses and all these farting noises in it — And the Pope just glares, dead silent.

We're busted, I'm sure, and excommunicated, too. But then wha'd'ya think: The Pope is whistling along! And next he's snapping his fingers. Tapping his toes. He's swaying. He's moving toward me … taking my hand … hand on my waist — and we're dancing! Mary Catherine Flynn from Fifty-seventh and Kingsessing is hoofing it up on the patio with the sainted Embodiment of Christ on Earth! This is sublime. This is rapture. This is heaven and I didn't have to die to get here.(…)

Polly Honeycombe

George Colman

Play
Comic
F
Teen
Classic

Polly, taking life's cues from novels, behaves in life as if she lived in one.

Novels, Nursee, novels! A novel is the only thing to teach a girl life, and the way of the world, and elegant fancies, and love to the end of the chapter. (…) Do you think, Nursee, I should have had such a good notion of love so early, if I had not read novels? — Did I not make a conquest of Mr. Scribble in a single night at dancing? But my cross papa will hardly ever let me go out. — And then I know life as well as if I had been in the beau monde all my days. I can tell the nature of a masquerade as well as I had been at twenty. I long for a mobbing-scene with Mrs. Scribble to the two-shilling gallery, or a snug party a little way out of town, in a post-chaise — and then I have such a head full of intrigues and contrivances! Oh, Nursee a novel is the only thing! I tell you what, Nursee. I'll marry Mrs. Scribble, and not marry Mr. Ledger, whether Papa and Mama choose it or no. And how do you think I'll contrive it? (…) I intend to elope! Yes, run away, to be sure. Why, there's nothing in that, you know. Every girl elopes, when her parents are obstinant and ill-natured about marrying her. It was just so with Betsy Thompson, and Sally Wilkins, and Clarinda, and Leonora in the *History of Dick Careless,* and Julia, in *The Adventures of Tom Ramble* and fifty others — did not they all elope? And so will I, too. I have as much right to elope as they had, for I have as much love and as much spirit as the best of them.

Pretzels and Longing

Linda Eisenstein

Play
Comic
F
25+
Contemporary

Maddie, on a bar stool, bemoans the sorry state of urban dating.

So I say to her, Rina, spare me the lecture. If you think it's sooo easy, meeting people in places other than bars, I am all ears! But you can skip the usual suspects. Because I have been down the list, girlfriend, I have tried the recommended places, many times, but they just don't seem to produce. (…) At the cafe bookstore, for example, if you make a precise looping maneuver between the Ani di Franco CD's and the Naiad mystery shelf, you can sometimes almost make eye contact with someone. As long as you don't stop too close to the Andrea Dworkin tracts. And people tell me that when a certain silky-haired folk singer in torn jeans plays there, the picking up is very good, but I almost always get the dates mixed up and instead it's some macho poet making rhymed couplets about carburetors. Not that I have anything AGAINST carburetors or fan belts, especially when they're being replaced by some hunky Queen Latifah look-alike in coveralls, but I draw the line at bad slam poetry. No, the cafe bookstore is out. And their mocha latte, puhlease, if I'm going to pay four dollars and eighty-two cents for a beverage it had better have more in it than whipped cream!

(She raises her glass, toasts her unseen companion.) Then Rina goes, why don't you go to the Center, I never see you there; it's a womyn-friendly alcohol-free space.

Oh, peachy, I say, that's a real upper, it's nothing but wall-to-wall support groups. Who wants to hear your own problems reflected back at you times 10. No it's not, she says, there are social events, too, and I say, Get real! Country line dancing, no THANK you, it's like bad aerobics with hay stuck in your teeth, even the Chlamydia Support Circle looks good next to that. All those groups, they're as demoralizing as therapy, only without the relief or the attention.

At least in a bar you get pretzels with your longing.

The Provoked Wife

Sir John Vanbrugh

Play
Comic
F
20s
Classic

Lady Brute provokes herself into behaving badly.

The surly puppy! Yet he's a fool for't. For hitherto he has been no monster, but who knows how far he may provoke me. I never loved him, yet I have been ever true to him, and that in spite of all the attacks of art and nature upon poor weak women's heart in favor of a tempting love. Methinks so noble a defense as I have made should be rewarded with a better usage. Or who can tell? Perhaps a good part of what I suffer from my husband may be a judgment upon me for my cruelty to my lover. Lord, with what pleasure could I indulge that thought, were there but a possibility of finding arguments to make it good. And how do I know but there may? Let me see. What opposes? My matrimonial vow? Why, what did I vow? I think I promised to be true to my husband. Well, and he promised to be kind to me. But he hasn't kept his word. Why then, I'm absolved from mine. Aye, that seems clear to me. The argument's good between the king and the people, why not between the husband and the wife? O, but that condition was not expressed. No matter, 'twas understood. Well, by all I see, if I argue the matter a little longer with myself, I han't find so many bugbears in the way as I thought I should. Lord, what fine notions of virtue do we women take up upon the credit of old foolish philosophers. Virtue's it own reward, virtue's this, virtue's that. Virtue's an ass...

The Rivals

Richard Brinsley Sheridan

Play
Comic
F
40+
Classic

While expressing her disdain for educating women "too much," Mrs. Malaprop makes the case against herself by mangling the English language.

Observe me, Sir Anthony — I would by no means wish a daughter of mine to be a progeny of learning. I don't think so much learning becomes a young woman. For instance — I would never let her meddle with Greek or Hebrew, or Algebra or Simony, or Fluxions, or Paradoxes, or such inflammatory branches of learning; nor will it be necessary for her to handle any of your mathematical, astronomical, diabolical instruments; but, Sir Anthony, I would send her, at nine years old, to a boarding school, in order to learn a little ingenuity and artifice. Then sir, she should have supercilious knowledge in accounts; and as she grew up, I would have her instructed in geometry, that she might know something of the contagious countries. Above all, she should not mispronounce or misspell words as our young ladies of the present day constantly do. This, Sir Anthony, is what I would have a woman know; and I don't think there is a superstitious article in it.

Ruling Passion

G. L. Horton

Play
Comic
F
50s
Contemporary

At the monthly gathering of the Duxbury Ladies Literary Society (founded in 1905), President Eleanor Holmes Witherspoon, costumed as Eleanor Roosevelt, calls the meeting to order.

Ladies! Ladies! Uh, thank you, Clara. Clara, that's enough! Stop the music, will you?

There now.

Hasn't this been fun? Like our July 4th parade! Now you might as well go back to your seats, girls, because we're not going to announce the winners until you're all settled. In the meantime, I want to take this opportunity to thank Leena Carlson, our program chairman. Stand up and take a bow, Leena, whoever you are! There she is! She's that Marilyn Monroe! *(ELEANOR leads the audience in applause.)*

Now there's been a nasty rumor going the rounds that Leena dreamed up this whole fantasy party so that she could show off that red sequin dress . The way I heard it, she paid four hundred dollars for it to wear on her anniversary, but when Bill saw that it was cut down to her appendix practically, he wouldn't let her out of the house in it! Not anywhere there's men! Not true, not a word of it. I happen to know that she borrowed this contest idea from the Chicopee Women's Guild, and the dress she got from her sister-in-law, who used to sing with a rock band. So shame on you gossip, whoever you are! (…)

I'm supposed to tell all you Jackie O's that the judges thought you were all very good, especially that one in the pink, with the blood on her stockings: but the ground rules that Dr.Engles set down for us say very plainly that our heroine can't be anybody who's married to somebody who's more famous than she is. So I'm afraid we have to rule that Jack was, no matter what he said to the French that time! Of course that eliminates you Nancy Reagans, too — and I suppose it'd even apply to me, if I were out there in the running! I knew I never should have married that upstart Franklin! (...)

Ruling Passion

G. L. Horton

Play
Comic
F
30s
Contemporary

This month, at the Duxbury Ladies Literary Society, they are saluting (and dressing up as) famous women in history.

So you're asking: "Why did I get up as Cleopatra?" Am I supposed to be honest? I mean, look at me! *(She does a bump and grind.)* Right!

OK, OK. It was after little Leroy was born. I decided I'd have to do something if I wanted to have a shape that I could do something with, if you get what I mean. Leroy was my third one, and he was a Caesarean. Which is kind of a coincidence, cause Cleopatra had a son Caesarion who was a Caesarean. Who was named after what isn't too clear, cause his Daddy Julius was Caesar, you know, and he . . .

Anyway, I signed up for this belly dance class, and I was great. I mean a real natural. The teacher talked me into buying this fourteen-carat costume cause I was so good, and she even got me a couple of gigs at that roadhouse out on Route #2. I used the name Sherrina, and I was what you would call a popular attraction. Even though what I made hardly paid for the sitter — to make the money, you have to encourage the guys to stuff money in your bra, and go out on "dates" and all like that, and I'm not that kind, — at least not when I'm married. Still, I got a real charge out of it, and shimming does wonders for the figure, you know? Then one of the guys my husband works with saw me out there and started mouthing off about it. So that was that, and I was stuck with this gold-plated shimmy suit. Then when I heard about this contest. I asked myself, "Who could I wear it and be?" My husband was OK with it, cause we're nothing but women here, and he suggested the Queen of Sheba. He teaches Bible class.

But I thought of Cleopatra. (…)

As for her being an example for women today? That Cleopatra was one girl who really had it. Think rock star, think mega-celeb! I mean, her word was law, at least in Egypt. Diss her, and you were dead meat. She was a high priestess, too, and a goddess — she could lock a guy away in hell for eternity. Plus, she slept with even bigger celebs — the most powerful guys in the whole world. They had it all, and there they were, pumping it into her! Think of the charge she must've got out of that, enough electricity there to illuminate the blooming Nile! Fireworks and a neon barge! She never had to pretend to be Goody Two-shoes either, like our gracious first lady. Bathing her ass in asses' milk, drinking pearls. As for her suicide — some people may cringe at that asp business. But I think it's the last word in class. She knew the party was over. So she wasn't about to stick around and let anybody make a fool out of her. That asp is class, man. A class act.

Screaming Violet

Deborah Grimberg

Play
Comic
F
40s
Contemporary

Fran, a working-class woman, discovers her moisturizer has side effects.

I was browsing through *Women's Weekly* the other night. Every morning before breakfast, Princess Diana, God bless her soul, used to get up and tap on her face like it was a piano. It brought all the blood to the surface of her skin and filled in the lines. That's it! From tomorrow onwards as God is my witness, I vow to forgo my bowl of Special K and will go at it like Beethoven pounding out his fifth symphony. Actually I have a wonderful moisturizer. I love love love it! Wrinkles be gone! It does make my face rather shiny though. I keep catching women checking their makeup in my forehead. The other day the checkout girl in Safeway asked if I wanted paper or plastic and then proceeded to rub the lipstick off her front tooth. And last summer I was responsible for the mass slaughter of several thousand green fly. It happened one very hot, muggy day in August. I had slapped on several layers of greasy, sticky sun block because I had to walk down the road to buy the paper, when a herd of green fly swarmed in blissful ignorance into the polluted mass on my face. Within seconds I had become a terrifying version of those sticky insect traps George hangs inside our greenhouse. My face had become an indiscriminate killer. It was a gruesome sight and one I was unaware of until I walked into the shop. The woman looked up from behind the cash desk, screamed and then walked very slowly backwards into the staff bathroom without taking her eyes off me. Oh it was embarrassing! I haven't bought the newspaper from that shop again. But I have to say the roses in North London are blossoming this year. I'm certain it's because there are far less green fly.

Seating and Other Arrangements

Barbara Kahn

Play
Comic
F
20s
Contemporary

At a Long Island railroad station, Amy plops down on the bench next to Gina, an unfortunate total stranger.

Are you going to New York? That was stupid. Of course, you are or you wouldn't be sitting *here*. You'd be sitting over *there*. Unless, of course, you came here just to sit — maybe cool off 'cause you live around here and just had a huge fight with your boyfriend or husband — oh, but then you wouldn't have luggage with you — unless, of course it was a really big fight and you decided to leave for good or at least for awhile to teach him a lesson . . . I'm sorry. It's just that I'm terrified of long train rides by myself. I imagine that I'll fall asleep and when I wake up, we'll be in some small town that looks exactly like where I grew up, only nobody there will recognize me, not even my family. I know what you're thinking. "That was on *The Twilight Zone*. Everyone saw that episode. That's a direct steal." You're right. Only I didn't steal it. I saw it on television when I was eight, and I ran all through the house, asking everyone — my parents, my sisters, everyone — "Who am I?!" And they just laughed. Except my father. He leaned over, pulled my ears and said, "You're Minnie Mouse." And I screamed — a real howl — and I ran into the living room and climbed up on the sofa so I could look in the mirror to make sure I was still me. It's funny how things like that stay with you. So, do you live here or there? I mean, are you coming or going? I'm sorry. I wasn't trying to pry. It's just that *I've* done all the talking, and I didn't want you to think that I'm the kind of person who just likes to talk about *herself*. I'm not. I'm really interested in other people. And I'm a pretty good judge of people, too. Like right now. I'll bet I can guess what you're thinking. You're probably saying to yourself, "Why didn't I bring the Walkman?" or "How can I casually open my suitcase to get to the book in there without appearing totally rude?" No. I'm wrong. What you're really wishing is that the station would be open late like it used to be, so you could go to the restroom and then sit down somewhere else when you come out. It's OK. Really. I understand.

Smashing

Brooke Berman

Play
Comic
F
20s
Contemporary

Clea goes on about Madonna to Nicky, a night clerk in a fleabag London hotel where she and her friend Abby are staying.

NO TALENT? How can you say no talent!? I'm going to pretend you didn't say that. What about postmodernism and appropriations? Gender iconography in the late twentieth century? She didn't just do yoga. She did Kabbalah. She did burning crosses. She vogued.

And she did Evita. The Argentines freaked, but controversy feeds her whole deal.

The tabloids say, Madonna: Has She Gone Too Far? But I say, Is there such a thing? Is there such a thing when you are Madonna and the world is your oyster because you never let anyone tell you who to be or what to do or what your limitations are? No. No. There is no such thing. Get into the groove. Open your heart. Express yourself, don't repress yourself. Music makes the people come together. The Bourgeoisie and the Rebel.

Yes. We have a lot in common. Her and me, not you and me though maybe you and me have a lot in common too, I don't know yet, but her and me, she and I, we have a bond. We're both from Detroit. And that's not all. The list goes on and on.

Loads of very creative people come from Detroit. Like Madonna and Diana Ross and me. And cars are made there. So you see. We are deeply connected by our Root Geography. And, OK this sounds fantastic but it's true — we were tigers in another life and she scratched my eyes out. It's OK though.

Three Weeks After Marriage

Samuel Foote

> **Play**
> **Comic**
> **F**
> **40+**
> **Classic**

Blind to her own abusive behavior, Lady Racket condemns another woman for the same thing. And you know that any monologue beginning with "Oh la!" has got to have something going for it.

Oh la! I am quite fatigued. I can hardly move. Why don't you help me, you barbarous man? (…) Dear me, this glove! Why don't you help me off with my glove? Pshaw! You awkward thing, let it alone! You aren't fit to be about my person. I might as well not be married, for any use you are of. Reach me a chair. You have no compassion for me. I am so glad to sit down! Why do you drag me to routs? You know I hate them. I'm out of humor. I lost all my money. I hate gaming. It almost metamorphoses a woman into fury. Do you know that I was frighted at myself several times tonight? I had a huge oath at the very tip of my tongue. (…) I caught myself at it, but I bit my lips and so I did not disgrace myself. And then I was crammed up in a corner of the room with such a strange party at a whist table, looking at black and red spots. Did you mind them? There was that strange, unaccountable woman, Mrs. Nightshade. She behaves so strangely to her husband, a poor, inoffensive good-natured, good sort of a good-for-nothing kind of man, but she so teased him — "How could you play that card? Ah, you have a head and so has pin! You are a numbskull, you know are — Madam, he has the poorest head in the world, he does not know what he is about — you know you don't — Ah, fie! I am ashamed of you." Why don't you hand me upstairs? Oh, I am so tired. (…) You awkward thing, let me alone!

True Story

Allison Williams

Play
Comic
F
17
Contemporary

The Geek, alone on prom night, considers watching TV.

Nobody gets surprised by TV.

Except when Marcy was babysitting and she was trying to get the Play-Doh out of the back of the wide screen TV where the little monsters put it when she was microwaving their Tater Tots —

Tater Tots? What the heck is a tater tot? Only in the U.S.A. would we eat food that has been — and I'm quoting from the package — extruded. No wonder the American race is doomed.

Oh. Me and Marcy's simple test to see if you're overweight. Stand by a window. Let your arms hang naturally by your sides. Look out the window. Are you in America? Then you're overweight! *(Cracks self up.)*

OK, *microwaving* their *Tater Tots* and the kids shoved Play-Doh, red Play-Doh, in the back of the TV and there was also a terrible rainstorm. And when Marcy was trying to pry it out — with a *plastic* knife, she's not stupid — lightning struck the tree next to the house! Which fell on the house which put out all lights all power to the entire neighborhood but one of the kids was reading with a flashlight so the neighbors saw the light and assumed all was well so that by the time the parents made it home (they had to wait for the storm it was so bad) Marcy had suffocated under the weight of the TV, which fell on her when the tree shook the house.

We were all pretty surprised by that TV.

True Story

Allison Williams

Play
Comic
F
25+
Contemporary

A Northwest Flight attendant as alpha female — others need not apply.

Sir, I'm afraid you're going to have to check that. No, I'm afraid it clearly does not fit into the overhead compartment. Sir, your Business Class ticket does not entitle you to an entire overhead compartment. Sir, I'm afraid I can't ask them to do that. Yes, I know you paid more than they did, but you do get a slightly wider seat and — I'm going to have to ask you to return to Business Class, Sir. Give me the bag! Drop it! Drop it! Now, sit!

Welcome to Northwest flight 19 with direct service from Minneapolis to Tokyo Narita. (…) Our flight today will take approximately twelve hours and fifteen minutes.

(…) Now, I'm going to ask that you put down your newspapers, books, magazines, and knitting, take out the information card from the seat pocket in front of you, and follow along as we detail the safety features of this Boeing 757.

All of you.

Now.

32-B, just because you're in the middle does not mean I can't see you!

That's better.

There are eight emergency exits on this aircraft. Please take a moment to locate the exit nearest you, remembering that the closest exit may be behind you.

The closest exit may be behind you.

I do not see heads turning!

In the event the cabin loses pressure, oxygen masks will drop from the ceiling. Place the mask over your mouth and nose, secure by pulling on the straps, and breathe normally. If you're traveling with small children, secure your own mask first.

And let the little beggars fend for themselves.

In the unlikely event of a water landing, your seat cushion can be used as a floatation device.

Did you know that no commercial aircraft has ever made a water landing in one piece? That means the chances you'll use your seat cushion are, well, none. However, if you do survive the impact — which is about the same as hitting a concrete parking lot — there may be a seat cushion floating near you. Place your arms through the straps and kick-paddle your way to shore. Which should only be about four hundred miles. In the event you reach the afterlife of your choice, there will be an entrance quiz on the safety features of this aircraft.

Ladies and gentlemen, I'm afraid the captain has just informed me that we have indeed missed the takeoff window and we are now fifty-seventh in line for takeoff. Since we have pulled away from the terminal, we are going to ask that all passengers remain seated, with their seat belts firmly fastened, for the approximately three hours and forty-one minutes remaining to takeoff. We'll be distributing cookies, juice, and water, to the passengers who can correctly identify the flight attendant serving them. People with more than one carry-on, children with video games that beep, and men who ask me if I want to join the Mile High Club will get nothing.

Thank you for flying with Northwest Airlines, and let me say that I'm especially pleased to be sharing this, my very last flight with Northwest, with such a lovely group of passengers. I will not be returning to Minneapolis with you, but instead will be joining the White Path Temple in Shiga Prefecture to begin my studies as a Buddhist nun.

Please remember, my vow of nonviolence does not begin until we land in Tokyo.

Enjoy your flight.

U.S. Drag

Gina Gionfriddo

> **Play**
> **Comic**
> **F**
> **20s**
> **Contemporary**

Allison is obsessed with coming up with a scheme to make as much money as fast as she can, with as little effort as possible.

I cried this morning. I was reading a book about JonBenet Ramsey. . . . This girl who babysat her a few times got $5,000 from a magazine. The lady who cleaned her house got $20,000. These magazines wrote just enormous checks to anyone who ever knew her. *(Pause.)* It just seems like you can get a lot of money if you're in the right place when something really bad happens. Like that woman who went to the hospital for a Caesarean and got a crazy doctor who carved his initials in her belly. She got millions of dollars. Just for having a scar. I would have a scar. It just seems unfair. Monica Lewinsky got to go to the Oscars and she wasn't in any movies! I want to go to the Oscars! There are all these people who are not as good-looking and smart as me and they are getting money and getting on TV and they didn't do anything except be nearby when something bad happened. It isn't fair! It just isn't fair! I don't have any money and nobody knows who I am! I want to do nothing and get money and have people know who I am! *(Silence.)* I'm sorry. It just . . . came out of me. I'm sorry.

vagina dentate

Clay McLeod Chapman

Short story
Comic
F
30s-40s
Contemporary

Sheldon, I think it's time you and I had a talk. Could you spare a moment for your mother, please? I've dedicated the last seventeen years of my life to raising you, all I'm asking for is five simple minutes. Three minutes. Two. I can help you get ready while we talk. Look at you. You can't leave the house looking like that. Your cumberbund is on all crooked. Let me at least fix your tie. Hold still for me. (…)

My little boy's not so little anymore, is he? You've grown up so fast. Seems like only yesterday you were tossing rocks at Nancy Lamia. Now you're taking her to prom. You believed she had cooties as a kid — which might not be so far from the truth, Sheldon. Don't disregard those adolescent instincts so soon, Son. They're there for a reason, Sweetie. Believe me. They just might end up saving your life one day. Because the older you get, the more your attitude toward girls will change. You might find yourself feeling curious over the opposite sex, which is fine. It's perfectly natural. (…) What a mother like me has to worry over, though — is that you be a thinking man. (…) Just because you're suddenly having these feelings for your female friends, doesn't mean you need to act upon them. Because once you're in over your head, honey — it becomes very difficult to find your way back up to the surface. Adults call cooties STDs, Sweetie. They don't go away once you grow up. We just gave them a better name. A young man like yourself has to worry over sexually transmitted diseases, unwanted pregnancies — or worse. Much worse. You can't just go around copulating with just anybody these days, sticking your little hoo-hoo inside some stranger's ha-ha. That's dangerous.

I know you're nervous about tonight, Honey. I am, too. It's not every night you have your senior prom. You want to mark the occasion. Make it special. But Sheldon, please — listen to me. Before you do anything you might regret for the rest of your life, there's something I need to share with you. Hidden inside every vagina is a little snapping turtle, tucked up, way up above the vulva. It lives within the uterus, just waiting for some young boy like yourself to come sticking his little man inside its home. As soon as you've slipped far enough in, can you imagine what happens? Can you? That snapper peaks out from its shell and bites right through you. Nips your kipper clear off. Before you can even think about pulling out, crack — it's too late. You've got no little man left. (…) They don't grow back once they're gone, honey. You'll be a eunuch for the rest of your life.

Just be a thinking man, Sheldon. That's all I ask. When prom's finally wound down and you're driving Nancy home, just remember what we talked about tonight — OK? Could you do that for your mother? Please, Sweetie?

You look so handsome, I think I'm going to cry. My little boy's become a man. (…)

Now let me get a picture of you before you go.

Valhalla

Paul Rudnick

Play
Comic
F
20s
Contemporary

Sally's engaged to be married, but she has strong feelings for another man, her fiancé's best friend, who's doing time in prison.

Some people think that I had — feelings for James Avery, but that is just not true. But before he — went away, he always used to say something which I will never forget. He would say that he'd been studying the situation since kindergarten, and that he'd made lists and charts and held a personal pageant, and that he had finally determined that I was the prettiest girl in all of Dainesville. And he said that the prettiest girl can give people hope, and brighten their day, and wasn't that just a wonderful thing to say? Especially for a delinquent? And ever since then, whenever I look in the mirror, I see Eleanor Roosevelt. Only, of course, pretty. I mean, Mrs. Roosevelt works so hard, trying to help the poor and the downtrodden, but can you imagine how much more she could do, if she were pretty? And of course, there's also inner beauty, but inner beauty is tricky, because you can't prove it. I've thought a lot about this, you know, about beauty and goodness, and all the different religions? I mean, Buddha is chubby — face it. And Confucius was all old and scraggly and, I imagine, single. And you're not even allowed to have a picture of Mohammed — was it the teeth? I don't know. But Jesus is always really pretty, with perfect skin and shiny hair, it's like God was saying, look to Jesus, for tips. But I know there's that German man, Adolf Hitler, and he thinks that everyone should be perfect and blue-eyed and beautiful, but that's wrong too, because then who would be the best friends? And I don't want to be vain or prideful, so I always remember what James said, in one of his letters. He said that there are only two things which really matter in life: youth and beauty.

Valhalla

Paul Rudnick

Play
Comic
F
40s-50s
Contemporary

*Tour guide Natalie Kippelbaum, from Long Island, wears a
gold lamé jogging suit, a leopard-skin fannypack, a majorly
highlighted hairdo, oversize eyeglasses, and hot-pink and
silver lamé sneakers.*

Hi! I'm Natalie Kippelbaum, and welcome to Temple Beth Shalom's
Whirlwind European Adventure Castles of Bavaria Plus Wine Tasting
and Wienerschnitzel Potpourri Tour. Yes. The bus will be here any second, so let's get started. And I know what you're thinking, you're going,
Natalie, from Long Island, what are you doing with Ludwig? Well, three
years ago, I hit bottom. First, my husband, he dies, from lung cancer.
Fun. But then, my daughter, she loses her job. Then my son, Debbie —
enough said. And I'm in my Hyundai, and I'm about to drive off a
bridge, like in a Hyundai that's even necessary, and then — I hear music.
Gorgeous, operatic music. You know — NPR. And I think, where is that
music coming from, I mean, where was it born? So I get on a plane, and
I'm here. And the minute I step into that grotto — I'm happy. I'm high.
And today we're going to see something even more beautiful, because in
1883, Ludwig decided to build his copy of Versailles. *(She pronounces
the word with a thick Long Island accent — "Versoy.")* That's right —
Versailles.

The Way of the World

William Congreve

Play
Comic
F
20s
Classic

Millament agrees to marry Mirabell — under these conditions ...

Good Mirabell, don't let us be familiar or fond, nor kiss before folks, like my Lady Fadler and Sir Francis; nor go to Hyde Park together the first Sunday in a new chariot, to provoke eyes and whispers; And then never to be seen there together again; as if we were proud of one another the first week and asham'd of one another for ever after. Let us never visit together, nor go to a play together. But let us be very strange and well bred: let us be as strange as if we had been married a great while; and as well bred as if we were not marri'd at all. (...) Liberty to pay and receive visits to and from whom I please, to write and receive Letters, without interrogatories or wry faces on your part. To wear what I please; and choose conversations only to my own taste; to have no obligation upon me to converse with wits that I don't like, because they are your acquaintance; or to be intimate with fools, because they may be your relations. Come to dinner when I please, dine in my dressing room when I'm out of humor without giving a reason. To have my closet inviolate; to be sole-empress of my tea-table, which you must never presume to approach without first asking leave. And lastly, where ever I am, you shall always knock at the door before you come in. These Articles subscrib'd, if I continue to endure you a little longer, I may by degrees dwindle into a Wife.

What's Rennet?

Sonia Fehér

Poem
Comic
F
40s
Contemporary

So, if your parents are hippies, like, does that make you one, too?

So we're drinking coffee and everyone's talking about TV shows from when we were kids — *Lost in Space, Good Times, Underdog* — and I don't know any of them, because WE didn't have a TV until I was ten and I find myself explaining again what it was like when I was a kid, just like I explain the names of my friends: Eliam, Xylon, Huckleberry Krishna, and Sylvan Rahma — his brother.

And they're looking at me, I'd say you know that look, but you probably *don't* — the one in which everyone steps closer or farther away because maybe I'm an ALIEN and the English I'm speaking has jumbled into a language they just can't understand.

In times like these, I feel like the ugly duckling following the wrong crowd and so what that I've been a vegetarian since birth — because my parents were meditating with a guru and believed the animals' souls got in the way of reaching the ethereal plane.

Am I a hippie because my parents were concerned when I got my first tattoo and now I'd never be able to hide from the FBI? Does it make me a hippie that after my first lesbian sleepover, my mom asked why I was so tired and my sister answered for me, in a dimly lit, otherwise sedate restaurant, "She's buttering the other side of the bread, Ma."

I could never understand the fear of coming out considering Mom asked, "Did you like it?" as my stepfather said, "She's taking after you, dear." I guess I'd been prepared for this every time my mom put out condoms for high school parties — to make sure we were having safe sex — or gave me Kama Sutra oils in my stocking at Christmas.

It all made sense to me until I left for college and my friends had been raised with church on Sundays instead of meditation meetings and mantras.

So my house has bells on the door to keep away evil spirits. So I think this plane is hell and I can only get out by improving my karma. What's wrong with full moons and sacred circles? Maybe we wouldn't need so many sleeping pills if everyone hung a dream catcher above the bed. (…)

OK, I'm a hippie. But I hate the Grateful Dead. I've never worn patchouli. I shave my legs and my armpits by choice. I drive a Japanese car. I have cable TV. And sometimes, when I really have no choice, I pretend that the cheese I'm eating isn't bound with cow intestines and that my leather jacket grew on a tree.

Where's My Money

John Patrick Shanley

> **Play**
> **Comic**
> **F**
> **20s-30s**
> **Contemporary**

Natalie, an accountant, is having a drink with Celeste, an out-of-work actress and old friend whom she hasn't seen in a while. While Celeste is something of a dreamy, ditzy romantic, Natalie is no-nonsense, all business.

All right, I'll just lay it out for you. (…) It's time for you to stop office-temping and doing Romeo's girlfriend in acting class and get a bona fide fucking job. It's two plus two. You have to drop the lollipop and pick up the car keys! Next issue. Kenny. This may sound tough, but I'm going to say it anyway. Kenny's your best bet. . . .

Yes, he's a loser. But what are you at this point? Maybe together you can pull your car out of the ditch and make some miles down the road. I know where you're at, Celeste. There's a million women like you. You don't want to look at your story 'cause you don't like your story, so you just close your eyes and tell yourself a fucking fairy tale. (…) The truth of your life is like a bad magazine. Boring story, lousy pictures. Which brings me to your mysterious, exciting, cheeseball stud. Who smacks you around because he's afraid of his wife. Do I even have to talk about this rodent? A married violent scumbug who slips you a Saturday Night Special for what? Valentines Day? You can't look at what this guy pegged the minute he smelled that thrift-shop essential oil you use for perfume. You're a pushover. Is this your notebook? . . .

What have you been writing? . . .

Poetry. You're going down in flames. Unless you get it together, they are going to pass you around like chicken wings.

White Elephants

Jane Martin

Play
Comic
F
20+
Contemporary

Giselle is welcoming the new arrivals to Heaven where, it turns out, all the wealthy white Republicans go.

Good morning, and to all our cherubim and seraphim inductees, we would like to welcome you to Republican Heaven. If you'll all just flap over here and hover for a minute or two, I'll give you the introductory. First of all, you'll be pleased to know liberals don't go to heaven; it's music we want around here — not whining. You may have noticed there are not black people here; that's not racism — that's interior design. Actually, we do have African Americans, but anyone who is black and Republican has to be so crazy we keep them in a separate space. This isn't about Apartheid; this is about mental health. After the period of acclimatization, many of you will become guardian angels. This means you look after people on earth who make more than $250,000 annually. They'll be up here with us eventually, and we don't want them damaged or scratched. Obviously, most harpists come from high-income families, plus seeing as we're here together for eternity, we prefer you've gone to cotillion. And, as we say here in Heaven, it's about manners, manners, manners.

Why Women Need Big, Strong, Rich Men

Lisa Marie Heitman

Essay
Comic
F
30+
Contemporary

I don't know if I'm getting older or if high heels are getting higher, but if this fashion trend continues, I'm going to need to marry a member of the World Wrestling Federation. Let me explain. When my heels were 1.5 five inches high (seventh grade?) I was attracted to the quiet, intellectual type. However, now that my heels are 5-plus inches high, I'm only dating men that can bench-press twice my body weight. Why? Because, if there's ever a fire at the mall, I won't be able to move fast enough to save myself. I'll die. I need to be with someone strong enough to carry me to safety. Right about now, I'm thinking Barney Rubble is hot.

I have other handicaps, too — handicaps that force me to exclude the Peewee Herman's in my life. It's not that I want to eliminate sensitive, compassionate men. It's just that my nails are so long that I can't even open a can of soda by myself. I need a man with brute strength, not a man who will give me a pep talk when I'm fighting to open a pad of butter at a five-star restaurant. Do you know my hair is flammable? It's true. I can't get anywhere near an open flame. I'm afraid.

I need to be kept at room temperature, too. This is why I must date a rich man, one that can afford to drive an air-conditioned car and live in an air-conditioned home. If I get too hot, the air pressure in my pump-up bra might get too high — I could blow a breast! On the other hand, if I get too cold, my breasts may appear much smaller. This makes me unhappy. It makes my date unhappy, too. Additionally, if I get either too hot or too cold, my mascara clumps and I can't open my eyes completely. This can't be safe.

Winner of the National Book Award

Jincy Willett

Novel
Comic
F
40+
Contemporary

Dork's mother actually named her Dork. What a dork!

Mother was always sending us out into the world with instructions on how to win friends, and it didn't take us long to figure out that she didn't have a clue. "When the other children call you by ... that name," my mother said to me (after the night Father explained to her about dorks), "you just look right at them and say, 'Do you know that when you call me ... that name ... you hurt my feelings very badly?' Just look right at them and say it straight. You'll be very surprised at how quickly they change their ways."

Mike Callahan, my nemesis, couldn't believe his luck. "Awwwww. I hurt your feelings. You gonna cry? HEY EVERYBODY! THE DORK IS GONNA CRY, BECAUSE HER *FEELINGS* ARE HURT..."

"All right. When they call you ... that name ... just answer to it, as though it didn't bother you at all. Don't give them the satisfaction of reacting to it. You'll spoil their fun, and in no time they'll get tired of teasing you and begin calling you by the right name."

Again I delighted the bullies and their sycophants, who, after two weeks, showed no sighs of boredom with their magical ability to make me acknowledge at their every whim that my name was a dirty word. In one way Mother was right: They did tire of using "dork" to get my weird, obliging attention, and soon they began calling me "asshole."

"When they call you ... that word," advised my dear mother, "you just look right at them and say, in a voice clear as a bell, "Sticks and stones may break my bones, but names will hurt me not.'"

The next day Mike Callahan called out to me in the playground during recess. "Asshole! Yeah, you! Watcha doin', Asshole?"

I walked over and stood in front of him and his semicircle of snorting admirers, and I said to him in a voice clear as a bell, looking right at him, "You are a stupid, ugly little boy, and an Irish Catholic, and when you grow up you'll belong to a labor union and live in a tenement and have ten kids and turn into a big stupid drunk."

Mike Callahan looked as if he had been axed in the center of his forehead. His face turned red and his eyes filled and he was apparently struck dumb. This was one of the happiest moments of my life.

A Woman of No Importance

Oscar Wilde

Play
Comic
F
30s
Contemporary

Mrs. Allonby has specific ideas about what constitutes The Ideal Man.

The Ideal Man! Oh, the Ideal Man should talk to us as if we were god-desses, and treat us as if we were children. He should refuse all our serious requests, and gratify every one of our whims. He should encourage us to have caprices, and forbid us to have missions. He should always say much more than he means, and always mean much more than he says. He should never run down other pretty women. That would show he had no taste, or make one suspect that he had too much. No; he should be nice about them all, but say that somehow they don't attract him. If we ask him a question about anything, he should give us an answer all about ourselves. He should invariably praise us for whatever qualities he knows we haven't got. But he should be pitiless, quite pitiless, in reproaching us for the virtues that we have never dreamed of possessing. He should never believe that we know the use of useful things. That would be unforgivable. But he should shower on us everything we don't want. He should persistently compromise us in public, and treat us with absolute respect when we are alone. And yet he should be always ready to have a perfectly terrible scene, whenever we want one, and to become miserable, absolutely miserable, at a moment's notice, and to overwhelm us with just reproaches in less than twenty minutes, and to be positively violent at the end of half an hour, and to leave us for ever at a quarter to eight, when we have to go and dress for dinner. And when, after that, one has seen him for really the last time, and he has refused to take back the little things he has given one, and promised never to communicate with one again, or to write one any foolish letters, he should be perfectly brokenhearted, and telegraph to one all day long, and send one little notes every half-hour by a private hansom, and dine quite alone at the club, so that everyone should know how unhappy he was. And after a whole dreadful week, during which one has gone about everywhere with one's husband, just to show how absolutely lonely one was, he may be given a third last parting, in the evening, and then, if his conduct has been quite irreproachable, and one has behaved really badly to him, he should be allowed to admit that he has been entirely in the wrong, and when he has admitted that, it becomes a woman's duty to forgive, and one can do it all over again from the beginning, with variations.

FEMALE
Seriocomic Monologues

Angels in America

Tony Kushner

Play
Seriocomic
F
50s
Contemporary

Hannah is Joe's Mormon mother. After her son calls her in the middle of the night to tell her that he is gay, she sells her house, flies to New York City, and gets lost. She is talking to a homeless woman on the streets.

Excuse me? I said excuse me? Can you tell me where I am? Is this Brooklyn? Do you know of a Pineapple Street? Is there some sort of bus or train or . . . ?

I'm lost, I just arrived from Salt Lake City. I took the bus that I was told to take and I got off — well it was the very last stop, so I had to get off, and I asked the driver was this Brooklyn, and he nodded yes but he was from one of those foreign countries where they think it's good manners to nod at everything even if you have no idea what it is you're nodding at, and in truth I think he spoke no English at all, which I think would make him ineligible for employment on public transportation. The public being English-speaking mostly. Do you speak English?

I was supposed to be met at the air port by my son. He didn't show and I don't wait more than three and three-quarters hours for anyone. I should have been patient, I guess . . . Is this Brooklyn?

The Bronx!?! Well how in the name of Heaven did I get to the Bronx, when the bus driver said . . . ? Can you just tell me where I . . . ? I don't know what you're . . .

Shut up. Please. Now I want you to stop jabbering for a minute, and pull your wits together and tell me how to get to Brooklyn. Because you know! And you are going to tell me! Because there is no one else around to tell me and I am wet and cold and I am very angry! So I am sorry you're psychotic but just make the effort! Take a deep breath! DO IT! *(Inhales with the crazy woman.)* That's good. Now exhale. *(Exhales with the crazy woman.)* Good. Now. How do I get to Brooklyn?

Blown Away

Lisa Walker

Essay
Seriocomic
F
Teens
Contemporary

After committing a murder to save her relationship with Charlie, Carol gets a bad case of the "if onlies."

We were in a bad mood. Charlie's dad wouldn't let him use the car, and we were both broke. Charlie never had money, because he spent his going to all the movies. My allowance had been suspended, because I slightly rearranged a letter my principal sent to my parents. He wrote them I had skipped school, and I slipped the words "ahead in" between "skipped" and "school." So what.

So anyway, you know how couples can get to taking things out on each other. Charlie and me, we'd been doing that for a while. Then there we were one day, just peckin' at each other, and it made me remember hearing how if you commit murder together, it's like the tightest thing you can do. So that's what we did. And now Charlie won't let me out of his sight, because he's afraid I'm unaware of my impact.

Some days I look back at what it was that got me to where I am right now. In an abandoned farmhouse with nothing but snakes and grasshoppers for outside company … except when Charlie eats the grasshoppers … just to make me mad. I try not to have regrets, but sometimes, usually when I'm hungry, I find myself wondering things. Like if Charlie had only been born with red hair. Then I never would have like him to begin with, and I wouldn't be here now. Or if I really had been skipped ahead in school, then I would have been too old to go out with Charlie, and I wouldn't be here now. What if Charlie's dad had given him the car that day? Then Charlie would have gone on about with his regular plan, which was to two-time me with Ariel Stillwater. If only murder wasn't a love cure.

The Brothers

Kathleen Collins

> **Play**
> **Seriocomic**
> **F**
> **27**
> **Contemporary**

At the top of the stairs in her home, Lena tries to prod her young husband from his bed, where he has remained since deciding his track career was over. She eventually sits and wonders aloud how she ended up with this guy.

I'm applying all my culinary skills to this meal, the least you could do is make it to the table. I'm asking you to walk a few hundred feet, crawl, if you have to, I don't give a damn how you get there . . . speak up, god-damn it, or else write me one of your notes . . . what's no use? What are you always crying about . . . you think you're the Prophet, Nelson the Negro Prophet leading his people through the Valley of Tears! Just get up and go to work! We could have a few drinks, a few kids, *then* you can die. Honest to God, Nelson, I'm gonna get old, how much longer you want to play this Job scenario . . . the whole damn race is Job, what makes you so special.

This could get bleak . . . me, a bottle of gin and a looney-tune col-ored man. Colored or not, I'm not built for despair . . . must be a high yaller impulse to keep things light. I'm descended from too long a line of sallow women who taught me to look stylish and shut my mouth . . . wear my skin like it was a precious jewel . . . wait for choice negro offer-ings to line up at my door. I was supposed to have myself a doctor, or a lawyer, why I chose Nelson is more than I can explain.

The Brothers

Kathleen Collins

Play
Seriocomic
F
30s
Contemporary

Marietta imagines this dialogue with Franklin, with whom she used to love gossiping.

Who? Lawrence and that sleek little Fieldsboro thing? That story's as clear as a bell, those two will most certainly marry, they have the same greedy high-pitched dreams . . . who else was there . . . old Bus? With a girl? *(Slightly embarrassed.)* . . . oh I guess I was hoping he'd ask me . . .never mind. Did you meet Rosie . . . I could have told you that, they don't like anyone who's brown. Tell me what Lillie was wearing . . . that sounds exactly like her with her "Frankie Boy" this and her "Frankie Boy" that, really, Franklin, that's a truly embarrassing name, only Lillie would think of such a thing out of her wide-ranging memory for the coy, romantic touch she calls you her Frankie Boy. *(She shakes her head disapprovingly.)* . . . I do like her, she's kind, even funny in a sweet, poetic way . . . and she certainly loves you . . . I don't know, that's her idea of romance, a singular adoration fixed forever on one chosen soul . . . I don't know love everlasting fits the hard Edwards mold for dreams. *(Suddenly uptight.)* I'm not jealous and I won't be teased like already I'm some spinster fool . . . who . . . oh . . . Bus . . . don't call him that, Franklin, he's nice and he has a good job with the railroad, too . . . you mock anyone who comes near my door . . . *(Mimicking him.)* "He's not good enough for you Marietta, not that scrawny negro fool." *(They laugh.)* . . . you're as bad as Pop . . . will he be among the first of the coloreds, he'd say . . . *(They begin to giggle.)* . . . poor Bus, I bet you scared him away. . . well, he is a little slow . . . and he's got big feet . . . *(They are really giggling now.)* And as Pop would say, he's a bit too colored for me. *(Laughing explodes out of her.)* . . . oh, Franklin, there's nobody but nobody I ever laugh with like you.

The Bubbly Black Girl Sheds Her Chameleon Skin

Kirsten Childs

Play
Seriocomic
F
20s
Contemporary

It's the early 1960s, and Viveca has decided to try to be as "white" as she can be. Here she is auditioning for a black role in a play, trying to "act black."

(She says angrily:) Hey, Director Bob! What do you think this is, camouflage? *(Getting control.)* OK — don't panic — black, black, black, black, black, black . . . lots of black people in the South . . . OK . . . southern accent, but not like a slave . . . 'cause if I do get this job, I don't want to offend the few black people that are gonna be in the audience any more than I have to . . . who has a southern accent? *(Thinks hard. Suddenly, an inspirational flash.)* Foghorn Leghorn! Ah say. Ah say. Ah say — Fawg Hone Lehg Hone! Yeah, that's good, but pitch it higher! *(High southern voice.)* Fawg Hone Lehg Hone! *(Snapping her fingers; in her own voice:)* That's it! I'm ready! . . . *(À la Foghorn Leghorn/Butterfly McQueen/Amos 'n Andy:)* Now Ah'm scramblin' — Ah say, Ah say, Ah say — Ah'm ska-ram-bull-in' up some eggs for buh-reck- fus', and here come — Ah say, Ah say, Ah say — here come mah boyfriend Ros-co, jes' a bu-rak-in' down mah kitchen doah. "Whu's wrong witcha, Ros-co?" Ah in — kwhy — red. "Wrong wit' me?" he says — *(Pointing accusingly, as if she is Rosco.)* "You da one — Ah say. Ah say, you da one dass' been lyin' down wit' da dawg-ketch-ah!" Well, Ah neither cared for his tone of voice, nor his bad breff all up in mah face — hunh! So Ah picked up — Ah say, Ah say, Ah say — Ah picked up da iron skillet from off'n da stove and, well — uh — anybody — Ah say, Ah say, Ah say anybody care for some eggs and buh-rains-ah?! *(Winks again, then grins expectantly into the audience.)* How was that?

Careless Vows

Marivaux

> **Play**
> **Seriocomic**
> **F**
> **18**
> **Classic**

I know these gentlemen a little. I notice that men are kind only when they are lovers. Their heart is the prettiest thing in the world, so long as hope keeps them in suspense. Submissive, respectful, attentive — for the little love you show them, your self-love is enchanted, it is quite delightfully served, quite surfeited with pleasure. And everything works for us — folly, arrogance, disdain, capriciousness, impertinence — everything we do is right, it's the law. We reign as tyrants, and our idolaters are always on their knees. But once you marry them, once the goddess becomes human, their idolatry ends at the point where our kindness begins. As soon as they're happy, they no longer deserve to be, the ungrateful wretches! (…)

Well, I shall sort that out, and the role of goddess will not bore me, gentlemen, I can assure you! What — young and lovely as I am, I should have less than six months in a husband's eyes before my face is thrown on the scrap-heap? From being eighteen, it would suddenly jump to fifty? No, thank you very much! That would be murder. My face will only age with time, and become uglier only by lasting longer. I want my face to belong only to me, I want nobody to see what I do with it, I want it to depend only on me. If I were married, it wouldn't be my face any longer, it would belong to my husband — he would abandon it, it would not please him, and he would forbid it from pleasing anybody else. I would rather not have one. No, Lisette, I have no desire to be a flirt, but there are moments when your heart speaks to you and you are very glad to have your eyes free. So, no more discussion. Take my letter to Damis, and let whoever wants line up under the yoke of matrimony.

Dear John

Steve Somkin

Play
Seriocomic
F
20+
Contemporary

*Rena crumples the letter she had been writing and picks up
a tape recorder. She stops and restarts the machine as her
thoughts and feelings shift.*

Dear John. Of course I know, Edward that your name is not John, but
this is a "Dear John" letter. I never want to see you again … I guess you
got that message when I threw your clothes into the hall … I must tell
you something. It's somewhat embarrassing … I hope as unpleasant for
you as it was for me … We two knew how to share pain, didn't we, my
darling? Let's do it one last time.

Steady, Rena, girl … woman. Deep breath. Let it flow. I cannot put
my words directly onto paper. On paper they look like translations from
a foreign language, grammatical exercises, contrived and stupid and
without feeling. I wish I were looking into your eyes, whispering in your
ear, holding you close in our bed. I never want to see you again.

Edward, I mean John, remember how we itched and scratched during our last week together? You said, "People who bitch together itch
together?" It was crabs. My doctor caught one of little things and gave
me a special shampoo to get rid of them. You must get treated too. If you
don't, God knows how many women will scratch away at their crotches …
needlessly. I don't resent your wanting other women, that's natural, I suppose … crabs. Cancer the Crab. Our relationship was like a malignant
cancer.

Stupid, stupid letter. He's over. Finished.

Dear Edward, comma. I am writing to inform you that in all prob-
ability you have a minor venereal infection called crab lice, full stop. This
is easily treated with a medication you can get from a pharmacy, full
stop. It is advisable that you inform anyone with whom you have had
sexual contact of the same, full stop. Eileen is probably … Full stop!
Eileen!

Dear Shithead, Eileen and her erotic acrobatics …! You have a serious venereal disease that, unless treated, will render you impotent for life. It's probably too late already, but with immediate medical attention … I would telephone to tell you, but I can't bear the sound of your voice!!

Over. It's over. Over. Over.

Dear Edward, I wonder, will there be any emotions I will not first have tasted while living with you? Trying to forget you is like trying to deny my heart. I regret that the end was so ugly. Perhaps it was the only way. Perhaps at a distance the good times will seem better for the contrast. Edward, you radiate success. But I need a man for whom I'm a companion, not merely one of his successes. Sincerely yours … With more than a little love, Rena. P.S., Check with your doctor about the itching, it's not serious. Good-bye, Eddie.

Empire Falls

Richard Russo

Novel
Seriocomic
F
15
Contemporary

*In Russo's Pulitzer Prize–winning novel, Tick is talking to her
father, owner of a small-town diner. Tick finds high school
and her ex-boyfriend, Zack, to be equally confusing institu-
tions.*

I made a new friend. (…) Candace Burke. She's in my art class. She stole
an Exacto knife today. (…) I guess she didn't have one. She starts all her
sentences with oh-my-God-oh-my-God. Like, "Oh-my-God-oh-my-
God, you're even skinnier than last year." (…) She's fat like I'm skinny. (…)
She lives with her mother and her mother's new boyfriend down on
Water Street. She says we've got a lot in common. I think she's in love
with Zack. She keeps saying, "'Oh-my-God-oh-my-God, he's *so* good-
looking. How can you stand it? I mean, like he was yours, and now he's
not."

(…) Here's the thing. Now that I'm not with Zack anymore, I don't
have a single friend.

(…) Oh-my-god-oh-my-god! I forgot Candace!

Hey for Honesty

Thomas Randolph

Play
Seriocomic
F
40+
Classical

Anus blames Plutus, god of wealth, for the female misfortune of aging and loss of sexual attributes. Too bad he can't blame Plutus for his name.

Heigho! Methinks I am sick with lying alone last night. Well, I will scratch out the eyes of this same rascally Plutus, god of wealth, that has undone me. Alas! poor woman, since the shop of Plutus, his eyes has been open, what abundance of misery has befallen thee! Now the young gallant will no longer kiss thee nor embrace thee; but thou, poor widow, must lie comfortless in a solitary pair of sheets, having nothing to cover thee but the lecherous rug and the bawdy blankets. O, that I were young again! How it comforts me to remember the death of my maidenhead! Alas! poor woman they condemn old age, as if our lechery was out of date. They say we are cold: methinks that thought should make 'um take compassion of us, and lie with us — if not for love, for charity. They say we are dry: so much the more capable of Cupid's fire; which young wenches, like green wood, smoke before they flame. They say we are old: why, the, experience makes us more expert. They tell us our lips are wrinkled: why that in kissing makes the sweeter titillation. They swear we have no teeth: why, then, they need not fear biting. Well, if our lease of lechery be out, yet methinks we might purchase a night-labourer for his day's wages. I will be revenged of this same Plutus, that wrongs the orphans, and is so uncharitable to the widows.

Hot Flashes, Cold Horses

David Lavine

Play
Seriocomic
F
50
Contemporary

Duchess, an aging porn star desperately fighting for a come-back is in town filming the Encyclovideo Erotica, a video compendium of sexual positions that will hopefully put her back on the map. She speaks with an accent of indeterminate origin.

My men wanted here because the scenes are beautiful, but who've woulded thought to make the Encyclovideo in *this* place? Cheap, they said. (…)Ago years ago — but not so many as you will think — things were a tat successfuller and I would not to have arrive here out for project such as this, but — oh! — this is my perhaps return ticket at the life I once had, you know? The Encyclovideo! And me — internationally acclaimed by my performances! *(With a wink.)* If you view those types of films, and I feel certain you do on opportunity you will surely know me, I believe it. You know me (…) Oh, I fear my cosmetics smushy after so crying and fretting. Too tired. Baggies under eyes, eh? (…) They report that I fight poorly uphill age and decay, but no, no, no, I know naked the truth. Silly things. "The Duchess's flesh hangs like my nana's stockings outside on the drying line." "The Duchess has seen more rides than the Derby of Kentucky, put the old nag onto a pasture." "Why'd the Duchess screw a lightbulb? Because there's no one left who wanted to do so with her!" *(She breaks down and sobs.)* Forgive me again. (…)Eh. There is no utility to cry atop milky spills, yes? The most we will do is do our most and continue with life . . . *(She digs in her purse again and pulls out a vial of pills.)* I am too distressed, too distressed, too distressed. *(She pops several and dry-swallows them. To Mindy.)* Can I offer you a coping device? Sedavil? They are prescription strength, but sometimes you must eat several before enjoying appropriate relief. *(She gives him a few and he happily downs them.)* So good, yes? (…) I am still young, you know, I am still womanly, my bones are still strong and unhollow, no? The men don't know any nothing! Knock, knock! Stone like I am! *(Sotto again.)* But one day my ovarians are soon like sun-dried tomatoes. And we in this your free nation do not only accept and make salad with these like my old motherland — we medicate!

Johnnieruth

Becky Birtha

Short story
Seriocomic
F
Teen
Contemporary

Weighing the benefits of being alone, versus being with some dumb ol' boy.

Last summer, I used to ride with the boys a lot. Sometimes eight or ten of us'd just go cruising around the streets together. All of a sudden my mama decide she don't want me to do that no more. She say I'm too old to be spending so much time with boys. (That's what they tell you half the time, and the other half the time they worried cause you ain't interested in spending more time with boys. Don't make much sense.) She want me to have some girlfriends, but I never seem to fit in with none of the things the girls doing. I used to think I fit in more with the boys.

But I seen how Mama might be right, for once. I didn't like the way the boys was starting to talk about girls sometimes. Talking about what some girl be like from the neck on down, and talking all up underneath somebody clothes and all. Even though I wasn't really friends with none of the girls, I still didn't like it. So now I mostly just ride around by myself. And Mama don't like that neither — you just can't please her.

This boy that live around the corner on North Street, Kenny Henderson, started asking me one time if I don't ever be lonely, cause he always see me by myself. He say don't I ever think I'd like to have me somebody special to go places with and stuff. Like I'd pick him if I did! Made me wanna laugh in his face. I do be lonely, a lotta times, but I don't tell nobody. And I ain't met nobody yet that I'd really rather be with than be by myself. But I will someday. When I find that special place where everybody different, I'm gonna find somebody there I can be friends with. And it ain't gonna be no dumb boy.

Johnnieruth

Becky Birtha

Short story
Seriocomic
F
Teen
Contemporary

An unexpected discovery swings Johnnieruth from shock to "carpe diem."

This one night when I was sitting over in that corner where I always be at, there was this lady standing right near my bench. She mostly had her back turned to me and she didn't know I was there, but I could see her real good. She had on this shiny purple shirt and about a million silver bracelets. I kinda liked the way she look. Sorta exotic, like she maybe come from California or one of the islands. I mean she had class — standing there posing with her arms folded. She walk away a little bit. Then turn around and walk back again. Like she waiting for somebody.

Then I spotted this dude coming over. I spied him all the way cross the Plaza. Looking real fine. Got on a three-piece suit. One of them little caps sitting on a angle. Look like leather. He coming straight over to this lady I'm watching and then she seen him too and she start to smile, but she don't move till he get right up next to her. And then I'm gonna look away, cause I can't stand to watch nobody hugging and kissing on each other but all of a sudden I see it ain't no dude at all. It's another lady.

Now I can't stop looking. (. . .) I really know I oughtta turn away, but I can't. And I know they gonna see me when they finally open they eyes. And they do.

They both kinda gasp and back up, like I'm the monster that just rose up outta the deep. And then I guess they can see I'm only a girl, and they look at one another — and start to laugh! Then they just turn around and start to walk away like it wasn't nothing at all. But right before they gone, they both look around again, and see I still ain't got my eye muscles and my jaw muscles working right again yet. And the one lady wink at me. And the other one say, "Catch you later." (. . .)

I wheel on outta the Plaza and I'm just concentrating on getting up my speed. Cause I can't figure out what to think. Them two women kissing and then, when they get caught, just laughing abut it. And here I'm laughing too for no reason at all. I'm sailing down the boulevard laughing like a lunatic, and then I'm singing at the top of my lungs.

Kimberly Akimbo

David Lindsay-Abaire

Play
Seriocomic
F
30s
Contemporary

*Pattie is the mother of a teenaged girl who has a disease
that causes her to prematurely age. Pattie is pregnant again,
and she speaks into a tape recorder with a message for her
unborn child.*

OK, here we go. Let's see. Record. (…) Hello, darling. This is your
mother speaking. You're in my belly right now. And sometimes you kick
me. Isn't that precious? Now listen to me, sweetheart, because people are
going to tell you awful things about me. You mustn't believe them.
People lie. They are hateful cocksuckers. All of them. People spread
vicious lies when victims aren't around to defend themselves. Remember
that when I'm dead and someone tells you I was a demonic bitch. You
stand up and tell them that I was sweet and funny and you have the tapes
to prove it. It's always good to have evidence, sweetheart. That's why I'm
making you this tape. I wanna make sure you get your info from the
horse's mouth, because I'm gonna drop dead any second. *(Beat.)* On the
bright side, I just got my carpal tunnel operation, so I may be able to use
my hands before I die. We'll see. All those years in Secaucus took their
toll. Sixteen years I worked in the Sunshine Cupcake Factory, pumping
cream into those Ding-Dong knockoffs. Sixteen years of squeezing that
Goddamn cream gun. That's one of the reasons we moved away from
Secaucus. Not the main reason, but one of them. *(Beat.)* I hope I get to
breast-feed.

Lady Windermere's Fan

Oscar Wilde

Play
Seriocomic
F
40s
Classic

Mrs. Erlynne sought through blackmail to claim her daughter, whom she abandoned as a baby, and who has now married a rich man. When her scheme backfires, Mrs. Erlynne admits her defeat.

[I've come here] to bid good-bye to my dear daughter, of course. Oh, don't imagine I am going to have a pathetic scene with her, weep on her neck and tell her who I am, and all that kind of thing. I have no ambition to play the part of a mother. Only once in my life have I known a mother's feelings. That was last night. They were terrible — they made me suffer — they made me suffer too much. For twenty years, as you say, I have lived childless, — I want to live childless still. *(Hiding her feelings with a trivial laugh.)* Besides, my dear Windermere, how on earth could I pose as a mother with a grown-up daughter? Margaret is twenty-one, and I have never admitted that I am more than twenty-nine, or thirty at the most. Twenty-nine when there are pink shades, thirty when there are not. So you see what difficulties it would involve. No, as far as I am concerned, let your wife cherish the memory of this dead, stainless mother. Why should I interfere with her illusions? I find it hard enough to keep my own. I lost one illusion last night. I thought I had no heart. I find I have, and a heart doesn't suit me, Windermere. Somehow it doesn't go with modern dress. It makes one look old. And it spoils one's career at critical moments. (…)

I suppose, Windermere, you would like me to retire into a convent, or become a hospital nurse, or something of that kind, as people do in silly modern novels. That is stupid of you, Arthur; in real life we don't do such things — not as long as we have any good looks left, at any rate. No — what consoles one nowadays is not repentance, but pleasure. Repentance is quite out of date. And besides, if a woman really repents, she has to go to bad dressmaker, otherwise no one believes in her. And nothing in the world would induce me to do that. No; I am going to pass entirely out of your two lives. My coming into them has been a mistake — I discovered that last night.

The Last Cigarette

Sherry Kramer

Play
Seriocomic
F
20s
Contemporary

Meg's roommate is insane. She is driving Meg insane. Meg is trying to summon the guts to avenge herself.

(Meg lights a cigarette, the last in the pack.) Did you ever notice how the sound of the hot water changes when it gets hot? I did.

I noticed a lot of other things besides.

One day I woke up and noticed that most of those things made me angry.

Then I noticed something else.

That if I took a long, hot shower, I wasn't angry anymore. (…)

(Meg smiles.) What if I'm going to take that shower now. What if I've already taken it, and don't know. What if I'm getting angrier and angrier and they could heat up the Canadian side of Niagara Falls to the boiling point, keep the American side running cold, put handles on the side, throw me a big bar of soap, and it still wouldn't calm me down. What then?

Because you know why I'm angry? You really want to know?

My roommate Wendi steals my cigarettes. She steals my cigarettes and it creates a rage in me greater and more terrifying than the rage created in me by the thought of early death caused by many forms of cancer, even though I don't have any of them and even if I did they could be diagnosed in time and I could probably be saved. Unless it was head cancer. Or throat cancer. Or lung cancer.

(Meg stamps out her cigarette.)

Which I also do not stand a good chance of getting, if I stop.

But that's not why I'm going to stop.

I am going to stop because when Wendi steals my cigarettes, she doesn't steal all of them. She steals all of them but one.

I take it only as a sign of the influence of a civilization on even the criminally insane that Wendi never takes my last one. It has nothing to do with consideration. Compassion. Courtesy. Wendi has left all those things far behind. Trains can't stop her. Bullets can't stop her. She threatens to leap from tall buildings in a single bound. Medical science can't help her. Deep hypnosis can't reach her. But the myth of the last cigarette stops her. Dead, every time.

If she would just take the last cigarette, maybe I wouldn't be so angry. But no, she takes nineteen and stops. She opens a fresh pack, empties them all out, and replaces one.

I want to kill Wendi.

(Pause.)

Or maybe I'll just take a shower instead.

Lovers

Brian Friel

Play
Seriocomic
F
16
Contemporary

Pregnant Mag talks idly to her distracted fiancé, Joe.

I read in a book that there are one million two thousand nuns in the world. Isn't that fierce? Imagine if they were all gathered in one place — on an island, say — and the Chinese navy was let loose at them — cripes, you'd hear the squeals in Tobermore! I have a wicked mind, too. D'you ever think things like that, Joe? I'm sure you don't. I think that women have far more corrupt minds than men, but I think that men are more easily corrupted than women.

Food! — I don't care if I never see another bite ever again. My God, I thought I was going to vomit my guts out this morning! And this could keep up for the next seven months, according to Doctor Watson. The only consolation is that *you're* all right. It would be wild altogether if you were at it too. Sympathetic sickness, they call it. But it's only husbands get it. Maybe you'll get it this day three weeks — the minute we get married — God, wouldn't that be a scream! D'you know what Joan O'Hara told me? That all the time her mother was expecting Oliver Plunket, her father never lifted his head out of the kitchen sink. Isn't it crazy! And for the last three days he lay squealing on the floor like a stuck pig and her mother had to get the police for him in the end. I love this view of Ballymore: the town and the fields and the lake; and the people. When I'm up here and look down on them, I want to run down and hug them all and kiss them. But then when I'm down among them I feel like doing that *(She cocks a snook into JOE's face.)* into their faces. I bet you that's how God feels at times, too. Wouldn't you think so?

Well, I'll tell you something: there are occasions in my life when I know how God feels. And one of those occasions is now. At this moment God feels … expansive … and beneficent … and philanthropy.

Mama Day

Gloria Naylor

Novel
Seriocomic
F
30s
Contemporary

She reads him the riot act for staying out the night before.

Twice in less than twenty-four hours you ended up sprawled out on the bed with me having to undress you, and it was getting to be a bit much. That mess Dr. Buzzard brewed up was known to take paint off a wall — it had to be almost two hundred proof *after* he cut it down. What could have possessed you? Trying to be macho, no doubt. But you woke up after your wild drinking spree feeling a lot better than you deserved to. You had Mama Day to thank for that: She said just force two aspirin and a pint of water down your throat and you wouldn't have a hangover in the morning. Personally, I wanted you to suffer, especially when you got up arrogant and lying through your teeth about the condition you'd been in. Yes, I was always exaggerating and downright spiteful because you had gone out and had a little fun alone without clinging to my side. And, oh, now, you weren't going to humor me by having tea and dry toast for breakfast. You felt fine this morning because there had been absolutely nothing wrong with you last night. You insisted on pancakes and I *soaked* them with butter. You didn't stay arrogant long, did you. I didn't even bother repeating myself about your stomach muscles being paralyzed — you couldn't have heard me any with your head buried in the toilet.

Normal Girl

Molly Jong-Fast

Novel
Seriocomic
F
20s
Contemporary

A brief look into a fast young life.

A blind mention on page six in less than a day — now, that's a party.

Just Asking: What nineteen-year-old wonder brat Jewish Nicole Kidman look-alike had a party at her socialite mother's Greenwich house? And was found freebasing in the living room far past dawn?

Maybe it says the wrong thing about me. I think I need a publicist.

What little of the house remains is destroyed. I don't know how things got so out of hand, but then again, I can't say I'm all that surprised. My mother's white carpets are obscured by gray ash from cigarettes; everything breakable from the Ming dynasty is broken. All this serves as a sure sign that the weekend is over and it's time to make another mess in some other state. I decide to pack up the hangover and go, before any of the remaining guests' tans get a chance to fade. I make a mental note to liquidate my trust fund for the purpose of paying Mom's decorator to do a fast something with the house. She has four days to do her magic before Mom comes up again. But I'm sure she can find some good fabric and carpeting to disguise the mess.

Omnium Gatherum

Theresa Rebeck and Alexandra Gersten-Vassilaros

Play
Seriocomic
F
30s-40s
Contemporary

Julia, a guest at a sumptuous dinner party, excuses herself to use the bathroom. When she returns, she regales the dinner guests with a description of the room's opulent décor.

(Charged, a little angry.) Girl, you have to see it! I mean, it's big! . . . There I was, all by myself, you know, and I suddenly became aware of this kind of infinite chorus line reflection of me in every single mirror! I mean, I was just surrounded by ME, hundreds of "ME's" just sitting there. And, well, I started to feel sorry, so sorry, like I wanted to apologize but I didn't know to whom. *(Suddenly.)* I mean, it's really less of a bathroom and more of a shrine to our own shit, isn't it? . . . I was down there and I thought of my mother and the little excursions we'd take to Bloomingdales. We'd go up to the eighth floor where there were these little mock rooms, all decorated to the hilt, and she'd oohh and ahhh, I mean this was way better than a trip to the museum for her, it was more like an archeological foray into white people's lives only you didn't have to make small talk and pretend you were cozy. See, she wished that all that luxury could be mine one day, 'cause that was a sign of real achievement to her. But for me, hanging out in that ballroom you call a bathroom, well, it just made me feel so far away from her and so far away from anything real — look, no offense, Suzie, but don't you think having a gloriously appointed bathroom is the strangest barometer of fulfillment you could ever imagine?

Perfect Body

Cynthia Meier

Original Monologue
Seriocomic
F
30s
Contemporary

"Warm, sensuous, full-figured blonde . . . " the ad began. I got lots of responses. Men, I soon discovered, had a different idea of what full-figured meant than those of us who have used those euphemisms for years. Euphemisms like chubby, Rubenesque, *overweight*. I always want to ask, over *whose* weight?

But before I met my husband, I still used euphemisms and full-figured was one of them. Seventeen men responded to my ad in the *Tucson Weekly*. I met nearly all of them. Many were surprised by my size and were politely uninterested and I never saw them again. Some I dated over a period of months. The most amazing experience was with a man who suggested we meet at TGIFridays. (I should have taken a clue from that.) When we met, he said, "You said you were overweight, but I didn't know you meant *that* overweight." I burst into tears, cursing that I'd bought what was to be our first and last round of drinks, and we sat down to talk. Pretty soon, he was consoling me, saying, "It's OK. I used to be a cocaine dealer."

In all of these encounters, I learned three things:

1. Never use euphemisms.
2. Rejection has nothing to do with who I am.
3. Never go to TGIFridays.

The Perfect Fight

Jenny Lee

Essay
Seriocomic
F
20s
Contemporary

A recently married woman describes the "perfect fight" that, like the "perfect storm," can leave a trail of rubble in its wake.

Now comes the trigger moment, the thing that causes the perfect storm to erupt. I have heard from others that the trigger moment is always a smallest, trite, not-a-big-deal thing, but given the background of the slow internal buildup and the extraneous short-term buildup, it's understandable how the wrong look or word or action could be the match that ignites the whole thing. Our trigger moment was completely absurd and involved the wrong drink. I had just gotten home and was sitting on the couch fuming over my really awful, wretched day. Cosmos came in a few minutes later from an equally really awful, wretched day. He said, "I stopped at the deli and bought drinks." No hello. No kiss. He opened his own Diet Coke and handed me the bag. Inside the bag was a Sunkist orange soda. I have nothing against orange soda, and I can see why it's popular for its fizz and its tangy taste, but it just so happened that I personally do not care for orange soda. In fact, I probably hadn't had an orange soda in maybe twenty years. So I just staring at it, and the only words that came out of my mouth were "Orange soda?" So he said, "What's wrong with orange soda?" meaning I should feel lucky that he got me anything at all. And I said, "Have you ever seen me drink an orange soda?" in a tone that meant "proceed with extreme caution." He said, "I don't know, probably not," meaning I dare you to keep going. So I said, "Then what on earth would possess you to buy me a Sunkist orange soda when you should know that the only soda I drink is Diet Coke." Meaning I was about to lose it. He said, "I dunno," meaning today of all days I will not deal with your crap. So I'm wondering how I managed to marry the most oblivious, unobservant man in the world.

Did he not care to know my drink of choice when I can name every drink he likes and put them in the order of his preference depending on his mood, what he's eating, and where we are. And so began the perfect fight.

Picasso

Ellyn Maybe

Poem
Seriocomic
F
20+
Contemporary

The speaker recognizes herself in a Picasso painting and reflects on socially prescribed standards of beauty.

I found a year that likes my body
       1921
girl sitting on a rock
Picasso painted a woman
with my thighs

walking around the museum
it hit me how Rubenesque
is not just some word
for someone who likes corned beef

there I was
naked on the edge of something
overlooking water
or was it salt

it was weird
nobody was screaming fat chick at the frame
nobody was making grieving sounds
but the girl in the painting looked sad

as though she knew
new ears were smudging
a forced liposuction
with rough acrylic

the caption said

girl sitting on rock

not woman who uses food to help cope
for the lack of empathy in her sphere

not the gyms are closed and there are
better muscles to develop

not girl one calorie away
from suicide

just flesh on a rock

her eyes dripping
question marks onto
girl looking into a mirror

(. . .)

I like titles
their vocabulary of oil
the girl on the rock
whispered to me

go girl

I love museums
call me old-fashioned
but I like face-to-face
conversations.

Says I, Says He

Ron Hutchinson

Play
Seriocomic
F
20s
Contemporary

In an Irish pub, Bella cuts the men down to size with her saucy tongue.

Shall I tell you Jigger's problem? Like his brother. Like the other hero in the family. Scared shitless at the thought of an honest bit of fanny. At the age of nothing and a half he thumbs up the skirt of one of me dolls and finds to his amazement it not the same at the business end as down the front of his wee trousers — Upshot being the sort of chiseler he was — his ma finds him hanging the bog lid up and down on it, trying to chop it off. Which has put a dent in his entire bloody apparatus to this day. You know the truth of it yourself, Maeve. Petey's only got it in the gab and Jigger when he can feel the weight of that thing in his hand. Just strutting their stuff, the two of them, and not a blind bit of notice should be taken of the pair. A couple of pop-eyed lugs who couldn't hold down jobs as doormats if times was straight. It's the likes of yourself who build them up for heroes. Eeejits. A right dopey pair of bookends, both. Now, your man my brother — he's a different case entirely. There's more than a bit of suss behind that piggy eye of his.

The School of Beauty and Charm

Melanie Sumner

Novel
Seriocomic
F
Teen
Contemporary

As the car she is sitting in hurtles down a mountain road, Louise concludes she is going to die, and her last thoughts turn to her one true love, her seventh-grade English teacher, Mr. Rutherford.

My death was for my English teacher, Mr. Samuel Rutherford III. I loved him.

(…) He was not married, but I knew that the chances he'd ask a seventh-grader for a date were slim. In order to get his attention, without being obnoxious, I sat about thirteen inches from his desk and absorbed every word he uttered. Consequently, I learned English grammar, but being recognized as a good student fell far short of my mark. Then I switched strategies. I wrote papers with my left hand, so that they were illegible, and when called on in class, I gaped, mouth open, eyes wide, as if struck dumb by a sudden brain tumor.

This worked. (…) He looked at me, hard. His eyes were blue. (…) Slowly, the fire in my chest flickered up to my neck, and then my cheeks, spreading out to my ears. Love! How could I tell him? He had to know my scorching agony — it was him! He was burning in me, burning and burning. (…) "You're slacking off," he said. "Any reason?"

I gazed back at him. This was the moment. I could say, "Mr. Rutherford, I lust for you." My face was on fire; my palms sweated; my loins ached. I opened my mouth. "Kiss me," I wanted to say, and then he would stand up from his swivel chair, lift me onto the broad, battered old desk, and deflower me.

(…) At last, my words came out. I said, "I dunno."

"I suggest you get off your butt and get back to work," he said, and that was the end. His face closed. He was done with me. I was a child.

Screaming Violet
Deborah Grimberg

Play
Seriocomic
F
40s
Contemporary

Fran, a working-class woman, has upper-class sightings.

You know George I think I've got my famous-person syndrome again. Everywhere I look I think I see someone famous. This morning I went to the adult education center to do my flower-arranging course and the new teacher looked just like Dame Judi Dench — every time I asked her a question about my marigolds, I felt obliged to curtsy. Then I went to the Women's clinic because they're doing mammograms there all week. And who do you think it was that told me to take off my blouse and "pop my breasts" onto the metal shelf … Shirley Maclaine! I'd just seen her on the TV at the Academy Awards.

Oh, it was awkward, having a woman whose work I so admire, take photographs of my you-know-whats. And if that wasn't enough, I was standing at the bus stop when Michael Caine went past on a bicycle. Well, it was all too much for me, I had to pop into Starbucks and have a hot cup of tea and a scone and who was standing in front of me ordering a skinny soy, Grande latte with a touch of nutmeg — Elvis! Oh I must say he does look well, George, he's lost a lot of weight, his little white trousers fit him so much better now, they're not nearly so snug around the hips.

Smugglers Three

David Lavine

Play
Seriocomic
F
20s-30s
Contemporary

Kiki, not exactly Mensa material, but well-meaning and warm-hearted, attempts to torture her whore-mongering boyfriend with her fantasy future husband.

You're going to see me on the Paris boulevard with my new husband and you're going to eat your fucking heart out. And he's going to be a successful artist and poet, by the way, not some half-assed pill-smuggling drunk. You're going to walk by with your cheap French whores and the crabs they gave you and I'll be wearing high French fashions and sipping, um, Evian *("EEE-ve-ahn")* at my private table in the Eiffel Tower and I'll just be *laughing* about how pitiful you are. "Look at that asshole," I'll say. "Look at that asshole that just crawled out of the sewer. He's a half-assed pill-smuggling drunk." *(Beat.)* But it'll be in French, because I'll have the language down in no time. And my husband'll laugh, too. And then he'll put down his sketch pad because he'll be sketching me for a fifty-story full-color national monument the king is paying him a billion dollars to build and it's going to be of me, so every time you go out to find more whores, no matter where you are, you're going to see me — and so my gorgeous talented husband and I will be laughing and he'll put down his sketch pad and he'll kiss me. So softly, so gently, a gentleness you've never known. And I'll soak it in, straight into every corner of my heart. But I'll still be laughing, and that's all you'll hear. And every second you'll be wishing to high heaven that you never let me go because I'm the *best* fucking thing that ever happened to you.

Spell #7

Ntozake Shange

> **Play**
> **Seriocomic**
> **F**
> **20s-30s**
> **Contemporary**
>
> *In this scathing send up, Natalie inhabits the mind and body of a white girl.*

… today i'm gonna be a white girl/ i'll retroactively wake myself up/ ah low & behold/ a white girl in my bed/ (…) what's the first thing white girls think in the morning/ do they get up being glad they ain't niggahs/ do they remember mama/ or worry abt gettin to work/ do they work?/ do they play isadora & wrap themselves in sheets & go tip toeing to the kitchen to make maxwell house coffee/ oh i know/ the first thing a white girl does in the morning is fling her hair/

so now i'm done with that/ I'm gonna water my plants/ but am i a po white trash white girl with a old jellyjar/ or am I a sophisticated & protestant suburbanite with 2 valium slugged awready & a porcelain water carrier leading me up the stairs strewn with heads of dolls & nasty smellin white husband person's underwear/ if i was really protected from the niggahs/ i might go to early morning mass & pick up a tomato pie on the way home/ so i cd eat it durin the young & the restless. (…) coming from bay ridge on the train i cd smile at all the black & puerto rican people/ & hope they can't tell i want them to go back where they came from / or at least be invisible.

(…) i'm still in my kitchen/ so i guess i'll just have to fling my hair once more/ but this time with a pout/ cuz i think i haven't been fair to the sisterhood/ women's movement faction of white girls/ although/ they always ask what do you people really want. as if the colored woman of the world were a strange sort of neutered workhorse/ which isn't too far from reality/ since i'm still waiting for my cleaning lady & the lady who takes care of my children & the lady who caters my parties & the lady who accepts quarters at the bathroom in sardi's (…) cd you hand me a towel/ thank-you caroline. i've left all of maxime's last winter clothes in a pile for you by the back door. they have to be cleaned but i hope yr girls can make gd use of them.

oh/ i'm still not being fair/all the white women in the world don't wake up being glad they aint niggahs/ only some of them/ the ones who don't ... [say] i know i'll play a tenor horn & tell all the colored artists i meet/ that now i'm just like them/ i'm colored i'll say cuz i have a struggle too.

(...) I'm still in my house/having flung my hair-do for the last time/ what with having to take twenty valium a day/ to consider the ERA/ & all the men in the world/ & my ignorance of the world/ it is overwhelming. i'm so glad I'm colored. boy i cd wake up in the morning & think abt anything. i can remember emmett till & not haveta smile at anybody.

Storage

Lisa Samra

Original monologue
Seriocomic
F
20s-30s
Contemporary

ok so i go home to visit my mother for christmas and there are no christmas decorations up because my brother who lives thirty minutes away and works two minutes away from my mother's doesn't ever come over or offer to do anything for her she's seventy-one and christmas is very important to her because she likes it so much plus my father left her alone and went golfing in arizona the last christmas before he died so i go home and she says that we're going to take all the christmas stuff and other stuff down from the crawl space above the linen closet which is up high which is why she can't do it herself (…) so we take all the linens and things down from the upper levels of the linen closet and i have to lift myself up to the top shelf and remove the special hidden wall from the back of the closet the whole space is full of junk, dusty and in bags just shoved up in there i take things out and hand them down to her and i notice that there are lots of nut type things rolling around and falling off of things i take out and i say to her what are these did some wreath fall apart or something and then i look closer and the nuts have holes in them where they have been eaten and my mother says oh yeah there might be a dead squirrel and i say WHAT and i start getting nervous and itchy and she says that karen my sister was visiting two weeks ago and thought she heard something making noises in the wall and now the sound is gone my mother says so it might be dead and i start freaking out and taking the stuff out more quickly and she is not taking the bags and boxes from me quickly enough and i say hurry up here's another bag and then i get everything out and i say well that's it and she says here's a flashlight see if there's a squirrel and i take it and see nothing but i am not wearing my glasses and she pops her head up and looks and says there it is in the back it's dead get it out of there and i scream NO WAY and she says i'll get you a broom and i'm waiting up there while she goes and gets the broom and dustpan from downstairs and i'm looking around at the ceiling of the crawl space wondering if it has any friends and if they will be disturbed if we remove this dead squirrel that i can't see my breathing is heavy now and she comes with the broom and says to throw the dustpan to the back of the space and use the broom to push the dead squirrel on to the dustpan and bring it out i say what if it's not dead what if it's sleeping she says it's not sleeping i throw the dustpan over there and scream i'm sweating and screaming the whole time and i push the thing i can hardly see on to the dustpan i did it i say and she says bring it out and i scream again and pull the dustpan closer and closer to me get something to put it in i say so i can put it right in it and she gets a wastebasket from the upstairs bathroom here she says ok here goes i scream and pull it closer i can see it now but i close my eyes and i reach out my hand to grab the handle and i grab it and with my eyes closed i pull it out here i say take it and i flip the dustpan over into the wastebasket take it away i scream she goes downstairs and puts it in the garbage in the garage and she comes back upstairs and i say that was so terrifying did you look at it of course she says it had very pretty fur it must have been dead only two weeks or so and i screamed again and she said you think that's bad i found your father dead in the bathroom.

To Die for Want of Lobster

Kato McNickle

Play
Seriocomic
F
26
Contemporary

Lena and Bobby have returned after the memorial service for Jack, whose remains are in the urn.

It. Bobby. It's an it. It's an urn and inside is a bunch of dust. It was an excellent choice. Hides a lot. But you shouldn't tug on it or it might end up on the floor along with the remains of your brother — all over the place. It might hurt the resale value of the house. So. Where do you want to dump it? It's best to get it out of the way. Move straight ahead. Finish. Get rid of the body *(Sorting through the mail.)* There's always the toilet. Burial at sea. I had a goldfish once and that's how it all ended. Here's a letter for you. From your school. Want to take a look?

Well, I want to see what it is. Doesn't school start soon? Look at that. Sorry to lay more bad news on you, but it looks like you're fired. Guess the homicide was a little much for them. *(Picks up a pack of cigarettes.)* Even if the grand jury did rule it as an accident. Thanks to me. Wasn't I grrreat? *(Puts cigarette in mouth — lights.)* What a killer, being up there. Asked so many questions. On the news. I was fantastic. That is my true calling. What a rush. Now I know why my father loved the law. My father was a lawyer — you know.

Anyway. I'm so glad I've got you Bobby. And you're lucky you've got me. Together we're practically unstoppable. You've got something for me. Stability. I've always wanted that. Some stability. Peace of mind. Once we sell the house it will be beautiful. We'll have money. I can show you Europe, especially Greece. You'll love Greece. We can meet some Greek men. We can tease them and make them spend their money on us. It'll just be the grandest thing. I guess you're just what I needed. Bobby? What're you doing? Come down here so we can decide what to do with Jack. *(She takes the lid off the urn and looks inside.)* Big ol' pile of Jack. Hello, Jack. Can I buy you a drink. You're looking a little parched. Poor Jack. *(Flicks cigarette ash into urn.)* Poor, poor Jack.

Tophet Point

Chris Shaw Swanson

Play
Seriocomic
F
20s
Contemporary

By relating a childhood experience, Sara gains insight into her present relationship.

This adventure with Professor Brian — this reminds me of my first near-sex experience. I was around eight or nine and Suzie Parisi, my best friend who I thought was rich because she told me her family belonged to a country club, finally invited me to swim at her club — the YMCA. Pool rules dictated that women wear bathing caps, so I borrowed my mother's, a very stylish number with a huge water lily attached to the top of it. When I got to the pool, I realized that all the female country clubbers were wearing plain old white bathing caps. I also realized that I had to go to the bathroom, (…) so Suzie pointed to a stairway, and told me she hoped everything came out OK. When you're rich, you don't have to be original.

So off I galloped up the steps until I reached a black metal door. Swinging it wide open, I bounded right into a sea of so many naked male bodies, I was frozen dead in my tracks. (…) I can't remember seeing even one face. (…) After an eternity, I unfroze enough to turn and stumble down the steps, groping my way back to the pool. (…) First, Suzie was very sympathetic, then she begged me for penis details. I, of course, had only one overriding concern — being recognized and ridiculed when I returned to the pool. Suzie assured me no one would spot me. Then I realized her gaze was fixed on something over my head. Yes. The water lily would be my waterloo. (…)

That was a long foolish time ago. But to this day, when I'm with a group or just a few other people, or one scholarly stud, and I start sensing I'm the odd woman out, which I almost always sense even when the people or stud seem to like me, I can almost feel that big old water lily begin to sprout on my head. And once again, I try to muster enough strength and courage to convince myself that I do belong here — right here — right now — with these people — or at least somewhere in this general space and time and crowd. Kissing — Unshackling — Depth — it all comes so easy to Brian. And maybe, with a few more lessons from him, just maybe everything really can come out … OK.

True Story

Allison Williams

Play
Seriocomic
F
17
Contemporary

The Geek, holding a purse, promises to avenge her promless evening. Carrie ain't got nuthin' on her.

I understand school shootings. I mean, I don't say, "Hey, good idea! Let's all solve our problems with violence!" But I understand the feeling of wanting to kill everyone in my school or even just a select few to set an example. You can only be spit on so many times. The nice thing is, these days, everyone's so afraid of guns that I probably won't even have to shoot anyone.

Am I a psychopath?

No!

I am a sociopath.

A psychopath will kill you in front of a cop. A sociopath waits until the cop leaves. Most serial killers are sociopaths. Mass murderers tend to be psychopaths.

Charles Manson? Psychopath.

John Wayne Gacy? Sociopath.

Waco? Psychopaths on both sides.

Ted Bundy? Sociopath.

Ted Bundy was hot. Blond hair, blue eyes, tan, skied. You know how he got the girls in the car? He wore a fake cast and pretended he couldn't get a piece of furniture loaded. He was so sweet, so nice, they just wanted to help.

Psychopaths, now, those would be your wild-eyed unwashed. Sociopaths tend to live next door to people who think they're just swell.

Rob says it's all about Prom. If you're popular and pretty and handsome and you go to parties on boats and at lakeside cabins where there's lots of beer and girls with cheerleader poms in the trunk, and you finish your high school career by having a *great prom* … *You* are *fucked* because

God figures, OK, my job's over, you're launched, out you go! But if you have a lousy prom …

God spends the rest of your life making it up to you.

(Pats purse.) I'm gonna have a great life.

White Linoleum

SuzAnne C. Cole

Play
Seriocomic
F
20s
Contemporary

Sally, a young housewife, at first thrilled with her white floor, becomes obsessed with keeping it clean.

Our first house! I'm so excited. I love everything. You know what room I like the best? My pure white, sparkling kitchen! (…) My wonderful, dazzling, white linoleum!

(Time lapse indicated by pause and change in SALLY's mood.) People ask how I do it, keep my house so nice and all. Especially this floor. It sure is harder to clean than I expected. I had no idea how red the clay was around here — or how much of it two boys, one dog, and one grown man — who should know better — could track in. Thank goodness for Clorox, Comet, and sudsy ammonia. My best friends!

(Time lapse.) Three AM. Three pairs of rubber gloves. Five toothbrushes. One gallon of bleach. I'm so tired. But it was worth it. My floor is really, truly clean. And I'm going to keep it that way. From this moment on, this family has some new house rules:

1. Except for meals, the kitchen is now off-limits to everyone but me.
2. No one is allowed to wear shoes in the kitchen-socks only. No, make that white socks only.
3. No more red or purple food will be served in this kitchen.

(Time lapse.) Don't you just love picnics? We have them every day — at every meal! We're the only family on the block that has picnics for breakfast. The family says they're cold, but I say that's nonsense. It's healthy to eat outside.

(Time lapse.) I know the boys will miss the dog, … but Sparky had been rolling in the mud, and when I turned around and saw his muddy paw prints all across my beautiful white linoleum, I tell you, something

just snapped inside me. I grabbed the boys' ball bat and I ... (...) When the boys come in from school, I'm going to say Sparky ran away.

(Time lapse.) I told my husband over and over again that he couldn't asphalt the driveway, that I'd never be able to get that sticky black stuff off my beautiful white floor. So what does he do? He asphalts the driveway! Now I can't let anyone in! Wait a minute! He's coming up the driveway. Just let him try to walk on my floor!

(Pretends to hold up and aim a shotgun.) "Hi honey, I'm home" my ass.

MALE
Comic Monologues

The 72-Ounce Steak

Sherry Kramer

Play
Comic
M
30s
Contemporary

*Brent, a truck driver, uneducated but not unintelligent,
proudly tells this story to a woman he once slept with and
knows to be desperately in love with him.*

You let them know, right when you walk in under the big cow, through
the swinging doors, so they give you the special table. (…) They've got
this real sharp knife hanging on the wall behind the table, and maitre d'
knows how to use it in an emergency, so you have to sign this release saying if he botches it, if he tries to save you and he botches it, you agree
not to sue.

(…) You got to eat the 72-ounce steak, the tossed salad, the shrimp
cocktail, the vegetable medley, the twice baked potato, and the pie a' la
mode, all in an hour.

You eat it all in an hour, you don't have to pay.

You get it down, they carve your name with a branding iron on a big
wooden plaque.

(…) They let you order it any way you want …Well. I ordered it
extra well. I mean you go to McDonald's, you get a quarter pounder,
that's a quarter pounder before cooking, right, and what do you get, you
get nothing, right? So I figured, seventy-two times ounces, that's four
and half pounds, that's eighteen times nothing.

(…) You talk about your fatal errors. You talk about your fatal flaws.
Everybody has them.

Seventy-two ounces of shoe leather. Seventy-two ounces of gristle
and fat and flesh, charred beyond recognition. Seventy-two ounces of
open-hearthed, petrified prime … I was able to rip the thing in half. I
had to stand up to do it — they let you stand up. I was reminded, and
inspired, by a painting I once saw of Jacob wrestling with the angel. It
was a lot like that.

(…) My waiter sounded the first quarter. I'd barely made it past the outer crust on the pointed end. I started to panic. The waiter reached across and wiped my forehead with the napkin he had draped over his arm. (…) I took up the chunk of meat in my hands. I dove into, buried my face in it, determined to eat my way through to the light.

The bell rang. It had a far-off sound, as if it were coming from another world. I stayed where I was, chewing, ripping, swallowing, submerged. Again the bell. Fifteen minutes left. I stuffed the rest of the flesh down my throat. I gagged, kept on swallowing, come one, come on, you can do it. My fists struck the table. One. Two. I was in trouble.

(…) The tossed salad. That looks easy. Sure, that will go down, all that dressing. Two handfuls in, swallow…two pieces of eat, don't chew, no time to chew, just swallow, swallow. *Damn you, swallow.* Another. Swallow. Another.

The baked potato. Yes. Won't fit. *Won't fit.* Tear it in half.

Vegetables. Don't forget your vegetables.

OK. OK. What? What?

One minute? One?

One minute! Apple pie — where's that bitch — that apple pie — Jesus Christ — *Thirty seconds?* Two slices left — swallow, swallow — fifteen seconds — one piece left, one — get it in — get it in! *swallow!!!* Five seconds — five — four — three — two — one — *swallow!!!*

The bell!!! The bell!!!

Mac McClellan himself came over to congratulate me. My waiter hugged me, and went off to heat up the branding iron.

They blew the whistle, so everybody stopped eating during the engraving ceremony, and when it was over, everybody cheered.

Now I ask you. Have you ever heard a story like that before?

Actor!

Frederick Stroppel

> **Play**
> **Comic**
> **M**
> **20s**
> **Contemporary**

> *In this surreal satire spoofing the acting life, a young actor is about to give his first performance.*

An actor? Who respects actors? All they do is make believe. *(The actor slips on a robe and a bejeweled turban.)* I mean, this is just silly. Look how supremely foolish I appear. And all those parents and teachers out there are supposed to believe I'm from a different time, a different culture, a different world, just because I say so? I just can't take it seriously, I'm sorry. This can't be a man's work, to pose and pretend and …

(Spotlight hits actor. He immediately reacts, and he goes into his speech with shaky confidence.) "I, too, have followed the star to this poor babe's stable." *(The spotlight goes off. Excited:)* My God! That was incredible! All alone, just me, in front of all those people. And they were listening! I could feel it! I moved them. Lord, I'm getting chills! I want to do that again! I can't wait till tomorrow! But tomorrow will be better. This was only a surface reading. I have to get under the skin off my character. Who is Gaspar? Was he a tall man, did he stoop? Where did he glom all this frankincense? Did he convert, or was this just a one-time fling? So many questions!

Alien Idiots

Richard Krzemien

Original monologue
Comic
M
20+
Contemporary

William holds a cup of coffee, stands in front of a bookstore waiting for it to open. He looks up at the heavens, then down.

I'm scared. *(WILLIAM drinks his coffee. Clears his throat. He waits, looks left and right expecting something to happen. Nothing happens.)* There's a lot of idiots out there. Most people are stupid and lack vision. They suck and they're everywhere. Stand in line at the grocery store. The bank. The gas station. Just look at what happens on the freeway. It's a suckfest. People need an I.Q. exam before they drive. Below an I.Q. of 90 … most roads would be off limits. Anything with a curve or a stop sign — "figget about it."

(Beat; sips his coffee.) But, what if that's a universal principle. Like gravity, or time and space. What if stupidity exists throughout the universe. What if like, every alien race has a huge percentage of idiots like we do. Imagine a universe filled with alien Jerry Lewises or French people? Got that?

(Beat.) OK. So, the aliens are out exploring the galaxy because that's what they do. But the real smart aliens never leave their planet because they're too smart. Instead, they stay home eating Soylent Green or something. Therefore, most of the traveling aliens would be the idiots.

(Sips coffee.) So imagine being abducted. I bet that's why most people repress their close encounters. You lie there looking up thinking, wow, they've got Windows version 10,000 or something — which finally doesn't crash. They've discovered the meaning of life. Then you suddenly realize these "things" — about to stick some probe up your ass — are the idiots of the intergalactic highway. How can you trust them? You can't. You see? That's why I'm scared.

Amphitryon

John Dryden

Play
Comic
M
20+
Classic

Amphitryon's servant, Sosia, rehearses the message he has been asked to deliver.

Well! The greatest plague of a serving-man is to be hired by some great lord! They care not what drudgery they put upon us, while they lie lolling at their ease a-bed, and stretch their lazy limbs in expectation of the whore which we are fetching for them. The better sort of 'em will say Upon my Honor at every word; yet ask 'em for our wages, and they please the privilege of their honor, and will not pay us, nor let us take out privilege of the law upon them. There's conscience for you! (…) Now am I to give my lady an account of my Lord's victory; 'tis good to exercise my parts before hand, and file my tongue into eloquent expressions, to tickle her ladyship's imagination *(Setting down his lantern.)* This lantern, for once, shall be my lady, because she is the lamp of all beauty and perfection. Then thus I make my address to her: *(Bows.)* Madam, my lord has chosen me out, as the most faithful, though the most unworthy of his followers, to bring your ladyship this following account of our glorious expedition. Then she: — "Oh, my poor Sosia *(In a shrill tone.)* "how am I overjoyed to see thee!" — She can say no less — "Madam, you do me too much honor, and the World will envy me this glory." — Well answered on my side. — "And how does my lord Amphitryon?" — "Madam, he always does like a man of courage, when he is called by honor." — There I think I nicked it. — "But when will he return?" — "As soon as he possibly can, but not so soon as his impatient heart could wish him with your ladyship." — "But what does he do, and what does he say? Prithee tell me something more of him." — "He always says less than he does, madam, and his enemies have found it to their cost." — Where the devil did I learn all these elegancies and gallantries?

Anton in Show Business

Jane Martin

Short play
Comic
M
35+
Contemporary

Don Blount is a tobacco company executive in charge of charitable arts donations.

Don Blount of Albert & Sons Tobacco calling for Martha Graham ... Then why is it called the Martha Graham Dance Company? Oh. No, I knew that. Little joke. Listen, the grant's in the mail. Yes. Well, it's our pleasure to support a dance company of your caliber and if you might find an opportunity to mention to the chairman of your board that we'd be thrilled if she'd tell her brother the congressman to stop sodomizing the tobacco industry just because he's personally in the pocket of the HMOs, I think you'd find your grant is definitely renewable. My pleasure. *(Don hangs up the phone, picks it back up, and dials.)* Mom, it's Don. Your son Don. I need the favor, Mom. I know we did it yesterday, but I'm feeling a little alienated ... a little remote. Wonderful. Good. I knew I could count on you. Momma. Ready? All right, light it up, Mom. Inhale, Mom. Would I encourage you to smoke if there was any danger? That's right, I wouldn't. I would never harm my mom. I must be a good person if I would never harm my mom. If I'm a good person, it must be all right to do what I do. Thanks, I feel a lot better. Put it out now, Momma. Everything's all right. I feel damn good. Go back on the oxygen, Ma. See you Sunday.

Anton in Show Business

Jane Martin

> **Short play**
> **Comic**
> **M**
> **40s-50s**
> **Contemporary**
>
> *Joe Bob is a white southerner, chairman of the Board of
> Directors of a small professional theater company. He's had it
> with artsy-fartsy pretensions.*

Damn woman! You got no more sense than a hog on ice! I been pourin'
my money an' the money of my friends down your double-talk rathole
since Jesus was a pup, so my wife could drag me down here to see plays
nobody can understand with a buncha people I would never invite to
dinner, on the basis it creates some quality of life I'm supposed to have
since I figgered out how to make some money. Half the time, that stuff
doesn't have a story, and it's been five years since you done one takes
place in a kitchen, which is the kind all of us like. The rest of the time
it's about how rich people is bad and Democrats is good and white people is stupid and homosexuals have more fun an' we should get rid of the
corporations an' eat grass an' then, by God, you wonder why you don't
have a big audience! Now you just blew 15 percent of your budget 'cause
you riled up the tobacco interest, plus you got the colored rattlin' on my
cage, and as of this precise minute, you are out of luck, out of work an'
outta San Antonio, Texas. See, I am closin' us down, lockin' the door, an'
then, by God, we can go back to hittin' each other up to give to the
United Way where it will, by God, do some poor handicap some actual,
measurable good, an' I won't have to hear anybody say "aesthetic" from
one year to the goddamned next! Now, vaya con Dios, darlin'.

The Arkansas Tornado

Kathleen A. Rogers

Play
Comic
M
58
Contemporary

Franklin Wilford recalls how he got his nickname.

I's about eighteen, nineteen. Had a gig in some two-dog town over in Georgia. Miss Nancy Yancey's honky-tonk and barbecue. Miss Nancy was some kind of woman — three-hundred-pound retired lady wrestler. Things got dull she'd put on this Scarlet O'Hara get up and take on all comers — best two outta three falls.

I's over there with the Silmer twins, Bud and Beau.

Friday night we bunk down in the barn. We don't know until morning we're sharing quarters with Miss Nancy's pet hog, Clark Gable. And Old Clark went and helped himself to a midnight snack — Beau's banjo. Now old Beau, he's always one to hold a grudge, and he took a powerful hatred to that animal. So, being the brains of the operation, I come up with a plan.

Saturday night the joint is jumping. I got Miss Nancy to put on her costume and go a few rounds with a mystery contender.

Well, to make a long story short, Clark Gable hadn't liked it much when I tied some of Miss Nancy's spare ringlets round his head, and he didn't like it much when I tied a big pink ruffle round his middle, and he didn't like it at all when I pulled him into that honky-tonk.

Miss Nancy takes one look at old Clark and starts in on the biggest hissy fit in the history of Georgia. Clark Gable don't like that the most of all, knocks me for a loop, and tears through the place, like, well, like a hog in a honky-tonk.

Oh, it was some sorry sight all right. But we don't stay around to assess the damage, 'specially not after one of the patrons discharges his firearm into the ceiling. We just loose out of there and are over the border into Alabama before we even take a breath to laugh. That was a night. Bud and Beau's the ones started calling me the Arkansas Tornado. On account of the general destruction I 'spect. Don't tell Granny Mabel. She thinks it's on account of my guitar playin'. Though I 'spect she knows more about me than I've ever let on to her.

The Bachelor's Soliloquy

Anonymous

> **Original monologue**
> **Comic**
> **20+**
> **Classic**

This contemporary take on Shakespeare's famous soliloquoy may qualify as a classic choice.

To wed, or not to wed — that is the question:
Whether 'tis nobler in a man to suffer
The slings and sorrows of that blind young archer;
Or fly to arms against a host of troubles,
And at the altar end them. To woo — to wed —
No more; and by this step to say we end
The heartache, and the thousand hopes and fears
The single suffer — 'tis a consummation
Devoutly to be wished. To woo — to wed —
To wed — perchance repent! — ay, there's the rub;
For in that wedded state, what woes may come
When we have launched upon that untried sea
Must give us pause. There's the respect
That makes *celibacy* of so *long* life;
For who would bear the quips and jeers of friends,
The husband's pity, and the coquette's scorn,
The vacant hearth, the solitary cell,
The unshared sorrow, and the void within,
When he himself might his redemption gain
With a fair damsel. Who would beauty shun
To toil and plod over a barren heath;
But that the dread of something yet beyond —
The undiscovered country, from whose bourne
No bachelor returns — puzzles the will,
And makes us rather bear those ills we have
Than fly to others that we know not of!
Thus forethought does make cowards of us all,
And thus the native hue of resolution

Is sicklied o'er with the pale cast of thought,
And numberless flirtations, long pursued,
With this regard, their currents turn awry
And lose the name of marriage.

The Bad-Tempered Man

Menander

Play
Comic
M
50+
Classic

Cnemon, the bad-tempered man of the title, thinks the world would be an OK place if it didn't have people in it. (Asclepios is the god of Medicine; his name is used here as a sort of oath.)

Now Perseus was a famous man. What luck he had!
First, he had wings — could fly about in the air. That meant
He never had to meet a soul that walks on earth.
Second, he had an invaluable possession, with which
He could turn everyone who annoyed him into stone.
If only I had that power now! There'd be nothing
More plentiful anywhere than fine stone statues
As it is — by Asclepios, life grows impossible.
People come trespassing on my ground and chat to me.
I've taken to spending my days on the public highway, have I?
Why, I don't even work this bit of land any more,
I've given it up, to avoid the people who pass by;
And now — they hunt me up to the hilltops. Curse them all,
There are too many *people!* — Oh, for pity's sake, there's another,
Standing at my front door! (…)
Where can one get away from *people?* Even if a man
Wanted to hang himself he couldn't do it in private.

Benefit

Eric Bogosian

Play
Comic
M
40s
Contemporary

An aging rock and roller is a guest on a talk show.

I used to do quite a few drugs … But you know, Bill, drugs are no good for anybody. I've seen a lot of people get really messed up on drugs, I've seen people die on drugs. *(Lights cigarette, inhales deeply.)* (…) You see, Bill, that's the insidious thing about drugs — you don't realize … uh … I mean, you're having such a good time, you don't realize what a bad time you're having. (…) I got straight while I was on tour. Woke up one morning … typical tour situation: luxury hotel room, I don't even know where I am … beautiful naked girl lying next to me in the bed, I don't know who she is, I don't know how she got there … champagne bottles all over the floor, cocaine on every horizontal surface. I hardly have the strength to pick up my head. So I pick up the remote control and I flip on the telly.

And I was saved, Bill, I was saved.

You have a man on in this country, on TV all the time. Saved my life. White hair. A genius … Donahue, Donahue was on … What he said really hit me. He said: "If you haven't met your full potential in this life, you're not really alive." The profoundness struck me like a thunderbolt. I thought, "That man is talking about me. He's talking about me."

(…) I straightened up and I went cold turkey. Had all my blood changed. And I feel like I've been reborn. I can say today, "I like myself today. I'm not such a bad guy, in fact, I'm an amazingly wonderful human being." I'm honest enough to say that today. I've really come to terms with my own brilliance — it's not a burden anymore.

(…) A lot of the kids watching right now buy our albums, learn the lyrics, memorize them, live their lives by them. So I know that everything I have to say is very, very important. And I'd like to say this about drugs: *(He looks directly and "meaningfully" at the audience.)* I've done a lot of drugs. I had a lot adventures on drugs. Some of my music has been inspired by drugs. In fact, I think it's safe to say I had some of the best times of my life on drugs.

That doesn't mean *you* have to do them.

(…) The next time someone offers you drugs, remember you can always just … turn them in.

Thank you, Bill. Good night. *(Peace sign.)* Cheers.

Bigfoot Stole My Wife

Ron Carlson

Short story
Comic
M
30+
Contemporary

The problem is credibility.

The problem, as I'm finding out over the last few weeks, is basic credibility. A lot of people look at me and say, sure Rick, Bigfoot stole your wife. It makes me sad to see it, the look of disbelief in each person's eye. Trudy's disappearance makes me sad, too, and I'm sick in my heart about where she may be and how he's treating her, what they do all day, if she's getting enough to eat. I believe he's being good to her — I mean I feel it — and I'm going to keep hoping to see her again, but it is my belief that I probably won't.

In the two and half years we were married, I often had the feeling that I would come home from the track and something would be funny. Oh, she'd say things: *One of these days I'm not going to be here when you get home*, things like that, things like everybody says. How stupid of me not to see them as omens. When I'd get out of bed in the early afternoon, I'd stand right here at this sink and I could see her working in her garden in her cut-off Levis and bikini top, weeding, planting, watering. I mean it was obvious. It was too busy thinking about the races, weighing the odds, checking the jockey roster to see what I now know: He was watching her too. He'd probably been watching her all summer.

So, in a way it was my fault. But what could I have done? Bigfoot steals your wife. I mean: Even if you're home, it's going to be a mess. He's big and not well trained.

Birth

Bless ji Jaja

Play
Comic
M
60s
Contemporary

Fred defends himself to his wife, who wishes he wouldn't watch so much TV.

No, no, hold on cause you think I'm blowing hot air. Allow me to make you gain more respect so you can stop disrespecting this vital piece of furniture here. Now, let me take you back to early 19 and 63. Birmingham, Alabama, and the local police commissioner, Bull Connor. Now picture attack dogs, fire hoses, mace, and swinging batons. Scenes of brutality and racial intolerance. Now when those scenes were finally shown on what, the television? The tel-e-vis-ion did things start to change? Yes, they did. (…) By spring those televised demonstrations led to national legislation which led to what? The de-seg-re-gation of rest-rooms, water fountains, lunch counters, theaters, and more importantly for you, what? (…) The desegregation of what? …

Fitting rooms! So you wouldn't have to buy a dress, come home, try it on, have it not look like it does on those anorexic window man-nequins, and then you not be able to take it back. (…) [T]o what do we owe the end of that indignity? Tel-e-vision. So what do I have in my liv-ing room? (…) Not a fire hydrant. Not a dog leash. But what? A big screen, remote control, picture-in-picture, Technicolor, tel-e-vision … My television. It keeps me informed. It let's me know what struggles are still to be fought.

Black Thang

Ato Essandoh

Play
Comic
M
20s-30s
Contemporary

Jerome talks to his best friend Sam, who has recently started dating a white woman.

You know what your problem is man? Lack of ambition. You're not see-ing the big picture my friend. This is not about you and one white chick. This is about you and all the white chicks. This is God saying, "Go forth my son and plunder the white man's natural resources." You owe it to yourself. You owe it to us. Power to the people! That's what I'm talking about. I mean look at you man. Ya fine-ass Mandigo-looking mother-fucker. How are you not fucking every minute of the day? I mean you're so good-looking I'd fuck you. And I don't mean that in the gay way. I mean it in the prison way. If we were in lockdown, I'd be fucking the shit outta you right now. Shit I'd let you fuck me. That's how good-looking you are.

Black Thang

Ato Essandoh

> **Play**
> **Comic**
> **M**
> **20s-30s**
> **Contemporary**

Jerome, talking to his friend Sam, tells the story of an encounter with an Indian woman he met at a sneaker store.

I knew this Indian chick once. You know, red dot on the forehead and all that shit. Her name was Sipi. Worked at the Foot Locker on Flatbush. (…) Sold me all kinds of shit. Socks, Tees, my Knicks hat. Damn, I would just go in there sometimes, not even wanting to buy shit. Just check her out. She had this shy smile, the way she looked at me, all shy and shit. I think she was sweating me too. You know. (…) So I rolled up in there, had my pumps on, had my Knicks hat on with matching Reebok suit. Yeah, you know the deal. And I rolled up in there and I said "A yo Sipi come here girl!" And she was all embarrassed and shit. Talking about "Can I help you sir?" And I was like "Yeah you can help me … what's up with that red dot on your forehead girl somebody poke you or what?" You know, just trying to break the ice and shit. And she looked at me for a second … and started to cry. And I'm like "Naw Sipi baby don't cry I was just teasing. Shit I like the red dot!" And that was the truth. I was cool with the red dot. But she just kept crying like I stole her suede Pumas or something. So the manager, probably her father or some shit comes out and says to me *(Mimicking Indian manager.)* "My friend. You must leave. You must leave right now my friend." And I'm like: "Yo can't I apologize? Can I say I'm sorry?" "No my friend you must leave. You must leave right now my friend. Or I call the cops." Shit what's this friend shit? You ain't my friend motherfucker! You ain't my friend! How are you gonna call the cops on your friend? So anyway, they kicked me out. Banned me from Foot Locker. Imagine that? Ban a brother from Foot Locker? That shit ain't right …

The Boor
Anton Chekhov

Play
Comic
M
30s
Classic

Smirnov, the proprietor of a country estate, has loved pas-sionately and disastrously. He'll now have no more of it.

I don't understand how to behave in the company of ladies. Madam, in the course of my life I have seen more women than you have sparrows. Three times have I fought duels for women, twelve I jilted and nine jilted me. There was a time when I played the fool, used honeyed language, bowed and scraped. I loved, suffered, sighed to the moon, melted in love's torments. I loved passionately, I loved to madness, loved in every key, chattered like a magpie on emancipation, sacrificed half my fortune in the tender passion, until now the devil knows I've had enough of it. Your obedient servant will let you lead him around by the nose no more. Enough! Black eyes, passionate eyes, coral lips, dimples in cheeks, moon-light whispers, soft, modest sights — for all that, madam, I wouldn't pay a kopeck! I am not speaking of present company, but of women in gen-eral; from the tiniest to the greatest, they are conceited, hypocritical, chattering, odious, deceitful from top to toe; vain, petty, cruel with a maddening logic and in this respect, please excuse my frankness, but one sparrow is worth ten of the aforementioned petticoat-philosophers. When one sees one of the romantic creatures before him he imagines he is looking at some holy being, so wonderful that its one breath could dis-solve him in a sea of a thousand charms and delights; but if one looks into the soul — it's nothing but a common crocodile. But the worst of all is that this crocodile imagines it is a masterpiece of creation, and that it has a monopoly on all the tender passions. May the devil hang me upside down if there is anything to love about a woman! When she is in love, all she knows is how to complain and shed tears. If the man suffers and makes sacrifices she swings her train about and tries to lead him by the nose. You have the misfortune to be a woman, and naturally you know woman's nature; tell me on your honor, have you ever in your life seen a woman who was really true and faithful? Never! Only the old and the deformed are true and faithful. It's easier to find a cat with horns or a white woodcock, than a faithful woman.

Boy's Life
Howard Korder

Play
Comic
M
20s
Contemporary

Phil can't seem to get it together with the ladies. The equally neurotic Karen was his latest disaster.

I would have destroyed myself for this woman. Gladly. I would have eaten garbage. I would have sliced my wrists open. Under the right circumstances, I mean, if she said, "Hey, Phil, why don't you just cut your wrists open?" Well, come on, but if seriously … We clicked, we connected on so many things, right off the bat, we talked about God for three hours once. I don't know what good it did, but that intensity … and the first time we went to bed, I didn't even touch her. I didn't want to, understand what I'm saying? And you know, I played it very casually, because, all right, I've had some rough experiences, I'm the first to admit, but after a couple weeks I could feel we were right there, so I laid it down, everything I wanted to tell her, and … and she says to me, she says … "Nobody should ever need another person that badly." Do you believe that? "Nobody should ever … !" "What is that? Is that something you saw on TV? I put my heart on the table, you give me Dr. Joyce Brothers? "Need, need," I'm saying I love you, is that so wrong? Is that not allowed anymore? *(Pause.)* And so what if I did need her? Is that so bad? All right, crucify me, I needed her! So what! I don't want to be by myself, I'm by myself I feel like I'm going out of my mind, I do. I sit there, I'm thinking forget it, I'm not gonna make it through the next ten seconds. I just can't stand it. But I do, somehow, I get through the ten seconds, but then I have to do it all over again, cause they just keep coming, all these … seconds, floating by, while I'm waiting for something to happen, I don't know what, a car wreck, a nuclear war or something. That sounds awful but at least there'd be this instant when I'd know I was alive. Just once. Cause I look in the mirror, and I can't believe I'm really there. I can't believe that's me. It's like, my body, right, is the size of, what, the Statue of Liberty, and I'm inside it, I'm down in one of the legs, the gigantic hairy leg, I'm scraping around inside my own foot like some tiny fetus. And I don't know who I am or where I'm going. And I wish I'd never been born. *(Pause.)* Not only that, my hair is falling out, and that really sucks.

Calling Wanda

Megan Gogerty

Play
Comic
M
20s
Contemporary

Kevin swoons, proving once again that stalkers are people, too.

Her name is Wanda. Isn't that a pretty name? Wanda. I get goosebumps. Wanda Wanda Wanda. *(Real fast:)* WandaWandaWandaWandaWanda WandaWandaWanda. She's a professional. I'm going to call her again tonight. No, I know what you're thinking. You're thinking, last month, right? That one time with Delores, right? That whole stalking bit, but see, this is different. Wanda is different. She wants me to call her back. So it's OK. She and I are connected spiritually. She said so. She is so alive. Me, I'm not living. I am dead. Well, I'm not dead-dead. I'm breathing, I'm passing food, but I'm not really alive, y'know? I'm — I'm existing. Wanda. She's … she's amazing, is what she is. I think — Whoah. *(Hand to chest.)* Guys, feel my chest. I'm having palpitations. Palpitations of love!

Casina

Titus Maccius Plautus

Play
Comic
M
45+
Classic

Lysidamus, a self-described curmudgeon smitten with Casina, is transformed by love.

Ah, yes, yes, there's nothing in the world like love, no bloom like its bloom; not a thing can you mention that has more flavour and more savour. Upon my soul, it's most surprising that cooks, with all their use of spices, don't use this one spice that excels them all. Why, when you spice a dish with love it'll tickle every palate, I do believe. Not a thing can be either salt or sweet without a dash of love: It will turn gall, bitter though it be, to honey — an old curmudgeon to a *(Self-consciously.)* pleasing and polished gentleman. It is more from my own case than from hearsay I draw this conclusion. Now that I'm in love with Casina, how I have bloomed out! I'm more natty than nattiness itself. I keep all the perfumers on the jump; wherever there's a nice scent to be had, I get scented, so as to please her. *(Preening himself.)* And it seems to me I do please her. *(Pauses.)* But my wife does torment me by — living! *(Glancing toward his house; stiffens.)* I see her, standing there with a sour look. And unless she's gone deaf, she's heard every word. Well, I suppose I must greet this bad bargain of mine with some smooth talk. *(To audience, hopefully.)* Unless there's anyone here who would like to substitute for me. *(Vainly waits for reply; turns to his wife, fondly.)* And how goes it with my dear and my delight?

The Casket Comedy
Titus Maccius Plautus

Play
Comic
M
20s
Classic

Alcesimarchus, tortured by love, begs our sympathy.

I do believe it was Love that first devised the torturer's profession here on earth. It's my own experience — no need to look further — that makes me think so, for in torment of soul no man rivals me, comes near me. I'm tossed around, bandied about, goaded, whirled on the wheel of love, done to death, poor wretch that I am! I'm torn, torn asunder, disrupted, dismembered — yes, all my mental faculties are befogged! Where I am, there I am not; where I am not, there my soul is — yes, I am in a thousand moods! The thing that pleases me ceases to please a moment later; yes, Love mocks me in my weariness of soul — it drives me off, hounds me, seeks me, lays hands on me, holds me back, lures, lavishes! It gives without giving! beguiles me! It leads me on, then warns me off; it warns me off, then tempts me on. It deals with me like the waves of the sea — yes, batters my loving heart to bits; and except that I do not go to the bottom, poor devil, my wreck's complete in every kind of wretchedness! Yes, my father has kept me at the villa on the farm the last six successive days and I was not allowed to come and see my darling during all that time! Isn't it a terrible thing to tell of?

Changes in the Memory After Fifty
Steve Martin

Essay
Comic
M
50+
Contemporary

The lapses of memory that occur after fifty are normal and in some ways beneficial. There are certain things it's better to forget, like the time Daddy once failed to praise you, and now, forty years later, you have to count the tiles in the bathroom — first in multiples of three, then in multiples of five, and so on, until they come out even — or else you can't get out of the shower. The memory is selective, and sometimes it will select 1956 and 1963 and that's all. Such memory lapses don't necessarily indicate a more serious health problem. The rule is that if you think you have a pathological memory problem you probably don't. In fact the most serious indicator is when you're convinced you're fine and yet people often ask you, "Why are you here in your pajamas at the Kennedy Center Honors?"

Let's say you've just called your best friend, Joe and invited him to an upcoming anniversary party, and then, minutes later, you call Joe back to invite him to the same party again. This does not mean that you are "losing it" or are "not playing with a full deck" or are "not all there" or that you're "eating with the dirigibles" or "shellacking the waxed egg" or "looking inside your own mind and finding nothing there," or any of the other demeaning epithets that are said about people who are peeling an empty banana. It does mean, however, that perhaps Joe is no longer on the list of things that you're going to remember. This is Joe's fault. He should be more memorable. He should have a name like *El Elegante*.

The Clawfoot Interviews

Werner Trieschmann

Play
Comic
M
Teen
Contemporary

Angus, a hyper teenager, pitches his movie idea as Olivia tries to sell a clawfoot bathtub.

… so the girl is in the tub, you see. But she's like not the Creature yet. Her hair's all wet and shit and hangin' down and she's got this scowl, like you know somethin' is going on, somethin' is happenin' to this chick. And the power chords are getting wicked at this point, downright evil. Cut to the band and we're whipping our hair back and forth like this, then cut to the Doctor. The Doctor's eyes are buggin' out to here 'cause he doesn't know what the hell he's got on his hands. You know, like what is this thing he made and what can he do about it now, but then you can see that he thinks what the hell, it's too late at this point, science or his karma got seriously out of whack and let things get to this point. So WHAT THE HELL, you know. So cut to his hand throwing the switch and then cut to the tub where the girl is shakin', water is bubblin' and smoke is everywhere. And we're at the climax, laying down some heavy shit, and the Doctor with a big friggin' ax comes up behind the Creature and cuts its head off. The End. Righteous, huh? The point is you can't fool with nature, or if you do you gotta like kill stuff with an axe. This clawfoot bathtub will be awesome! The name sounds wicked, ya know? Anyway, after we shoot the video, the band is goin' on the road. You can come.

The Clouds

Aristophanes

Play
Comic
M
45+
Classic

Pheidippides has just been beating his father, Strepsiades, with a stick, right there, in front of everyone at the banquet. Strepsiades has just asked the young upstart to sing his defense of his actions for the guests. The smarty-pants son refuses.

You hear that?
                    A cricket-concert!
His exact words.
                    And then he started sneering at Simonides!
Called him — get this — Puny Pipsqueak Hack!
                                        Was I *sore?*
Brother!
        Well, somehow I counted to ten, and then I asked him
to sing me some Aischylos "a poet of colossal stature." —

Yup,
"the most colossal, pretentious, pompous, spouting, bombastic bore
in poetic history."
                    I was so damn mad I just about went through
the
roof.
But I gritted my teeth together, mustered up a sick smile
and somehow managed to say, "All right, son, if that's how you feel,
then sing me a passage from one of those highbrow modern plays
you're so crazy about."
                    So he recited — you can guess — Euripides!
One of those slimy tragedies where, so help me, there's a brother
who screws his own sister!
                    Well, Ladies, *that* did it!

I

jumped up,
blind with rage, started cursing at him and calling him names,
and he started screaming and cursing back and before I knew it,
he hauled off and — *wham!* — he biffed me and bashed me and
        clipped me
and poked me and choked me and —

                                        Euripides! A GENIUS??

The Clouds

Aristophanes

Play
Comic
M
45+
Classical

What's an Ancient Greek father to do? This is Strepsiades.

> Why, you ungrateful brat, I *raised*
> you!
> When you were a baby I pampered you! I waited on you hand and
> foot!
> I understood your baby talk. You babbled GOO and I obeyed. Why,
> when you whimpered WAWA DADA, who brought our water?
> DADA did.
> When you burbled BABA, who brought your Baby Biscuits?
> DADA did.
> And when you cried GOTTA GO KAKA DADA, who saved his
> shitty darling?
> Who rushed you to the door? Who held you while you did it? Damn
> you,
> DADA did!
>
> And in return you choked me.
> and when I shat in terror,
> would you give your Dad a hand,
> would you help me to the door?
> No, you left me there alone
> to do it on the floor!
>
> *Yes, to do it on the floor!*

The Clouds

Aristophanes

Play
Comic
M
45+
Classic

Unable to sleep, Strepsiades mulls over his entire life.

Great gods! will these nights never end? Will daylight never come? I heard the cock crow long ago and my slaves are snoring still! Ah! 'twas not so formerly. Curses on the War! Has it not done me ills enough? Now I may not even chastise my own slaves — they never wake the whole long night, but, wrapped in five coverlets, fart away to their hearts content. Come! let me nestle in well and snore too, if it be possible ... oh! misery, 'tis vain to think of sleep with all these expenses, this stable, these debts, which are devouring me, thanks to this fine cavalier, my own son, who only knows how to look after his long locks, to show himself off in his chariot and to dream of horses! And I, I am nearly dead, and my liability falling due ... Slave! light the lamp and bring me my tablets. Who are all my creditors? Let me see and reckon up the interest. What is it I owe? ... Twelve minæ to Pasias ... What! twelve minæ to Pasias? ... Why did I borrow these? Ah! I know! 'Twas to buy that thoroughbred, which cost me so dear. Oh! curses on the go-between who made me marry your mother! I lived so happily in the country, a commonplace, everyday life, but a good and easy one — had not a trouble, not a care, was rich in bees, in sheep and in olives. Then forsooth I must marry the niece of Megacles, the son of Megacles; I belonged to the country, she was from the town; she was a haughty, extravagant woman, a true Cœsyra. On the nuptial day, when I lay beside her, I was reeking of the dregs of the wine-cup, of cheese and of wool; she was redolent with essences, saffron, tender kisses, the love of spending, of good cheer and of wanton delights. I will not say she did nothing; no, she worked hard ... to ruin me. Later, when we had this boy, what was to be his name? 'Twas the cause of much quarrelling with my loving wife. She insisted on having some reference to a horse in his name. I wanted to name him after his grandfather. She used to fondle and coax him, saying, "Oh! what a joy it will be to me when you have grown up, to see you, like my father, Megacles, clothed in purple and standing up straight in your chariot driving your steeds toward the town." And I would say to him, "When, like your father, you will go, dressed in a skin, to fetch back your goats from Phellus." Alas! he never listened to me and his madness for horses has shattered my fortune.

The Constant Couple

George Farquhar

Play
Comic
M
30+
Classic

Sir Harry babbles on about virtue.

(Aside.) This is the first whore in heroics that I have met with. *(Aloud.)* Look ye, madam, as to that slander particular of your virtue, we shan't quarrel about it; you may be as virtuous as any woman in England, if you please; you may say your prayers all the time. But pray, madam, be pleased to consider what is this same virtue that you make such a mighty noise about. Can your virtue bespeak you a front row in the boxes? No; for the players can't live upon virtue. Can your virtue keep you a coach and six? No, no, your virtuous women walk a-foot. Can your virtue hire you a pew in church? Why, the very sexton will tell you, no. Can your virtue stake for you at picquet? No. Then what business has a woman with virtue? Come, come, madam, I offered you fifty guineas; there's a hundred. — The devil! Virtuous still! Why, 'tis a hundred, five score, a hundred guineas! Affront! 'Sdeath, madam! A hundred guineas will set you up at basset, a hundred guineas will give you an air of quality; a hundred guineas will buy you a rich escritoire for your billets-doux, or a fine Common Prayer Book for your virtue. A hundred guineas will buy a hundred fine things and fine things are for fine ladies, and fine ladies are for fine gentlemen; and fine gentlemen are for — Egad, this burgundy makes a man speak like an angel. Come, come, madam, take it and put it to what use you please.

Contest

Langston Hughes

Short story
Comic
M
60+
Contemporary

Simple satirizes the American Beauty Pageant.

They are always holding Beauty Contests all over America ... Why don't nobody ever hold an Ugly Contest?

... I would give [the winner] a great big prize, then put her under contract for all personal appearances on stage, screen, or at the Rockland Palace. I would charge one-thousand-dollars-a-day commission for the public to look at her — the Homeliest Woman in the Whole world. The Ugly Champion of the Universe! If ever she went up in a spaceship, she would scare the Man in the Moon to death before she had a chance to meet him. Miss Ugly would be so ugly she would be proud of herself, and her mama before her would be proud of her, as would her daddy when he learned how famous his daughter had got to be — pictured endorsing every filter-tipped cigarette, singing commercials for toothpaste, and posing for beer.

Seriously, I believe I will start such a contest, get me maybe a thousand entries, hire a big hall, Count Basie's Band, and have me an Ugly Parade instead of Beauty Parade, appoint Nipsey Russell and Jackie Moms Mabley as judges, and take a big pile of money. Besides, such a contest would make me famous, too — as the only man in the world with nerve enough call a *whole lot* of women ugly! "Jesse B. Semple, promoter of the Ugly Contest!" And if I found a woman uglier than I am a man, more homely than me, I would give her a special prize myself. A gold beer mug with my picture on it, engraved: TO YOU FROM ME, YOUR UGLY DADDY, JESSE B. SEMPLE, CONGRATULATIONS.

The Contrast

Royall Tyler

Play
Comic
M
20+
Classic

Plucky servant, Jessamy, gives a lesson in courting (as he has learned from his master).

Say to her! Why, when a man goes a-courting, and hopes for success, he must begin with doing, and not saying. When you are introduced, you must make five or six elegant bows. Then you must press and kiss her hand; then press and kiss, and so on to her lips and cheeks; then talk as much as you can about hearts, darts, flames, nectar, and ambrosia — the more incoherent, the better. If she should pretend — please to observe, Mr. Jonathan — if she should pretend to be offended, you must — But I'll tell you how my master acted in such a case. He was seated by a young lady of eighteen upon a sofa, plucking with a wanton hand the blooming sweets of youth and beauty. When the lady thought it necessary to check his ardor, she called up a frown upon her lovely face, so irresistibly alluring, that it would have warmed the frozen bosom of age; remember, said she, putting her delicate arms upon his, remember your character and my honor. My master instantly dropped upon his knees, with eyes swimming with love, cheeks glowing with desire, and in his gentlest modulation of voice, he said, "My dear Caroline, in a few months our hands will be indissolubly united at the altar; our hearts I feel are already so; the favors you now grant as evidence of your affections are favors indeed; yet, when the ceremony is once past, what will now be received with rapture will then be attributed to duty." The consequence? Ah, forgive me, my dear friend, but you New England gentlemen have such a laudable curiosity seeing the bottom of everything; — Why, to be honest, I confess I saw the blooming cherub of a consequence smiling in its angelic mother's arms about ten months afterwards.

The Country Wit

John Crowne

Play
Comic
M
25+
Classic

Ramble is stuck between a rock and a rather sweet place.

Into what villainous trap I am fallen, dull rogue that I was, not to know Isabella's voice, where were my ears, my senses? They were all in my pocket, I was tickled with my ravishing expectations into a perfect numbness to death. Now I am discovered in all my rogueries, and intrigues, and falsehoods, and must never hope to enjoy the sweet pleasure of lying or forswearing any more. I must now either repent, and become a downright plodding lover to Christina, or in plain terms, lose her. I must either forsake all the world for her, or her for all the world. Well, if I do forsake her, she has this to boast, I do not forsake her for any one woman, I forsake her for ten thousand. But what do I talk of forsaking her, will she not forsake me, after this discovery? And besides her own anger, will not Sir Thomas compel her? For he is horribly provoked against me, whatever the matter is. Well, I cannot bear the loss of Mrs. Christina, I had rather endure marriage with her than enjoy any other woman at pleasure. I must, and will repent, and reform, and now should an angel appear in female shape, he should not tempt me to revolt any more.

The Customs Collector in Baggy Pants

Lawrence Ferlinghetti

Play
Comic
M
Any age
Contemporary

In a ladies' washroom on an ocean liner, the customs collector addresses the ladies in the pay toilets.

Pardon me, ladies, forgive me for interrupting you at your devotions, but there is an urgent matter at hand, a pressing problem which will not wait, a certain famous diamond has been lost or stolen, and we have received cables containing certain information which led us to believe that this very diamond may very well be found upon persons of the female sex aboard this vessel, and so therefore this has necessitated my search of these private premises of you ladies (…) and if I now detect a certain sniggering and moaning in your midst, as if you were thinking that I have lost my marbles, I want you to know that my marbles are one thing which I have not lost, and in fact I have them right here, right here at hand, so to speak, and they are themselves gems of the very greatest worth, let me assure you, in case you should be beginning to doubt and deride my marbles, and I can assure you that each of them could bring you great things, and I always keep them hanging handy for just such occasions, on the ready, so to speak, yes, and I've got them here somewhere, if you will bear with me for a moment, I'm sure I had them with me, I always carry them wherever I go in this floating universe, in this fit of existence called life, for they are truly inseparable, these twin gems who will let nothing come between them, and yet, and yet whenever that great King of Diamonds rises up, as I have before described, whenever that great tyrant arises and goeth forth for the night then there is indeed great stress and strain created between my two little gems, but ladies I do not mean to regale you with old wives' tales as to the history of our customs, I merely mean to do my duty in the search for that lost treasure and in the collections involved therein, and therefore now I would ask you ladies one by one to allow me to investigate the problem to its very roots (…)

Dating Your Mom

Ian Frazier

Essay
Comic
M
25+
Contemporary

Dating your mother seriously might seem difficult at first, but once you try it I'll bet you'll be surprised at how easy it is. Facing up to your intention is the main thing: You have to want it bad enough. One problem is that lots of people get hung up on feelings of guilt about their dad. They think, Oh, here's this kindly old guy who taught me how to hunt and whittle and dynamite fish — I can't let him go on into his twilight years alone. Well, there are two reasons you can dismiss those thoughts from you mind. First, *every* woman, I don't care who she is, prefers her son to her husband. That is a simple fact; ask any woman who has a son, and she'll admit it. (…) When you and your mom begin going together, you will simply become part of a natural and inevitable historical trend.

Second, you must remember this about your dad: You have your mother, he has his! Let him go put the moves on his own mother and stop messing with yours. (…) It's not your fault that he didn't realize his mom for the woman she was, before it was too late. Probably he's going to try a lot of emotional blackmail on you just because you had a good idea and he never did. Don't but it. Comfort yourself with the thought that your dad belongs to the last generation of guys who will let their moms slip away from them like that.

(…) Once your dad is out of the picture — once he has taken up fly-tying, joined the Single Again Club, moved to Russia, whatever — and your mom has been wooed and won, if you're anything like me you're going to start having so much fun that the good times you had with your mother when you were little will seem tame by comparison.

Dick

Robin Rothstein

Original monologue
Comic
M
20s-30s
Contemporary

Richard, a waiter lacking in self-awareness, enters and approaches a table. He considers himself amusing and well-intentioned, but he ultimately comes off as obnoxious.

Good evening and welcome to *Il Piccolo Castello.* My name is Richard, and I will be your server this evening. So how are ya tonight? You both doin' good? New year treatin' ya good? *(He regards the couple, who say nothing back to him. He nods and smiles. Pause.)* OK. Great. Well, now that we've become acquainted, I would like to take this opportunity to make you aware of the fact that I am not just a waiter. I am actually an aspiring research scientist, and am currently working on my final thesis, which involves lab experiments with rare infectious diseases. Don't worry, I washed my hands before I cut your bread. *(He chuckles, then sneezes. He wipes his nose on his hand)* Okay. Great. So, we have two specials this evening … in addition to yourselves … which I would like to delineate, at this time. First off, for a mere twenty-two dollars, our talented chef has prepared an awesome seared salmon, which he adorns with a pungent lemon relish and capers, and serves over a bed of sautéed escarole. This special is so a must have! As you probably already know, salmon is not only an excellent source of iodine — a known goiter deterrent — but also contains your cancer-crushing Omega-3 fatty acids. And on top of that, holy cow you get the escarole, which will provide you with the roughage you need for healthy digestion and cohesive bowel movements! Now that's special, huh! *(Pause.)* OK. Great. So, our other special this evening is a fabulous orecchiette pasta, which in Italian means *(He tugs lightly on one of his earlobes.)* "little ears." The orecchiette is tossed in a tomato cream sauce comprised of prosciutto and hot pepper, and is being offered at the bargain price of sixteen dollars. *(He turns to one of the guests.)* Now ma'am, you seem as though you're probably in about your second trimester about now, so I would encourage you to stay away from the pasta considering it does have hot pepper. *(Pause. Listens.)* Oh. (…) Well, I've got great news for you! On the lighter side, I would like to point out that we proudly feature a fabulous steamed vegetable medley over organic risotto, which is conveniently equal to "one bread!" (…) Would either of you care for a nice glass of vino Italiano while you're deciding? *(To woman.)* Or perhaps a Diet Coke?

The Discovery
Frances Sheridan

Play
Comic
M
35+
Classic

Sir Harry Flutter shares his marital woes with his lordship.

Upon, my soul, my lord, I have been so stunn'd this morning with the din of conjugal interrogatories, that I am quite bated — do, let me lounge a little on this couch of yours. I came home at three o'clock, as I told you, a little tipsy, too, by the by, but what was that to her, you know for I am always good humored in my cups. To bed I crept, as softly as a mouse, for I had no more thought of quarreling with her then, than I have now with your lordship. — La, says she, with a great heavy sigh, It is a sad thing that one must be disturbed in this manner; and on she went, mutter, mutter, mutter, for a quarter of an hour, I all the while lying quiet as a lamb, without making her a word of answers. At last, quite tired of her perpetual buzzing in my ear, Prithee, be quiet, Mrs. Wasp, says I, and let me sleep (I was not thoroughly awake when I spoke). Do so, Mr. Drone, grumbled she, and gave a great flounce. I said no more, for in two minutes I was as fast as a top. Just now, when I came down to breakfast, she was seated at the tea table all alone, and looked so neat, and so cool, and so pretty, that, e'gad, not thinking of what had passed, I was going to give her a kiss; when up she tossed her demure little face. You were a pretty fellow last night, Sir Harry, says she. So I am every night, I hope, Ma'am, says I, making her a low bow. Was not that something in your manner, my lord? — Pray where were you till that unconscionable hour, says she? At the tavern drinking, says I, very civilly. And who was with you, Sir? Oh, thought I, I'll match you in your enquiries; I named your lordship, and half a dozen more wild fellows (whom, by the way, I had not so much as seen), and two or three girls of the town, added I, whistling, and looking another way. Down she slapped her cup and saucer. If this be the case, Sir Harry *(Half sobbing.),*

I shall desire a separate bed. That's as I please (…) No, it shall be as I please, sir. — It shan't madam; It shall, Sir; and it shan't and it shall, and it shall and it shan't was bandied backwards and forwards till we were both out of breath and passion.

The Doctor in Spite of Himself

Molière

Play
Comic
M
40+
Classic

Amid a series of misunderstandings, Sganrelle, a peasant woodcutter, finds himself elevated to the role of doctor. His patient, Lucinde, is faking dumbness to avoid marrying a nobleman. Together, they seek to deceive Lucinde's father. (Performance note: At times, this speech flies.)

Young lady, please, give me your little hand.
Ah, yes, this pulse gives me to understand,
Your daughter's dumb. Yes, sir, that's her affliction!
I feel it with a sudden, strong conviction!
Great doctors diagnose these things at once.
Some other folk might hem and haw for months,
Suggesting it was this, or it was that,
But I can see at once, and tell you flat,
What might not be so evident to some,
But to my eyes, it's clear your daughter's dumb.
In my opinion it comes from a humor,
And from experience we may assume her
Debilitation stems from out the gall,
A state which comes from humors which we call
Unhealthy. There are vapors which arise from
Emission of the influence which drys from
The onset of the maladies which sat in,
Diseases which, you know … Do you know Latin?
Hmm? No? No? Not a word?
So, vapors by the humors are so stirred,
And pass from liver's region on the left,
Unto the right, where heart is there bereft.
The vapors there fill ventricles, waylaid
Amid a portion of the shoulder blade.

And since such vapors ... follow closely, please,
The vapors often carry on the breeze,
And ... please, I beg you, pay your best attention ...
This breeze can blow a most malign intention,
Which comes from ... please, now, follow this most close ...
It all, you see, stems from too big a dose:
Acidity within the diaphragm;
Forms a concavity which makes a dam,
The edge of which may then begin to feel loose
As ... nequer, potarinum quipsa milus.
And that is why your daughter is now mute!

Well, yes, that's true; you are, Sir, most astute
The time was when the heart was on the left,
With liver on the right. You are most deft.
And yet we now have changed all that around,
Advances that we've made are quite profound.
(...)
A moment, sir. Allow me to prescribe.
She suffers from a noxious diatribe.
I think that I know just the remedy.
To bring her back from such extremity.

Dominic

Rob Matsushita

Radio play
Comic
M
20s
Contemporary

Dominic can make one phone call. Maybe he should have called his lawyer.

Don't hang up — don't hang up!

Please don't hang up.

It's Dominic.

Don't hang up — don't hang up!

I think it's important for you to know that this is my *one* phone call.

Well, because I could have called *anyone*. And I called *you*. So I think that should count for something.

Yes, it should!

Don't hang up — don't hang up!

Look. OK. I'm just … I'm really embarrassed about the whole thing. And I just wanted to know if we can put it past us —

Don't hang up — don't hang up!

OK, OK … bad choice of words. I just wanted to …

"Where did I get the gun?" What the hell does that have to do with anythi —

Don't hang up — don't hang up!

I got it from this guy — you know, I probably shouldn't say while I'm *here*, and all.

Well, they could be listening.

No, I'm not being *paranoid!* I'm in a *police station!* They could —

Don't hang up — don't hang up! Please don't hang up.

OK, look:

Where I got the gun doesn't matter. I'm just sorry I …

Well, OK, I'll explain.

You just made me mad, sweetie. Really, really mad.

No, no, It was my fault. I'm sorry about what I said to your father. I was wrong to say it — he and I usually argee on stuff, and —

Yeah, I guess I'm sorry I hit him, too.

But you shouldn't have said to me —

Don't hang up — don't hang up! Please don't hang up. OK? OK?

You ... were right to say what you said. I was just angry.

And I really thought you were working today.

Well, I thought you were.

I mean, thank God you weren't. If you were, then ...

I'm just glad you didn't work today.

I'm glad you're alive.

It sounds weird to say out loud, but thank God I thought that other girl was you, otherwise ...

I just wanted you to know that I'm glad I killed the wrong girl.

Hello?

Hello?

Um.

Um, Officer? Does it still count as my one phone call if I call the same person back?

Um, OK, go ahead and check.

I'll just wait here.

Duane

Rob Matsushita

Radio play
Comic
M
20s
Contemporary

Duane, a fool for love, apologizes to Jody-Jo. This will play best if it's sincere, folks.

Um, hi.

Uh, I guess this is gonna be more of an apology than anything else, so I'll just hit you with it.

Jody-Jo, I am very sorry for the things I said to you at The Ground Round last Saturday.

But, y'know. With what you told me?

It was a lot to take in.

I mean, I knew you had news. I had an idea it wasn't going to be good news, so ...

Well, OK, I might have been OK with you sleeping with another woman. That would be one thing.

And, OK, that you had a serious relationship with her upset me.

I don't know why, really.

And then I called you ... that name. That no one should be called.

I guess I'm sorry for that, too. I guess.

So, I'm thinking now that I overreacted.

To *that* news.

Looking back, I would have held back if I'd have known there was more.

Like the fact that you were a *man* when you were in that relationship.

And if the lady who got hit with my clam sauce is listening? I'd like to apologize to her, too.

I don't know if I should have seen it coming. I mean, I've seen your baby pictures and all.

Like I said, maybe I overreacted. After all, you were *born* a girl, so it's not like it makes me gay for being attracted to you.

I don't think.

I mean, I've given this a lot of thought. I hope you realize that.

And I hope you also realize that, what with you being born a girl, having a sex change operation to make you a man, then having another sex-change operation to make you back into a girl again …

… Well, you can see why I thought you might have some commitment issues.

But I've done some real thinking on this, Jody-Jo, and I really want you to come back to me.

Because I love you, and I want you to be my wife.

Or, you know, whatever.

Dumb as a Brick

Keith Knight

Comic strip
Comic
M
30s
Contemporary

I am so stupid. So damn stupid. Lemme explain …

About twenty-five years ago, I was watching this flick called *The Swarm*. The swarm was this movie about a big swarm of Africanized killer bees that invades the U.S. and kills everyone in its path. It wasn't the film itself that was so scary … it was the real-life news story that followed that was really frightening: "Killer bees are real!! But don't worry … they are in South America right now and it will be at least 20 years before they reach California …"

The news story prompted me to announce my first, big, life decision at the dinner table the following evening: "I don't know much, but this I know: I will NOT be living in California in the 1990s!"

Well, it's twenty-five years later and I just read about some guy in Southern California that was fatally attacked by a swarm of killer bees. And I just celebrated my ninth anniversary of moving to California.

How the hell could I have screwed up so bad? I blame my parents. They tried in vain to talk me out of moving to California from Boston: "Wait!! You've got no money!!! You don't know anyone out there!!"

All they had to say was "What about the killer bees?" and I would've stayed.

I called them up last week to bitch them out and demanded they come up with a way for their only son to protect himself. They said if I encounter a swarm of them, coat myself in honey and throw a brick at them. They said it works for bears, too.

The Fawn

John Marston

Play
Comic
M
25+
Classic

Nymphadoro. His name says it all.

Faith, Fawn, 'tis my humor, the natural sin of my sanguine complexion: I am most enforcedly in love with all women, almost affecting them all with an equal flame. If she be a virgin of a modest eye, shamefaced, temperate aspect, her very modesty inflames me, her sober blushes fire me; if I behold a wanton, pretty, courtly, petulant ape, I am extremely in love with her, because she is not clownishly rude, and that she assures her lover of no ignorant, dull unmoving Venus; be she sourly severe, I think she wittily counterfeits, and I love her for her wit; if she be learned and censure poets, I love her soul, and for her soul, her body; if she be a lady of professed ignorance, oh, I am infinitely taken with her simplicity, as one assured to find no sophistication about her; be she slender and lean, she's the Greek's delight, be she thick and plump, she's the Italian's pleasure; if she be tall, she's of a goodly form, and will print a fair proportion in a large bed; if she be short and low, she's nimbly delightful, and ordinarily quick-witted; be she young, she's for mine eye, be she old, she's for my discourse, as one well knowing there's much amiableness in a grave matron; but be she young or old, lean, fat, short, tall, white, red, brown, or black, my discourse shall find reason to love her, if my means may procure opportunity to enjoy her.

The Fawn

John Marston

Play
Comic
M
25+
Classic

Hercules makes a case for free love, for all.

Why should any woman only love any one man, since it is reasonable women should affect all perfections, but all perfection never rests in one man; many men have many virtues, but ladies should love many virtues; therefore ladies should love many men. For as in women, so in men, some woman hath only a good eye, one can discourse beautifully (if she do not laugh), one's well favored to her nose, another hath only a good brow, t'other a plump lip, a third only holds beauty to the teeth, and there the soil alters; some peradventure, hold good to the breasts, and then downward turn like the dreamt of image, whose head was gold, breast silver, thighs iron, and all beneath clay and earth; one only winks eloquently, another only kisses well, t'other only talks well, a fourth only lies well. So in men: One gallant has only a good face, another has only a grave methodical beard and is a notable wise fellow (until he speaks), a third only makes water well (and that's a good provoking quality), one only swears well, another only speaks well, a third only does well — all in their kind good; goodness is to be affected; therefore, they. It is a base thing, and indeed an impossible, for a worthy mind to be contented with the whole world, but most vile and abject to be satisfied with one point or prick of the world.

Good Evening

Peter Cook and Dudley Moore

Play
Comic
M
45+
Contemporary

Sometimes there are family secrets you'd rather not know.

Roger, here is your mother's signet ring she wanted you to have and wear for her. Took me two hours to get it off her bloody finger. And if you wouldn't mind wearing this black armband in memory of your Mother. I know she'd be pleased because she sewed it especially for you.

Roger, your Mother left this life as she lived it, screaming her bloody head off. I remember it very well, it was a Wednesday afternoon. Uncle Ralph had come in for a cup of tea, we hadn't seen him for twenty years and we were, you know, talking about when we used to walk over the cliffs at Leigh on Sea watching the boats come in — he's a boring bugger, that Ralph — once every twenty years is good enough for me. Anyway, Mother was lying very quietly, very still, almost at rest and suddenly, without a word of a lie, she sat bolt upright in bed, she went, "Aargh" *(Screams.)* Her false teeth hit the ceiling and that was it. Your mother never did anything by halves — both sets — POW — hit the electric lightbulb, the bulb fell to the floor, smashed, matron came running in, slipped on the broken glass, hit her head on the bedpost, killed outright … Nurse Oviatt, hearing the commotion, came roaring in from the President Roosevelt Memorial Ward, tripped over matron and went flying out the window. She fell five stories onto a car that was coming into the forecourt. It was an open car, she killed herself and the two passengers. The weight of the three dead bodies on the accelerator took that car roaring into the catering department, killed seven nurses, knocked ten orderlies into a huge vat of boiling potatoes. Well naturally, the valve on the vat got stuck and there was a tremendous explosion — and the first floor collapsed. Well, you can imagine what that did to the second and third floors. Anyway, son, I won't bore you with the details — suffice it to say, that I was the sole survivor. Nine hundred and eighty-seven people wiped out in a flash of your mother's teeth.

Half Asleep in Frog Pajamas

Tom Robbins

Novel
Comic
M
30s
Contemporary

Belford, a do-gooder, explains to a befuddled policeman why he needs help locating his lost monkey.

You ask me what kind of monkey is this lost monkey? Well, officer, if you know your monkeys, you'll have a good idea of Andre's description when I tell you he's a tailless macaque of the type commonly called a Barbary ape. An Old World monkey. About yea tall and yea wide. (...) Andre was not a new monkey. By which I mean, he was a previously owned monkey. And his previous master was a Belgian animal trainer turned bad. Turned jewel thief, to be frank. *Famous* jewel thief. Or would that be *infamous*? (...) You may have heard of the guy. Kongo van den Bos. No? Really? Well, in any case, it was entirely Kongo's fault. (...) Andre was just doing what Kongo van den Bos — I'm surprised you never heard of him in your line of work — taught him to do. (...) He was caught red-handed in Saint-Tropez — that's a town on the Riviera, not the sort of spot where I normally hang out, ha-ha — and it was at that time that the authorities finally realized he had trained this monkey to do his dirty deeds for him. (...) I guess there was a big to-do over it, because the authorities wanted to put Andre to death. (...) I've always loved animals, officer. Somebody mistreat a dog, it'd really get my dander up. This French monkey was so cute, and its life had been so unfair. (...) At first, they wouldn't even listen to me, but I was persistent. You learn that in salesmanship. Persistent and polite. (...) I don't know which the chief got the most tired of, the controversy, the media, or me on his doorstep, but one day, after about a month of hard lobbying, he called me in and said in perfect English, "If you can get this damnable brute out of France by tomorrow night, it is yours." (...) You see, I was convinced I could reform him. And I did. (...) Lord, how I prayed and prayed over that monkey! And I taught Andre to pray, too. OK, you can look at me funny, but for the last year and a half, Andre has been kneeling down beside me every night at bedtime and bowing his head, and folks may say, "Monkey see, monkey do" but I believe sincerely there's more to it than that. Andre is devout. He is. You should see the way the little rascal reacts to pictures of Jesus Christ. I know, I know, it's only a dumb animal, but who's to say Andre does not have a soul, a little monkey soul? Sure, he's been retrained, but I'm prepared to go further than that. Andre's been *reborn*.

Half Asleep in Frog Pajamas

Tom Robbins

Novel
Comic
M
40s
Contemporary

Larry Diamond, tattooed ex-stockbroker and mind-blower, reacts to Gwendolyn's egotistic brush off.

Future? Oh, I get it. You mean you don't foresee a pot of gold at the end of our juicy rainbow. You mean that our intimacy isn't likely to yield a dividend. You disappoint me, Gwendolyn. I hoped you might have a watt or two more light in your bulb than those poor toads who look on romance as an investment, like waterfront property or municipal bonds. Would you complain because a beautiful sunset doesn't have a future or a shooting star a payoff? And why should romance "lead anywhere"? Passion isn't a path through the woods. Passion *is* the woods. It's the deepest, wildest part of the forest, the grove where the fairies still dance and obscene old vipers snooze in the boughs. Everybody but the most dried up and dysfunctional is drawn to the grove and enchanted by its mysteries, but then they just can't wait to call in the chain saws and bull-dozers and replace it with a family-style restaurant or a new S and L. That's the payoff, I guess. Safety. Security. Certainty. Yes, indeed. Well, remember this, pussy latte: we're not involved in a "relationship," you and I, we're involved in a collision. Collisions don't much lend themselves to secure futures, but the act of colliding is hard to beat for interest. Correct me if I'm wrong. (…) It's disappointing because I was rather hoping we could have done some business together: I've got a plan … But it's probably best I do it on my own. As for the, uh, sex part, those things happen. No regrets. As long as you're disease-free. You *are*, aren't you?

An Indignation Dinner

James David Corrothers

Poem
Comic
M
30+
Classic

This poem was written around 1900.

Dey was hard times jes fo' Christmas round our neighborhood one year;
So we held a secret meetin', whah de white folks couldn't hear,
To 'scuss de situation, an' to see what could be done
Towa'd a fust-class Christmas dinneh an' a little Christmas fun.

Rufus Green who called de meetin', ris an' said: "in dis here town,
An' throughout de land, de white folks is a'tryin' to keep us down."
S' 'e: "Dey bought us, sold us, beat us; now dey 'buse us 'ca'se we's free;
But when dey tetch my stomach, dey's don gone too fur foh me!

"is I right?" "You sho is, Rufus!" roared a dozen hungry throats.
"Ef you'd keep a mule a-wo'kin', don't you tamper wid his oats.
Dat's sense," continued Rufus. "But dese white folks nowadays
Has done got so close and stingy you can't live on what dey pays.

"here 'tis Christmas-time, an', folkses, I's indignant 'nough to choke.
Whah's our Christmas dinneh comin' when we's mos' completely broke?
I can't hahdly 'fo'd a toothpick an' a glass o' water. Mad?
Say, I'm desp'ret! Dey jes better treat me nice, dese white folks had!"

Well, dey 'bused de white folks scan'lous, till old Pappy Simmons ris,
Leaning' on his cane to s'pote him, on account his rhematis,
An's' 'e: "Chillun, whut's dat wintry wind a-sighin' th'ough de street
'Bout yo' wasted summeh wages? But, no matter, we mus' eat.

"Now, I seed a beau'ful tuhkey on a certain gemmun's fahm.
He's a-growin' fat an' sassy, an' a-struttin' to a chahm.

Chickens, sheeps, hogs, sweet pertaters — all de craps is fine dis year;
All we needs is a committee foh to tote de goodies here."

Well, we lit right in an' voted dat it was a gran' idee,
An' de dinneh we had Christmas was worth trabblin' miles to see;
An' we eat a full an' plenty, big an' little, great an' small,
Not beca'se we was dishonest, but indignant, sah. Dat's all.

Life Without Leann

Larry Doyle

Essay
Comic
M
25+
Contemporary

Though written originally as a "newsletter" from a jilted lover, imagine the speaker in a more immediate situation. In front of a video camera?

By the time you receive this, it will have been more than five hundred days and nearly seventy-five weeks since Leann and I broke up, and, while I cannot proclaim our long ordeal ended, I am pleased to report some encouraging developments in that direction.

LEANN WATCHER OF THE WEEK … Kudos (and a two-year subscription to this newsletter) for Mike, of Evanston, Ill., who so eloquently and informatively captures a brief encounter he had with Leann on Jan. 6.

"Leann has lost some weight," Mike writes, "but she is no less beautiful for it. She says she has been exercising, taking classes, doing this, doing that. It appeared to me that she was struggling to fill some void. Your name didn't come up, but it wasn't so much what she said as what she didn't say."

THE STRUGGLE CONTINUES … If only it could all be such good news. But unfortunately, OPERATION: TERRIBLE MISTAKE has not been the success I anticipated, and I'm afraid a new strategy may be required.

As you may recall (LWL #57), the operation's objectives were to: (1) apply societal pressure; (2) foster emotional uncertainty; (3) precipitate reevaluation; and ideally (4) achieve reconciliation. The following conversation starter was suggested:

LEANN, I WAS SO SORRY TO HEAR ABOUT YOU AND LARRY. YOU MAKE SUCH A WONDERFUL COUPLE, SO I DON'T MIND TELLING YOU, I THINK YOU ARE MAKING A TERRIBLE MISTAKE. THIS IS MY OWN PERSONAL OPINION ON THE MATTER.

Unfortunately, a number of well-meaning individuals took this suggestion rather more literally than intended, and repeated it verbatim to Leann, creating a cumulative effect other than the one desired.

I have now received word through an intermediary that Leann requests I "call off the zombies." I will honor her wishes, as always, though I must emphasize that I cannot be held responsible for the behavior of individuals acting on their own initiative.

Love Tricks

James Shirley

> **Play**
> **Comic**
> **M**
> **50+**
> **Classic**

The thought of an impending wedding makes Rufaldo young again.

'Tis now early day; fie, what a long night hath this been! The sun went drunk to bed the last night, and could not see to rise this morning. I could hardly wink, I am sure, love kept me waking; and the expectation of this my wedding day did so caper in my brains, I thought of nothing but dancing the Shaking of the Sheets with my sweetheart. It is certain I am young, everybody now tells me so, it did appear by Selina's consenting so soon to love; for when I had but broke the ice of my affection, she fell head over heels in love with me. Was ever man so happy as I am? I do feel, I do feel my years dropping off, as the rain from a man that comes dropping. I do feel myself every day grow younger and younger still. Let me see, an hundred years hence, if I live to it, I shall be new out of my teens, and running into years of discretion again. Well, I will now to Master Cornelio's and bid them good morrow with a noise of musicians; and to see, at the very talking of music, how my heart leaps and dances at my wedding already! I have bespoke the parson to marry us, and have promised him a double fee for expedition. Oh, now I am so proud of my joy, my feet do not know what ground they stand on.

The Mathematics of Change

Josh Kornbluth

Play
Comic
M
35+
Contemporary

Josh likens his day at Princeton to a mathematical function.

Let's start with functions, why don't we?

A function is a transformative experience. It's kind of like a machine — you go into the function machine and you get ... changed. Well, you don't go into the machine — usually x goes into the machine. Mathematicians describe this situation as "f of x." X goes into f, the function machine, and it gets transformed into ... y. No one knows the reason for this — why x almost always gets transformed into y. But let's just accept it for now.

And x is the kind of thing you'd want to put inside a transformative machine, because x is a variable. You wouldn't want to put, say, c inside the machine, because c is a constant. And a constant is ... constant. You go up to a constant: "How're ya doing today, constant?" "Fine." Next day: "How're ya doing?" "Fine." Next day: "Fine." It's a constant!

But a variable: "Well, how're ya doing today, variable?" "Oh, pretty good." Next day: "Great!" Next day: "Lousy!" You know, it's a variable!

And mathematicians have focused on what happens to x when it's inside the machine, and what happens after it emerges. Less attention, I think, has been paid to that moment just before x enters the function machine. As it stands there, at the threshold of some new experience, not knowing what's about to befall it. Standing there — trembling, tremulous ...

Standing, or sometimes ... sitting — sitting in folding chairs arrayed neatly all along the great North Lawn of the Princeton University campus. We were the incoming freshmen of Princeton, and this was our first day at college. They had announced over the loudspeaker: "Incoming freshmen!" We all ducked.

Mexican American

Rick Najera

> Play
> Comic
> M
> 20-30s
> Contemporary

Rick's twelve-step testimony takes on characteristics of a split personality. No, it doesn't. Yes, it does. No, it doesn't.

I love commercials. They are so educational. They let me know what I need. I got a lot of needs 'cause I'm Mexican-American. (…) My American side needs football. My Mexican side needs bullfights … I know, it's very violent and barbaric, but I love football. I need Mexican food. And American food. My Mexican side needs *carne asada*. My American side needs New York steak, which is basically bland *carne asada*. I love Mexican food. When I see that Rosarita Refried Bean commercial, my Mexican side just wants to take that Rosarita woman and put her on a kitchen table and wango, wango, wango! And have twelve children through her. But my American side would like to get to know her better, talk to her, establish some honesty, communication, and then wango, wango, wango! And have 2.5 kids with her. My American side would like to hang out with his friends, and that's called a fraternity. But when my Mexican side hangs out with his friends, it's called a street gang! (…) I call myself Mexican so I won't forget my past, and American because that's what I am. When do I get to call myself an American? When do I get to drive past San Clemente and not get stopped by a guy in a green uniform on top of my trunk looking for illegal aliens? I'm going to say something very controversial. I love folklorico dancing. I don't think it's boring at all. Whenever I see a hat in front of me … *(A Mexican hat is thrown in front of him.)* Gotta dance! *(Tries to dance, but can't.)* Oh, my God, I've lost my rhythm. My American side is invading my central nervous system. *(In a Mexican voice.)* "You colonizing bastards." *(In a yuppie tone.)* "Go back to Mexico, dude." *(Mexican voice.)* "I din't cross the border. The border crossed me." *(Yuppie voice.)* You beaner. *(Mexican voice.)* You Gavacho. *(Yuppie voice.)* You wetback. *(Mexican voice.)* Wetback? Nobody calls me a wetback. I'll kill you. *(He chokes himself. Yuppie voice.)* Help me, help me! The Mexican is going to kill me. Help, help! Somebody call the border patrol!

The Minor

Samuel Foote

Play
Comic
M
30+
Classic

Smirk relates how he came to be an auctioneer.

… did you hear, Sir George what first brought me into the business?
Quite an accident… You must have known my predecessor, Mr. Prig, the
greatest man in the world, in his way, ay that ever was or ever will be;
quite a jewel of a man; he would touch you up a lot; there was no resist-
ing him. He would force you to bid, whether you would or no. I shall
never see his equal. Far be it from me to vie with so great a man. But, as
I was saying, my predecessor, Mr. Prig, was to have a sale, as it might be,
on a Saturday. On Friday at noon (I shall never forget the day) he was
suddenly seized with a violent colic. He sent for me to his bedside,
squeezed me by the hand, "Dear Smirk," said he, "what an accident! You
know what is tomorrow: the greatest show this season; prints, pictures,
bronzes, butterflies, medals and mignonettes; all the world will be there,
Lady Dy Joss, Mrs. Nankyn, the Duchess of Dupe and everybody at all.
You see my state, it will be impossible for me to mount. What can I do."
It was not for me, you know , to advise that great man … At last, looking wistfully at me, "Smirk," says he, "do you love me?" "Mr. Prig, can
you doubt it?" "I'll put it to the test," says he. "Supply my place tomorrow." I, eager to show my love, rashly and rapidly replied, "I will."
Absolute madness. But I had gone too far to recede. The point was, to
prepare for the awful occasion. The first want that occurred to me was a
wig. But this was too material an article to depend on my own judgment.
I resolved to consult my friends. I told them the affair: "You hear, gentlemen, what has happened: Mr. Prig, one of the greatest men in his way
the world ever saw, or ever will, quite a jewel of a man, taken with a violent fit of colic; tomorrow, the greatest show this season: prints, pictures,
bronzes, butterflies, medals and mignonettes; everybody in the world to
be there; lady Dy Joss, Mrs. Nankyn, Duchess of Dupe and all mankind;
it being impossible he should mount, I have consented to sell — They
stared. "It is true, gentlemen. Now I should be glad to have your opin-
ions as to a wig."

Monster in a Box

Spalding Gray

Play
Comic
M
40+
Contemporary

In his one-man tour de force, Gray shares a 'special' acting experience.

Often, when you do a long run of a play, in this case *Our Town,* you have what I like to call a unifying accident, in which something so strange happens in the play, that it suddenly unites the audience in the realization that we are all here together at this one moment in time. It's not television. It's not the movies. And it probably will never be repeated ever again. It happened as I was speaking of the dead and I say, "And they stay here while the earth part of them burns away, burns out … They're waitin' for something they feel is comin'. Something important and great …" As I say this, I turn and gesture to them, waiting, and, just as I turn and gesture, the little eleven-year-old boy playing Wally Webb projectile vomits! Like a hydrant it comes, hitting some of the dead on their shoulders! The other dead levitate out of their chairs, in total shock, around him and drop back down. Franny Conroy, deep in her meditative trance, is slowly wondering, "Why is it raining on stage?" The little boy flees from his chair, vomit pouring from his mouth. Splatter. Splatter. Splatter, I'm standing there. My knees are shaking. The chair is empty. The audience is thunderstruck! There is not a sound coming from them, except for one little ten-year-old boy in the eighth row. He knows what he saw and he is LAUGHING!

At this point, I don't know whether to be loyal to Thornton Wilder and go on with the next line as written, or attempt what might be one of the most creative improvs in the history of American theater. At last I decide to be loyal to Wilder and simply go on with the next line, and I turn to the empty chair and say: "Aren't they waitin' for the eternal part of them to come out clear?"

My Heart and the Real World
Michael K. White

Play
Comic
M
30s
Contemporary

Leonard, brandishing his toy light saber, needs to get a life.

… allow me to introduce myself. I am Master Leonard Saterlee, Jedi trainer and martial arts expert and I'm making this instructional tape for use in schools, colleges, boardrooms, and such. This video will show you all you need to know about the ancient arts of the Jedi self-defense training. I have been certified by the Jedi council and the American Bureau of Martial Arts but I do not instruct in person, only via VHS long form videotape. My location, as you may understand is secret and well guarded because anyone of my knowledge and experience is a natural target for agents of the dark side.

(He resumes some energetic swordplay along with a few shaky kicks. When he's done, he's obviously winded.) Now you know what I'm talking about. You too can be a murderous killing machine to wreak vengeance on your enemies in Alaska … But let's not go into that. That's my business, not yours.

(He idly swings the light saber around to show he means business.) If you take my home video course, I can guarantee that you will be able to kill, maim, or disable any attacker or stalker.

(He suddenly pops off a series of moves which are like a cross between a disco dance and an epileptic seizure. When he stops he is sweating and panting. He faces the "camera" defiantly.) Upon completion of my course you will receive a dot matrix certificate which warrants you as having been under the tutelage of a Master Jedi trainer. The training will also include Jedi prayer worship, anticommunist talks, and light saber design. The cost of this training is not cheap. My knowledge is unique based upon my experience. I charge $100 per session …

(He trails off mesmerized by his own light saber. Suddenly he shrieks and starts stamping the floor, jumping around like a madman. This frenzy continues until we hear a piercing squeak, then LEONARD suddenly stops, going slack, like a marionette whose strings have just been cut. Winded…) Mouse. I hate mice. (…)

Never Tell

James Christy

Play
Comic
M
20s
Contemporary

Hoover relates a really good dream.

So I'm in this office, this really cool office. And I realize it's like a record company office, with gold records and shit all around. And I'm a big-shot record executive. And it's like I can do anything I want. Anything. I can call famous musicians or hook up with girls, whatever I want. So I'm sitting there deciding what I want to do, and Bob Marley walks in. Bob Marley. Now my dad played me Bob Marley records ever since I was like a baby so I know how big this is. But before I can think of anything to say he starts yelling at me and saying how I screwed him out of all this money in some record deal. And I'm trying to tell him no, you know, it isn't me, this isn't really my office, I'm just sitting here. But I can't get it out, I can't even talk. And he just keeps coming closer, behind the desk to where I'm sitting and right in front of me and I'm so scared. But at the same time, you know, I can't stop thinking how cool it is that he's talking to me. I also kind of knew in the back of my mind that he's dead, but that just made it that much cooler. So just as I'm starting to get scared that he's really going to fuck me up, I look down and I realize that I have this huge boner. And it freaks me out because I know you're not supposed to get boners in front of guys and it might make him even madder, but it's just happening and I can't do anything about it. So he looks down and he sees my boner, and he sort of smiles and stops being mad. Like he realizes he has the wrong guy. So then he just turns around and walks out. And when I woke up I was wet. So that was it, that was my first time. Bob Marley.

Never Tell

James Christy

Play
Comic
M
20s
Contemporary

Hoover at a party, drinking beer.

You see that guy over there? By the sink?

(He points.) He's got Kurt Cobain's pancreas.

(Swigs a beer.) No shit. Cobain's pancreas. He's always had this fucked up pancreas, some genetic thing, and he needed a new one, and for a long time he was on this waiting list because they're hard to come by and he wasn't, like, on the brink or anything. But one day his doctor called him up and told him to bring his ass in for surgery. He didn't know it was Cobain's pancreas until like two days later. He hadn't even heard he was dead yet, this candy striper chick comes up to him when he comes out of it and goes, "Dude, you're so lucky, you got Kurt's pancreas." And he's like, what the fuck, and she's like "yeah, don't tell anyone I told you, I could get in trouble, it's supposed to be confidential."

(Beat.) Can you imagine that shit? To wake up and find out: A) that Cobain's dead, and B) that you've got his fuckin' pancreas? Jesus Christ … Guess it worked out though. He's not supposed to drink anymore, but he does anyway and nothing's happened to him yet. Can't listen to Nirvana though.

The Old Bachelor

William Congreve

Play
Comic
M
50+
Classic

Fondlewife questions himself, whips himself into a jealous frenzy, then imagines a conversation with his wife.

Go in and bid my Cocky come out to me. I will give her some instructions; I will reason with her before I go. And in the meantime, I will reason with myself — Tell me, Isaac, why art thee jealous? Why art thee distrustful of the wife of thy bosom? Because she is young and vigorous, and I am old and impotent. Then why didst thee marry, Isaac? Because she was beautiful and tempting, and because I was obstinate and doting, so that my inclination was (and is still) greater than my power. — And will not that which tempted thee, also tempt others, who will tempt her, Isaac? — I fear it much. — But does not thy wife love thee, nay, dote upon thee? — Yes! — Why then — Ay, but to say truth, she's fonder of me than she has reason to be, and in the way of trade we still suspect the smoothest dealers of the deepest designs. — And that she has some design deeper than thou canst reach, th'hast experimented, Isaac. — But mum. Wife — have you thoroughly considered how detestable, how heinous, and how crying a sin the sin of adultery is? Have you weighed it, I say? For it is a very weighty sin, and although it may lie heavy upon thee, yet thy husband must also bear his part: for thy iniquity will fall upon his head. (…) Speak, I say. Have you considered what it is to cuckold your husband? *(Aside.)* Verily, I fear I carried the jest too far.

The Old Bachelor
William Congreve

Play
Comic
M
40+
Classic

Heartwell's got it bad for Sylvia, and he hates himself for it.

Oons, why do I look on her! Yet I must. Speak, dear angel, devil, saint, witch, do not rack me in suspense. Oh, manhood, where art thou! What am I come to? A woman's toy at these years! Death, a bearded baby for a girl to dandle. Oh, dotage, dotage! That ever that noble passion, lust, should ebb to this degree. No reflux of vigorous blood, but milky love supplies the empty channels and prompts me to the softness of a child, a mere infant, and would suck. Can you love me, Sylvia? Speak. Pox, how her innocence torments and pleases me! Lying, child, is indeed the art of love, and men are generally masters in it. (…) And a pox upon me for loving thee so well! Yet I must on — 'tis a bearded arrow, and will more easily be thrust forward than drawn back. But how can you be well assured? Take the symptoms and ask all the tyrants of thy sex, if their fools are not known by this parti-colored livery. I am melancholy when thou art absent; look like an ass when you art present, wake for you when I should sleep, and even dream of you when I am awake; sigh much, drink little, eat less, court solitude, am grown very entertaining to myself and (as I am informed) very troublesome to everybody else. If this be not love, it is madness, and then it is pardonable.

Picasso at the Lapin Agile

Steve Martin

Play
Comic
M
40+
Contemporary

Gaston, a non-artist, attempts to understand Picasso's creative process.

Well, you're a painter; you're always having to come up with ideas. What's it like? I mean, the only idea I ever came up with was when I had to paint my shutters. I had to figure out a color. And I thought about it for a long time. Should they be a light color or a dark color? For a while, forest blue seemed nice; then, I realized there was no such thing as forest blue. I tried to flip a coin but lost it on the roof. I started thinking, "What are shutters anyway, and what would their natural color be?" Then I realized that shutters don't occur in nature, so they don't have a natural color. Suddenly, I knew I was just moments away from a decision, just moments, finally. Then this gorgeous thing walks by, with ruby lips and a derriere the shape of a valentine. I swiveled my head around and snapped a tendon. That put the decision off for three days. Then I thought, "Maybe just take off the shutters"; I started to think about moving to a land where there are no shutters and, frankly, suicide. But then one day, I said to myself, "Green," and that was it. *(GASTON exits to the bathroom.)*

Picasso at the Lapin Agile

Steve Martin

Play
Comic
M
50+
Contemporary

Sagot, an art dealer, offers his insights into the "popular themes" in art. The kids with the big eyes, or the poker-playing dogs?

I know that there are two subjects in paintings that no one will buy. One is Jesus, and the other is sheep. Love Him as much as they want, no one really wants a painting of Jesus in the living room. You're having a few people over, having a few drinks, and there's Jesus over the sofa. Somehow it doesn't work. And not in the bedroom either, obviously. I mean, you want Jesus watching over you but not while you're in the missionary position. You could put Him in the kitchen maybe, but then that's sort of insulting to Jesus. Jesus, ham sandwich, Jesus, ham sandwich, Jesus, ham sandwich; I wouldn't like it and neither would He. Can't sell a male nude either, unless they're messengers. Why a messenger would want to be nude I don't know. You'd think they'd at least need a little pouch or something. In fact, if a nude man showed up at my door and I asked, "Who is it," and he said, "Messenger," I would damn well look and see if he has a pouch, and if he doesn't, I'm not answering the door. Sheep are the same, don't ask me why, can't sell 'em.

The Projectors

John Wilson

Play
Comic
M
20s
Classic

OK, don't sugarcoat it, Leanchops. What do you really think of your master?

Well! o' my conscience, there was never so unlucky a fellow as myself! Here I live with a master that has wealth enough; but so fearful, sad, pensive, suspicious a fellow, that he disquiets both himself and everyone else! Art, I have heard say, has but seven liberal sciences, but he has a thousand illiberal! There lives not a more base, niggardly, unsatiable, pinch-penny, nor a more gaping, griping, polling, extorting, devouring cormorant! A sponge sucks not up faster, and yet a pumice gives back easier! He shall watch you a young heir as diligently as a raven a dying horse, and yet swallow him with more tears than a crocodile! He never sleeps but he seals up the nose of his bellows, lest they lose breath, and has almost broke his brains to find the like device for his chimney and his throat! A gamester has not studied the advantage of dice half so much as he a sordid parsimony, which yet he calls thrift; and will tell you to a crumb how much difference there is in point of loss between a hundred dozen of bread broken with the hand and cut with a knife. The devil's in him, and I am as weary of him as of our last journey, which both of us perform'd on the same horse!

Psycho Beach Party

Charles Busch

Play
Comic
Male as Female, playing sixteen years old
Contemporary

Charles Busch's plays are satirical, campy and gender-bending. Here, Busch embodies Chicklet, his answer to Gidget, the star of the Annette Funicello/Frankie Avalon beach party movies.

Hi, folks, welcome to Malibu Beach. I hope you brought your suntan lotion cause here it's what you call endless summer. My name's Chicklet. Sort of a kooky name, and believe me, it has nothing to do with chewing gum. You see, I've always been so darn skinny, a stick, a shrimp, so when other girls turned into gorgeous chicks, I became a chicklet. Can't say I've always been thrilled with that particular nomenclature, but it sure beats the heck out of my real name, Florence. I'm supposed to meet my girlfriends, Marvel Ann and Berdine, here at the beach. Marvel Ann calls it a "man hunt." I don't know what's wrong with me. I like boys, but not when they get all icky and unglued over you. All that kissy kissy stuff just sticks in my craw. I don't know, maybe I need some hormone shots. I do have a deep, all-consuming passion. The mere thought fills me with tingles and ecstasy. It's for surfing. I'm absolutely flaked out about riding the waves. Of course, I don't know how to do it, not yet, but I'm scouting around for a teacher and when I do, look out world. You'll be seeing old Chicklet flying over those waves like a comet.

Red Diaper Baby

Josh Kornbluth

Play/Memoir
Comic
M
35+
Contemporary

In his staged memoir, Josh remembers Papa.

My father, [Paul Kornbluth], was a Communist.

He believed there was going to be a violent Communist revolution in this country — and that I was going to lead it. Just so you can get a sense of the pressure.

And anything my father told me I'd believe, because my father was such a physically magnificent man: He was big, and he had this great big potbelly — not a wiggly-jiggly, Social Democratic potbelly; a firm, Communist potbelly. You bopped it, it would bop you back. It was strong.

He had powerful legs, from running track at the City College of New York. And he had these beefy arms. And he was naked — virtually all the time; naked in the apartment. And all over his body he had these patches of talcum powder — you know, Johnson's Baby Powder — I guess because he was a big man and he would chafe. Especially around his private parts.

And he had me on the weekends. I would have loved to sleep late on the weekends, but I couldn't because my father wouldn't let me. He would wake me up.

This is how he'd wake me up: He'd come bursting into my room and then he'd stop in the doorway; and when he stopped, the talcum powder would come bouncing off of his balls — it was like the entrance of a great magician. And then he'd come running up to my bed, and looming over me he'd sing:

Arise, ye prisoner of starvation!

Arise, ye wretched of the earth!

I didn't know that was the "Internationale"; I didn't know that was the international Communist anthem. I thought it was my own personal wake-up song.

Check it out: "Arise, prisoner of starvation" — it's time for breakfast. "Arise, ye wretched of the earth" — it's five o'clock in the morning and I'm being woken up!

And if I didn't show the proper signs of life right away, my father would lean down over me — and his long, graying hair would straggle down, his beard would flutter down into my nose — and he'd yell, "Wake up, Little Fucker! Wake up, Little Fucker!"

That was his nickname for me: Little Fucker. Nothing at all pejorative about it, as far as my father was concerned. For my dad, calling me "Little Fucker" was like calling me "Junior" … "Beloved Little One" … "Little Fucker."

I knew from an early age that one day I must grow up and become … a Big Fucker. And I assumed that that would be around the time that I would lead the Revolution. Because my dad had told me over and over that all the great revolutionaries were also great fuckers.

Remedial English

Evan Smith

Play
Comic
M
Teen
Contemporary

Vincent has been waiting for some time to see Sister Beatrice, a teaching nun at Cabrini Catholic Academy. His sits in the waiting room of her office.

Sister, I think it's very rude of you to keep me waiting like this. It's been fifteen minutes since you said, "I'll be finished in a minute," and unless I'm doing worse in algebra than I thought, you're off by fourteen minutes. Fourteen minutes may not seem like much to you — time moves pretty quickly after your hundredth birthday — but this is *supposed* to be my study hall. I have many important things to do during my study hall. I am developing a fascinating abstract pattern to fill the margins of my chemistry book, I'm right in the middle of *Lake Wobegon Days*, and I have almost finished my project of inserting the complete works of Judith Krantz into the library's card catalog. This is a school, after all, Sister. You of all people shouldn't want to see me wasting my time.

What did I do to merit such treatment? Is it because of that little tiff we had in English yesterday? Sister, we all say things in the heat of argument which we later regret. I'm sorry I called T. S. Eliot a "social-climbing Yankee papist." I don't even remember what I *meant* by that!

Have you forgotten all the good times we have had together? Don't you remember Dramatic Literature when I was a sophomore? We read aloud to the class … I was Jean … you were Miss Julie …

Oh, good grief, *please* don't tell me you found that Sister Beatrice Virgin Vote! God, how could I ever explain that? But if you *did* find it, you should at least be pleased with the results! Fifty-eight percent of my music class said that they thought you were a virgin. Sister, you've got to understand, such a large part of my life is spent in your company and yet I hardly know anything about you! You've got to expect a certain amount of healthy curiosity and speculation. Do you ever wish you hadn't become a nun? What would you have done instead? Do you have any regrets? *Are* you a …? Never any answers from this woman of mystery.

Romance in D

James Sherman

Play
Comic
M
40s
Contemporary

Charles Norton, a quiet and solitary musicologist, has vowed to remain lonesome. But he has befriended (and secretly fallen in love with) Isabel, a suicidal poet next door. In this scene, Charles has found Isabel after she has returned from an unhappy date with her ex-husband, and he forces himself to be unusually verbose.

I bought lox and bagels. Would you like some lox and bagel? (…) You know … You might find this interesting. You notice how I say, "lox and bagel?" Most people say, "bagels and lox," but think about it. Lox — no matter where you go — is eighteen, nineteen dollars a pound. Bagels are — well, they're not exactly a dime a dozen, but they're only about five dollars for a dozen. So given the relative merits of an insignificant lump of dough versus a thinly sliced treasure of fine smoked salmon … Why should the bagel get top billing? Huh? I ask you.

Which leads me to my second point. Why say "bagels and lox" as if the whole point of the exercise is to taste a bagel. It's the lox I want. So this is what I do. First of all, I never slice a bagel. I could slice through and cut that little fleshy part between my thumb and forefinger. So I just take the bagel and rip it in half.

Now, the cream cheese. You'll notice … I don't use cream cheese. You see the way people pile on the cream cheese? It makes me sick. It's a condiment! Most people, I could say, "Here's some bagel and lox," give them just a bagel with a mound of cream cheese on it, and they wouldn't even notice the lox was missing.

So now, the piece de resistance. I don't shove the lox between two halves of a bagel. I take a piece of bagel and wrap the lox around it. Getting the full flavor of the lox. And full value for my delicatessen dollar. Voila. Jewish sushi.

The School

Donald Barthelme

Short story
Comic
M
30+
Contemporary

Ever have one of those school years?

Well, we had all these children out planting trees, see, because we figured that … that was part of their education, to see how, you know, the root systems … and also the sense of responsibility, taking care of things, being individually responsible. You know what I mean. And the trees all died. They were orange trees. I don't know why they died, they just died. Something wrong with the soil possibly or maybe the stuff we got from the nursery wasn't the best. We complained about it. So we've got thirty kids there, each kid had his or her own little tree to plant, and we've got these thirty dead trees. All these kids looking at these little brown sticks, it was depressing.

It wouldn't have been so bad except that just a couple of weeks before the thing with the trees, the snakes all died (…) you remember, the boiler was shut off for four days because of the strike, and that was explicable. It was something you could explain to the kids because of the strike. I mean, none of their parents would let them cross the picket line and they knew there was a strike going on and what it meant. So when things got started up again and we found the snakes they weren't too disturbed.

With the herb gardens it was probably a case of overwatering, and at least now they know not to overwater. The children were very conscientious with the herb gardens and some of them probably … you know, slipped them a little extra water when we weren't looking. Or maybe … well, I don't like to think about sabotage, although it did occur to us. I mean, it was something that crossed our minds. We were thinking that way probably because before that the gerbils had died, and the white mice had died, and the salamander … well, now they know not to carry them around in plastic bags.

Of course we expected the tropical fish to die, that was no surprise. Those numbers, you look at them crooked and they're belly-up on the surface. But the lesson plan called for a tropical-fish input at that point, there was nothing we could do, it happens every year, you just have to hurry past it.

We weren't even supposed to have a puppy.

Sophistry

Jonathan Marc Sherman

Play
Comic
M
20s
Contemporary

The lovely Robin has just said, "Igor, please don't try to pick me up. This is not the time." Igor, who has quaffed a few, responds.

I wouldn't even know where to start, Robin, I swear. First of all, trying to find somebody safe on this campus, I mean, somebody who's relatively disease free, who hasn't slept with one of my friends, who isn't heavily involved with somebody, who isn't painful to look at or talk to, who actually likes guys — this is a next-to-impossible task. If I do find somebody like this, the odds that she will have any interest in me are not terrific. And, you know, I mean, I don't even know if I would allow myself to go after a person I respected, since I know the kind of guy I am. I know the thoughts I think. I know I would not want me to date my daughter, if I had a daughter. I know that I cease to become interested in nine out of ten women almost immediately after I've slept with them, and I've only slept with three women. I know I prematurely ejaculate on occasion. I know I sometimes prefer blow jobs to actual intercourse, yet I can't come up with a halfway logical reason for a woman to want to give one. I know I find sleazy women pretty attractive, and look at most women as objects. I know that white men have a hell of a historical legacy, what with enslaving blacks and treating women like cattle, so I feel ashamed to be a member of what is supposed to be the privileged class. And I know that sensitive guys sound good in theory, but in practice, most of the women I observe are attracted to men who treat them like shit. I know these things. So, you see, it would be very difficult for me to try to pick you up while retaining even minor amounts of dignity and truth and still enjoy myself a little … *(Beat.)* But I was standing over there, across the room, and I saw Willy try to pick you up, and I know he's pretty smashed tonight, and I just wanted to see if you were OK. *(Beat.)* Are you OK?

The Spellin' Bee

Paul Laurence Dunbar

Poem
Comic
M
40+
Classic

When handling dialect, less is more.

I never shall furgit the night when father hitched up Dobbin,
An' all us youngsters clambered in an' up the road went bobbin'
To school where we was kep' at work in every kind o' weather,
But where that night a spellin'-bee was callin' us together. (…)

The master rose and briefly said: "Good friends, dear brother Crawford,
To spur the pupils' minds along, a little prize has offered.
To him who spells the best tonight — or't may be "her" — no tellin' —
He offers ez a jest reward, this precious work on spellin'."
A little blue-backed spellin'-book with fancy scarlet trimmin',
We boys devoured it with our eyes — so did the girls an' women.
He held it up where all could see, then on the table set it,
An' ev'ry speller in the house felt mortal bound to get it.
At his command we fell in line, prepared to do our dooty,
Outspell the rest an' set 'em down, an' carry home the booty.
'Twas then the merry times began, the blunders, an' the laffin',
The nudges an' the nods an' winks an' stale good-natured chaffin'. (…)

So one by one they giv' it up — the big words kep' a-landin'
Till me an' Nettie Gray was left, the only ones a-standin',
An' then my inward strife began — I guess my mind was petty —
I did so want that spellin' book; but then to spell down Nettie
Jest sort o' went ag'in my grain — I somehow couldn't do it,
An' when I git a notion fixed, I'm great on stickin' to it.
So when they giv' the next word out — I hadn't orter tell it,
But then 'twas all fur Nettie's sake — I missed so's she could spell it.
She spelt the word, then looked at me so lovin'-like and mello',
I tell you 't sent a hundred pins a-shootin' through a fello'.

O' course I had to stand the jokes an' chaffin' of the fello's,
But when they handed her the book I vow I wasn't jealous.
We sung a hymn, an' Parson Brown dismissed us like he orter,
Fur, la! he'd learned a thing or two an' made his blessin' shorter.
'Twas late an' cold when we got out, but Nettie liked cold weather,
An' so did I, so we agreed we'd jest walk home together.
We both wuz silent, fur of words we nuther had a surplus,
'Till she spoke out quite sudden like, "You missed that word on purpose."
Well, I declare it frightened me; at first I tried denyin',
But Nettie, she jest smiled an' smiled, she knowed that I was lyin'.
Sez she: "That book is yourn by right"; sez I: "It never could be —
I — I — you — ah — " an' there I stuck, an', well, she understood me.
So we agreed that later on when age had giv' us tether,
We'd jine our lots an' settle down to own that book together.

Stick a Fork in It, Pal

Keith Knight

Comic strip
Comic
M
30s
Contemporary

Now that the dot-com boom is over and done with here in San Francisco, a whole lotta folks are wondering what the heck do they have to show for it? Well … I for one have plenty to show for it: assorted large produce from BigMelons.com, free garden tools from cheaphoe.com, fresh donkey meat from pieceofass.com. I've got literally a closetful of free stuff from all my favorite Web sites. But my biggest score was at the launch party for goneinsixmonths.com. While the company head was forking out tons of useless stock options, I opted to head to the food table and stock up on some useful forks.

My roommate was moving out and taking her silverware with her, so I was on the lookout for some replacements. After a few drinks I even went over and thanked the head cheese for hookin' me up; "Great frickin' party, bro."

Yeah, so the dot-com thing may be over, but every time I have a dinner party, I'm reminded of it. I just wish the boom lasted long enough for me to score some spoons.

The Virtuoso

Thomas Shadwell

Play
Comic
M
35+
Classic

*Sir Formal, an accomplished public speaker (he claims), finds
great significance in a common scene.*

I must confess I have some felicity in speaking. We orators speak alike
upon all subjects. My speeches are all so subtly designed that whatever I
speak in praise of anything with very little alteration will serve in praise
of the contrary. 'Tis all one to me. I am ready to speak upon all occasions. Now I am inspired with eloquence. Hem. Hem. Being one day,
most noble auditors, musing in my study upon the too fleeting condition of poor humankind, I observed, not far from the scene of my meditation, an excellent machine called a mousetrap (which my man had
placed there) which had included in it a solitary mouse, which pensive
prisoner, in vain bewailing its own misfortunes and the precipitation of
its too unadvised attempt, still struggling for liberty against the too stub-
born opposition of solid wood and more obdurate wire, at last, the pretty
malefactor having tired, alas, its too feeble limbs till they became languid
in fruitless endeavors for its excarceration, the pretty felon — since it
could not break its prison, and, its offense being beyond the benefit of
clergy, could hope for no bail — at last sat still, pensively lamenting the
severity of its fate and the narrowness of its, alas, too withering durance.
After I had contemplated a while upon the no little curiosity of the
engine and the subtlety of its inventor, I began to reflect upon the entice-
ment which so fatally betrayed the uncautious animal to its sudden ruin;
and found it to be the too, alas, specious bait of Cheshire cheese, which
seems to be a great delicate to the plate of this animal who, in seeking to
preserve its life, oh, misfortune, took the certain means to death, and
searching for its livelihood had sadly encountered its own destruction.

Wasp
Steve Martin

Play
Comic
M
35+
Contemporary

Father knows best?

You see, Son, a bicycle is a luxury item. You know what a luxury item is? (…) A luxury item is a thing that you have that annoys other people that you have it. Like our very green lawn. That's a luxury item. Oh, it could be less green, I suppose; but that's not what it's about. I work on that lawn, maybe more than I should and pour a little bit o' money into it, but it's a luxury item for me, out there to annoy the others. And let's be fair; they have their luxury items that annoy me. On the corner, that mailbox made out of a ship's chain. Now there's no way I wouldn't like that out in front of our house, but I went for the lawn. What I'm getting at is that you have to work for a luxury item. So if you want that bicycle, you're going to have to work for it. Now, I've got a little lot downtown that we've had for several years, and if you wanted to go down there on weekends and after school and, say, put up a building on it, I think we could get you that bicycle. (…)

Yes, I know, you're pretty excited. It's not easy putting up a building, Son, but these are the ancient traditions, handed down from the peoples of Gondwanaland, who lived on the plants of Golgotha. Based upon the precepts of Hammurabi. (…)

Son, we don't get to talk that much; in fact, as far as I can remember, we've never talked. But I was wondering several years ago, and unfortunately never really got around to asking you until now, I was wondering, what you plan to do with your life?

Where's My Money

John Patrick Shanley

Play
Comic
M
30s-40s
Contemporary

Sidney is a cynical divorce lawyer. He's talking to Henry, a potential client.

Manhood … It's a job. Done right, it's a tiring job. And women have a lot to do with what that entails. Sure, women create. (…) But there's another side. And it's not pretty. There's a Hindu deity in India named Kali. The god of destruction. It's a woman. She's got a bloody sword and an appetite for decapitation. In the West, we call her "The Devouring Mother." Creation, destruction. Every woman has these two sides to her, and every man must deal with these two sides. Creation, destruction. You gotta orient a woman in such a way so as to be facing her creative parts. You want the creative parts. The destructive parts … You want those to be facing away. (…) You've gotta point them. Like you would a bazooka. Like you would a chain saw. You don't hold a chain saw by the chain. Let me pull it together another way. Monogamy is like a forty-watt bulb. It works, but it's not enough.

MALE
Seriocomic Monologues

Afternoon Lovers
Vanda Wark

Play
Seriocomic
M
40+
Contemporary

Professor Arthur Robinson persuades his young colleague, Marion, to be a little friendlier for the good of the department.

These things take time, Marion. I've only been chairman for a year and a half. And to be frank, I can't do it all by myself. It wouldn't hurt if you were a little friendlier to some of the other committee members. Ol' Knudley's been awfully lonely since his wife passed. And then there's Anderson … I just know you could perk them up. Don't look like that. It could be fun. And it'd liven up this dead town for both of us. Nothing ever happens around here. You could, well, do it with them and then tell me about it. You'll be throwing a couple of extra votes your way and for us, well, it could be exciting. If you didn't make so much of it. You have no ties. Everyone would be discreet. I'd see to that. It'd be like a secret club. You know, Marion, sometimes when I'm conducting one of those god-awful departmental meetings, I just tune it all out and watch you sitting there in the back row. The way you always cross your legs with the left leg pressed precisely over the right knee. There you sit. The height of perfect decorum and I picture you naked. I get a hard-on just watching you all buttoned up and closed. So mysterious. And so deliciously naked right in the middle of that meeting. If I knew that just a select few, those on the tenure committee, were sitting there in that room seeing you naked like I do, it would be so exciting. And you could tell me all about your adventures and their strange perversions. I just know I would be able to make love to you the way I used to.

Baby with the Bathwater

Christopher Durang

Play
Seriocomic
M
Teen
Contemporary

Daisy is a very confused young woman. Young man. Wait.

When I was eleven I came across this medical book that had pictures in it, and I realized I looked more like a boy than a girl, but my mother had always wanted a girl or a best seller, and I didn't want to disappoint her. But then on some days, I don't know what got into me, and I just feel like striking out at them. So I waited till she was having one of her crying fits and I took the book to her, I was twelve then, and I said, "Have you ever seen this book? Are you totally insane? Why have you named me Daisy? Everyone else has always said I was a boy, what's the matter with you?" And she kept crying and said something about Judith Krantz, and then something about being out of shake and bake chicken, and then she said I want to die, and then she said perhaps you are a boy, but we don't want to jump to any hasty conclusions, so why don't we just wait and see if I menstruated or not. When I asked her what that word meant, she slapped me and washed my mouth out with soap. Then she hugged me and said she was a bad mother. Then she washed her mouth out with soap. Then she turned on all the gas jets and said it would just be a little while longer for the both of us. And then my father came home and he untied me and turned off all the gas jets and then when he asked her if dinner was ready she would lay on the kitchen floor and wouldn't move, and he said I guess not, and then he sort of crouched next to the refrigerator and tried to read a book, but I don't think he was ever really reading, because he never turned any of the pages. And then eventually, since nothing else seemed to be happening, I just went to bed.

Bang

Neal Lerner

Play
Seriocomic
M
30-35
Contemporary

Steve, on his cell phone, talks to his best friend's answering machine.

OK look, I know you're home, because I'm standing downstairs right outside your building, and all your lights are on. You who watches your Con Ed bill like a stock market ticker. Now come on. Ugh, look, I am not having this discussion with you on the phone. I mean, right now I am, but it's not appropriate. This is unfair. We must move through these things. You can't isolate yourself even if the day has overwhelmed. I mean, my God, you're not dying. I would think that would pep you up. That's certainly good news, right? Your prolapse is a two out of a possible five, and, I'm quoting here now, to be watched, not feared, and then something something something, blah blah blah (…) look Bill, I'm on your side — oooh, I'm running low on minutes. Now you listen to me, I do love you. I do care. I do know what you're going through, you know, as much as one can, certainly this phone call has illuminated certain things for me. And finally, I do expect to see you at my CD Release Party Slash Concert this Saturday. Seven sharp. Joe's Pub. Dress nice, you never know.

bear trap

Clay McLeod Chapman

Short story
Seriocomic
M
30s
Contemporary

Ma'am — do you mind calling the conductor? My arm's caught. The door doesn't want to open back up for me. I think the hatch might've hay-wired when I jammed my briefcase through. Something feels stuck. Could you just ask him to release the doors again? Ma'am? Please?

Excuse me. Sir? How about giving me a hand here? Just slip your fingers through the slit and try prying the doors apart. I'll tug this way if you tug that. Sir? Hello …

Jesus, my arm's about to pop out of its socket. I'm going to dislocate my shoulder if this door doesn't let go. I wasn't wanting to hold everyone up, here. I was simply trying to make it to work on time, just like the rest of you. I know, I know — I should've been patient and waited for the next train. But it's a little late to worry over that now. If I'd been a second sooner, I'd be crammed in there with the rest of you — but since it's my limb that's snagged here, it seems like we're all going to be a little late to the office today. Won't be just me who has to come up with some excuse over why they didn't clock in on time. This train's not going anywhere until I get my arm back.

So what's it going to be, people? Who wants to help me?

What the fuck is this? Don't just stand there, acting like you can't hear me. This is serious. I've lost the feeling in my fingers. My wrist's beginning to swell. I can't even tell if I'm still holding onto my briefcase or not. Please, for the love of God — just jostle my arm out. Shove my briefcase through the crack. Someone just help me. The subway won't be stalling at the station for much longer.

You're all just going to gang up on me like this? Make me pay for making you late? Fine. Go ahead. (…)

Fuck this subway. I count about a hundred steps in between me and the end of this platform. Who wants to bet I can chew through my own elbow before ramming into the wall? I'd rather be rendered a paraplegic by my own teeth than squeeze in there with the rest of you. This bear trap's not getting the best of me. Keep the briefcase. Hell, keep my fucking forearm if you want. Today, I'm nibbling my way to work.

Beeperless Remote

Van Whitfield

Novel
Seriocomic
M
29
Contemporary

Shawn Wayne, self-proclaimed good guy, uses particular criteria when searching for an ideal mate.

… the women I meet invariably fall into one of six categories.

The first one is the classic, "I'm just getting out of a bad relationship" babe. Guys know to run from these women. They're known as 1s, and to them, every guy is just an extension of the no-good man who just hurt them.

The second type of woman, a 2, is not really interested in relationships, but she doesn't mind dating (especially when the guy is treating). They're easy to spot. Their favorite line is, "I'm not really interested in having a boyfriend, but I do have friends."

(…) A 3 is a chick who's impossible to get with. She's so fine that she's just plain too good for anyone who doesn't have a major bankroll or significant power. 3s have radar and they can smell money and success a mile away which is why I never meet 3s.

(…) Kelly's a 4. And just like all 4s, she meets a guy, likes him, and immediately looks for reason to trash him. His biggest fault is that he's a man in the first place. 4s have a simple (yet universal) motto. Men are dogs.

(…) 5s are women who have a singular agenda. Marriage. (…) Most guys can round up another babe overnight (if they don't already have one in limbo). So "marry me or else" usually ends up as "or else." This makes most 5s a 1.

A 6 is the one perfect woman that God put on earth for every man … 6s are usually dumped to make room for a babe who's a total disaster. I don't know if I've met my 6, or if I ever will. I do know this. If she calls and leaves a message, I'll hurry to call her back.

As soon as SportsCenter goes off.

The Commissioner

Georges Courteline

Play
Seriocomic
M
40s
Classic

The Police Commissioner of Paris chastises his cowering assistant.

Good morning, Mr. Puny. Once again I must inform you that you do your work with the cleanliness and efficiency of a pig. If this goes on, I shall be compelled to ask the prefect to dismiss or demote you. Hundreds of times, Mr. Puny, I've told you to go through my mail ruthlessly, so that I can get my desk, my work and my thinking clear. And what happens? I might as well whistle through my ears for all the good it's done. Look at this. *(He picks a sheet of paper at random.)* "Complaint by a chambermaid about her employer, who tried to take advantage of her." What's this got to do with me? Get rid of it. *(He takes another sheet.)* "Complaint by a certain party against a cabdriver who used foul language." Amazing. Is this supposed to be for my attention? Get rid of it. Here's another one. A janitor with lazy ears and a tenant who had to wait for two hours in the rain. Let him talk to the landlord. I'm not a porter. Get rid of it. And here's a cook who's owed a week's wages. That's for the magistrate to settle, not me. And so is that. And that. And that. Get rid of them all. It looks to me, Mr. Puny, as if you're wrapped up in dreams of love, or else I've over-estimated your intelligence. This is the last straw. — Silence! I may have a big heart, but I won't have you taking advantage of me. Let this be a lesson to you. It's your last chance, for sure. Good morning, Mr. Puny.

Coriolanus

William Shakespeare

Play
Seriocomic
M
40+
Classic

Why one should not cross Coriolanus' friend, Menenius.

I am known to be a humorous patrician, and one that loves a cup of hot wine with not a drop of allaying Tiber in't; said to be something imperfect in favoring the first complaint; hasty and tinder-like upon too trivial motion; one that converses more with the buttock of the night than with the forehead of the morning. What I think, I utter, and spend my malice in my breath. Meeting two such wealsmen as you are, — I cannot call you Lycurguses — if the drink you give me touch my palate adversely, I make a crooked face at it. I cannot say your worships have delivered the matter well, when I find the ass in compound with the major part of your syllables; and though I must be content to bear with those that say you are reverend grave men, yet they lie deadly that tell you you have good faces. If you see this in the map of my microcosm, follows it that I am known well enough too? What harm can your bisson conspectuities glean out of this character, if I be known well enough too? You know neither me, yourselves, nor anything. You are ambitious for poor knaves' caps and legs. You wear out a good wholesome forenoon in hearing a cause between an orange-wife and a forset-seller, and then rejourn the controversy of threepence to a second day of audience. When you are hearing a matter between party and party, if you chance to be pinched with the colic, you make faces like mummers; set up the bloody flag against all patience; and, in roaring for a chamber-pot, dismiss the controversy bleeding, the more entangled by your hearing. All the peace you make in their cause is, calling both the parties knaves. You are a pair of strange ones. Our very priests must become mockers, if they shall encounter such ridiculous objects as you are. When you speak best unto the purpose, it is not worth the wagging of your beards; and your beards deserve not so honorable a grave as to stuff a botcher's cushion or to be entombed in an ass's pack-saddle. Yet you must be saying Marcius is proud; who, in a cheap estimation, is worth all your predecessors since Deucalion, though peradventure some of the best of 'em were hereditary hangmen. Good-e'en to your worships. More of your conversation would infect my brain, being the herdsmen of the beastly plebeians. I will be bold to take my leave of you.

The Country Wife
William Wycherly

Play
Seriocomic
M
40+
Classic

The perpetually jealous Pinchwife reviews his wife's corre-
spondences.

What, writing more letters? How's this? Nay, you shall not stir, madam.
"Dear, dear, dear, Mr. Horner" — very well — I have taught you to write
letters to good purpose — but let's see it. "First I am to beg your pardon
for my boldness in writing to you, which I'd have you to know, I would
not have done, had not you said first you loved me so extremely, which,
if you do, you will need suffer me to lie in the arms of another man,
whom I loath, nauseate, and detest" — Now you can write these filthy
words, but what follows — "Therefore I hope you will speedily find
some way to free me from this unfortunate match, which was never, I
assure you, of my choice, but I'm afraid 'tis already gone too far; however,
if you love me, as I do you, you will try what you can do, but you must
help me away before tomorrow, or else, alas, I shall be for ever out of
your reach, for I can defer no longer our — our" — (The letter concludes). What is to follow "our"? Speak, what? Our journey into the
country, I suppose. Oh, woman, damned woman, and love, damned
love, their old tempter, for this is one of his miracles: in a moment, he
can make those blind that could see, and those see that were blind, those
dumb that could speak, and those prattle who were dumb before, nay
what is more than all, make those dough baked, senseless, indocile animals, women, too hard for us their politic lords and rulers in a moment;
but make an end of your letter, and then I'll make an end of you thus,
and all my plagues together.

Crush Everlasting

Dave Ulrich

Original monologue
Seriocomic
M
20s-30s
Contemporary

A fast-talking, intense, obsessive young man describes what it means to have a crush.

The crush. Ah, the crush. You know the crush. The blood quickens and thins. The heat enveloping the head from the temples. Short breaths, ears tingling, throat tightens, limbs limp, feet numb, and balance suddenly conscious. Instant crush. This woman — This — woman … is all the more remarkable to me because I don't begin with hurdles, I don't just beg for her eyes, her attention — she gave them. She gave to me. Just gave them. Who does that? Who does that, that looks like her? To a guy like me? Who?

When you're crushing oh the world pops. So alive. So electric. So crisp. Everything. Inspiration flies forth, motivation springs to attention. You gesture, you make your point with force and confidence. When telling tales your voice lowers and booms as would send Charlton Heston cowering into the corner from awe of your command. Things rhyme! — right there, in your head! Colors are richer, you're more patient, forgiving, and you love — love … suddenly. And you don't want to lose it. Yet, you have to. You have to, to function. It's too much. Too strong. Too overwhelming to stay there. So hot the flame. You need … Orgasm. You have to.

The Fair Maid of the Exchange
Thomas Heywood

Play
Seriocomic
M
20s
Classic

Frank, resistant to love's transformations, succumbs.

I am not well, and yet I am not ill,
   I am, what am I? Not in love I hope?
   In love? Let me examine my self, who should I love? Who did I last
converse with, with *Phillis;* why should I love *Phillis?* Is she faire? faith so
so: her forehead is pretty, somewhat resembling the forehead of the signe
of the maidenhead ....What's her haire? faith two Bandora wiars, there's
not the simile: is it likely that I am in love? What next? her cheekes they
have a reasonable scarlet, never a Diars daughter in the townes goes
beyond her. Well, yet I am not in love. Nay, she had a mole in her cheeke
too: *Venus* mole was not a more natural; but what of that? I am *Adonis,*
and will not love. Good *Venus* pardon me, Let us descend: her chinne, O
Hellen, Hellen, where's our dimple *Hellen?* it was your dimple that
bewitcht *Paris,* and without your dimple I will not love you *Hellen,* No,
yet I am safe. Her hand, lets handle that, I saw her hand, and it was lily
white, I toucht her palme, and it was soft and smooth; and then, what
then? her hand did then bewitch me, I shall be in love now out of hand.
In love? Shall I that ever yet have prophan'd love, now fall to worship
him? Shall I that have feasted at lovers sighes now raise whirle-windes?
Shall I that have flowted ay-mees once a quarter, now practice ay-mees
every minute? Shall I defie hat bands, and tread garters and shoo-strings
under my feet? shall I fall to falling bands and be a ruffin no longer? I
must; I am now liege man to Cupid, and have read all these informations
in his booke of statutes, the first chapter, page *millefimo nono,* therefore,
hat band avaunt, ruffe regard your selfe, garters adue, shoo-strings so and
so; I am a poor enamorate, and enforc'd with the Poet to say, Love ore-
comes all, and I that love obey.

The Fairy Garden

Harry Kondoleon

Play
Seriocomic
M
30s
Contemporary

Mimi and his lover, Roman, are given to High Drama.

Oh get off my fucking back for five minutes won't you? I've got the whole night to push you away, must it start midday? Can't you relax? Can't you — if for no other reason than the sparkling change of pace it would bring — call off your sour marching band? Yes, I am better looking. Yes, I am more desirable — and that means just *that: more* people *desire* me, want me, fantasize about me, etcetera, than you. You aren't bad looking, Roman, and I've told you so and I've told you so and I've told you so. I've complimented you, I've repeated compliments I've overheard or thought I overheard, I've even invented compliments just to please you but *really* I don't care. I don't care that you think I'm performing sex acts with every man *you* find attractive. If you were more on the ball instead of constantly under it you might have noticed I have stopped all sex acts with you and anyone: I've had enough. I got too bored and expert, too distanced, too detached and deterred but you're too plain demented to understand. I want to wake up with my own hands on my own shoulders, so do not touch me, not as a joke, not as a jest, not as an anything, not now, not ever.

(…) [M]aybe it's time to say auf Wiedersehen or Toot-Toot Tootsie Good-bye or whatever droll distortion will suit the occasion.

(…) Call your therapist, Roman. He gets paid to listen to your prattle, I only get fatigued.

The Great Galeoto

Jose Echegaray

Play
Seriocomic
M
30s
Classic

Ernest, a frustrated writer, wrestles his writer's block to the desk.

(Poised to write.) Nothing — impossible! It is striving with the impossible. The idea is there; my head is fevered with it; I feel it. At moments an inward light illuminates it, and I see it. I see it in its floating form, vaguely outlined, and suddenly a secret voice seems to animate it, and I hear sounds of sorrow, sonorous sighs, shouts of sardonic laughter ... a whole world of passions alive and struggling ... They burst forth from me, extend around me, and the air is full of them. Then, then I say to myself: "Now is the moment." I take up my pen, stare into space, listen attentively, restraining my very heartbeats, and bend over the paper ... Ah, the irony of impotency! The outlines become blurred, the vision fades, the cries and sighs faint away ... and nothingness, nothingness fades, the cries and sighs faint away ... and nothingness, nothing ness encircles me ... the monotony of empty space, of inert thought, of idle pen and lifeless paper that lacks the life of though! Ah! How varied are the shapes of nothingness, and how, in its dark and silent way, it mocks creatures of my stamp! So many, many forms! Canvas without color, bits of marble without shape, confused noise of chaotic vibrations. But nothing more irritating, more insolent, meaner than this insolent pen of mine, nothing worse than this white sheet of paper. Oh, if I cannot fill it, at least I may destroy it — vile accomplice of my ambition and my eternal humiliation. Thus, thus ... smaller and still smaller. And then! How lucky that nobody saw me! For in truth such fury is absurd and unjust. No, I will not yield. I will think and think, until either I have conquered or am crushed. No, I will not give up. Let me see, let me see ... if in that way —

Imposters

Justin Warner

Play
Seriocomic
M
22
Contemporary

Andrew Delancey, a scientifically minded graduate student, is struggling to connect with his hyper-Catholic mother.

When Vincent and I were younger, my mother took us to Mass every Sunday. We weren't allowed to eat for an hour beforehand. So if Mass was at eleven, we had to finish breakfast by 9:59. Sometimes the deadline would pass, and we'd all have to stop in mid-forkful.

Eventually, of course, I asked my mother why we did this. She said that you needed to cleanse your body for an hour to get ready for Communion. I pointed out that Communion didn't happen until near the *end* of Mass, which normally lasted about an hour. So in essence, we had at least forty-five extra minutes to eat.

My mother, however, insisted that the hour was before the start of Mass, not Communion itself, because that's how she learned it. Well, that threw into question the whole idea of the cleansing time, because clearly it was *not* just an hour, but an hour plus whatever time it took to get to Communion, which for convenience's sake, we can call "x." Now "x" varied tremendously, anywhere from twenty-five minutes on a hot summer day when they cut the Mass short, to a couple hours on Palm Sunday. So given that the soul needed to cleanse for 1 hour plus x, and x is an independent variable, my final question to my mother was this: Is there some minimum value for x at which the soul can be considered cleansed, and if so, can we make adjustments in anticipation of longer Mass times?

After that we just ate whenever we wanted. It always frustrated me that my mom never thought that through. We could have saved ourselves a lot of aggravation. There's a certain lack of precision in my family.

Jails, Hospitals, and Hip-Hop

Danny Hoch

Play
Seriocomic
M
20s
Contemporary

Emcee Enuff is a successful rapper in a baseball cap, gold teeth, and Versace shades. This is his first appearance on the David Letterman Show.

I mean, look, I ain't perfect, Dave. I got faults and so do you. That's obvious. But this is what I'm trying to say: If you take all my fans all over the world and put them together in one room tell 'em Emcee Enuff is runnin' for president, they would vote for me! That's power! Man, I just did a tour in Japan, I'm standin' there in front of fifty thousand Japanese kids. I started singin' "Murder Every Day," right? They were singin' it with me! On some karaoke-type shit. They knew every word to that song. Every word! They was break-dancing' out there and everything. I said, This is some powerful shit. 'Cause last time I seen breakin' in this country … was in a Hershey's commercial. That's our culture man, Hip-Hop is alive!

I seen all that goin' on in Japan. I had an awakening Dave. It was ill too. Every night, I would hear my rhymes over and over in my head. Particularly this one line, "Break a bitch pussy, bust a nigga brain/ Break a bitch pussy, bust a nigga brain …" It just kept repeating itself … in my dreams. I got sick. And one morning I just woke up shakin' in a cold sweat, all fucked up and depressed, and … rich. And I got out of bed and I looked at myself in the mirror and I just said, "Where is the joy … Emcee Enuff?" You know? I'm a millionaire, why is my life filled with such … pain. Dave? I ain't gonna front, you got rappers that led ill lives or whatnot. They been to jail or whatever. But see, now they outta jail and they rappin' 'bout how great it is and everybody should go. And then 'cause they sayin' that, you got rappers that's never been to jail rappin' 'bout how they can't wait to get up in one. That's pain, Dave.

But lemme tell you, and you know this is true, Dave. Once you tasted a fresh tuna sashimi, melt in your mouth, you don't wanna go to jail.

Right, Dave? ... You see your mutual fund gain twenty points a year, you be like "Damn, I'm straight, I don't wanna go to jail." You walkin' down the hot white sands of Barbados or Jamaica or wherever on vacation, you got a fine woman's hand on yours. You go snorkelin' down there, and see all the little stuff on the bottom of the ocean, you like, "Damn — I didn't know this shit was here ... Wasup fish?" You like, "A'ight, yeah ... Here is the joy."

Kimberly Akimbo

David Lindsay-Abaire

Play
Seriocomic
M
30s
Contemporary

Buddy's wife is pregnant and has been recording her thoughts on a tape recorder. Here, Buddy gives it a try.

And the thing is, I don't think I'm very good with kids. I mean I like kids, I just never pictured myself as a father. I'm more of a bachelor-uncle type, you know? Which isn't to say I regret anything. I love Kim, and I'm happy you're coming but ... when you're young you imagine doin' a bunch of different things. Just ... crazy, unrealistic stuff but ... And then when Pattie got pregnant with Kim, it was like, "Oh, OK, I guess I do this then." Which was fine. Made things easier in some ways, you know, to not have any ... choices I guess. I mean, most guys in the world are just guys who go to work, right? Guys with kids. So there's no shame in that. Just being a regular person. *(Beat.)* Although I would still like to travel someday. That's something I'd like to do. I'll see these countries on TV and think, "Wow, that's a weird place. I'd like to see that in person maybe." Like Pamplona. That's in Spain, and the bulls run through the streets chasing everybody, and the guys scramble up the sides of buildings and jump in doorways and some people get gored. It looks fun. I'd like that. But you need money to see things, so ... *(Pause.)*

The Lady of Lyons

Edward Bulwer-Lytton

> **Play**
> **Seriocomic**
> **M**
> **20s**
> **Classic**
>
> *Melnotte, an impoverished painter, is wooing the wealthy Pauline, a young woman "above his station," as his mother points out.*

Do the stars think of us? Yet if the prisoner sees them shine into his dungeon, wouldnst thou bid him turn away from their lustre? Even so from this low cell, poverty, I lift my eyes to Pauline and forget my chains. *(Goes to her portrait.)* See, this is her image — painted from memory. Oh, how the canvas wrongs her! — I shall never be a painter! I can paint no likeness but one, and that is above all art. I would turn soldier — France needs soldiers! But to leave the air that Pauline breathes! What is the hour? — so late? I will tell thee a secret, mother. Thou knowest that for the last six weeks I have sent every day the rarest flowers to Pauline? — she wears them. I have seen them on her breast. Ah, and then the whole universe seemed filled with odors! I have now grown more bold — I have poured my worship into poetry — I have sent the verses to Pauline — I have signed them with my own name. My messenger ought to be back by this time, I bade him wait for the answer.

(…) She will admit me. I shall hear her speak — I shall meet her eyes — I shall read upon her cheek the swept thoughts that translate themselves into blushes. Then — then, oh, then — she may forget that I am the peasant's son!

(…) I foresee it all. She will tell me that desert is the true rank. She will give me a badge — a flower — a glove! Oh rapture! I shall join the armies of the republic — I shall rise — I shall win a name that beauty will not blush to hear. I shall return with the right to say to her — "See, how love does not level the proud, but raise the humble!" Oh, how my heart swells within me! — Oh, what glorious prophets of the future are youth and hope!

The Lady's Last Stake

Colley Cibber

Play
Seriocomic
M
30+
Classic

Lord George attempts to get himself off the hook regarding an unfortunate misunderstanding.

I'll tell you, Madam — about two years ago, I happened to make a country visit to my lady Conquest, her mother, and one day, at the table, I remember, I was particularly pleased with the entertainment, and upon enquiry, found that the bill of fare was under the direction of mademoiselle here. Now it happened at that time, I was my self in want of a housekeeper, upon which account I thought it would not be amiss, if I now and then paid her a little particular civility. To be short, I fairly told her, I had a great mind to have a plain good house-wife about me, and dropped some broad hints, that the place might be hers for the asking. Would you believe it, Madam, if I'm alive, the creature grew so vain upon it, so deplorably mistook my meaning, that she told me, her fortune depended upon her mother's will, and therefore she could receive no proposals of marriage without her consent. Now after that unfortunate blunder of hers, whether I ever gave my lady the least trouble about the business, I leave to the small remainder of her own conscience. Madam, if there's any faith in my sense, her only charms then were, and are still not in raising of passion, but paste. I own I did voraciously admire her prodigious knack of making cheesecakes, tarts, custards, and syllabubs. Whether I'm in love or no, I leave to your ladyship … In the meantime, I believe, our surest comfort will be to think well of ourselves, and let it alone.

The Liars

Henry Arthur Jones

Play
Seriocomic
M
50s
Classic

Sir Christopher dissuades his friend, Ned, from running away with Lady Jessica, a married woman.

Now! I've nothing to say in the abstract against running away with another man's wife! There may be planets where it is not only the highest ideal morality, but where it has the further advantage of being a practical way of carrying on society. But it has this one fatal defect in our country to-day — it won't work. You know what we English are, Ned. We're not a bit better than our neighbours, but, thank God! we do pretend we are, and we do make it hot for anybody who disturbs that holy pretense. And take my word for it, my dear Lady Jessica, my dear Ned, it won't work. You know it's not an original experiment you're making. It has been tried before. Have you ever known it to be successful? Lady Jessica, think of the brave pioneers who have gone before you in this enterprise. They've all perished, and their bones whiten the anti-matrimonial shore. (…) Do you think the experiment is going to be successful in your case? Not a bit of it. (…) First of all there will be the shabby scandal and dirty business of the divorce court. You won't like that. It isn't nice. You won't like it. After the divorce court, what is Ned to do with you? Take you to Africa? (…) Stay in England? In society? Everybody will cut you. (…) Take any of the other dozen alternatives and find yourself stranded in some shady hole or corner, with the one solitary hope and ambition of somehow wriggling back into respectability. (…) He's at the height of his career, with a great and honourable task in front of him. If you turn him aside you'll not only wreck and ruin your own life and reputation, but you'll wreck and ruin his. (…) If you care for him, don't keep him shuffling and malingering here. Send him out with me to finish his work like the good, splendid fellow he is. Set him free, Lady Jessica, and go back to your home. Your husband has been here. He's sorry for what is past, and he has promised to treat you more kindly in the future. He's waiting at home to take you out. You missed a very good dinner last night. Don't miss another to-night. (…) Go to him, and do, once for all, have done with other folly. Do believe me, my dear Ned, my dear Lady Jessica, before it is too late, do believe me, it won't work, it won't work, it won't work!

Lovers

Brian Friel

Play
Seriocomic
M
19
Contemporary

Joe entertains his wife, Mag, with how he procured their first flat, which oversees a busy slaughterhouse.

I signed the lease yesterday evening.

Old Kerrigan was so busy working he wouldn't take time off to go into the office; so we put the document on the back of a cow that was about to be shot and that's where we signed it. Cockeyed old miser!

I'm telling you. And crazy, too. In a big rubber apron and him dripping with blood. And cows and sheep and bullocks dropping dead all around him.

"Drive him up there! Another beast. C'mon! C'mon! I haven't all day. And what's bother you, young Brennan? Steady, there. Steady! Bang! Bang! Bang! Drag it away! Slit its throat! Slice it open! Skin it!"

Another beast! Get a move on! What am I paying you fellas for? You told me about the flat, Mr. Kerrigan. "Steady-bang! Bang! Dammit, I nearly missed — bang! — that's it. Drag him off. What are you saying, young Brennan? The lease? Oh, the lease! Oh, aye. Here we are." *(Joe produces an imaginary document from his hip pocket.)* "Best flat in town. Hell, it's all blood now." *(Joe wipes the imaginary document on his leg.)* "Come on! Another animal! There's a fine beast for you, young Brennan! Look at those shanks! Bang! Bang! Never knew what hit him! I sing here, son, don't I?" *(Joe pretends to write: but the pen does not work and he flings it away.)* "Hell, that doesn't write."

The Magic Realists

Megan Terry

Play
Seriocomic
M
Late teens
Contemporary

Don arrives at a job interview.

I'd like to've been here sooner — but I been sort of away from the action. You see, they kept feelin' like they have to put me in the cooler. And — well, the last time they stashed me there was on account a — *(Relating the story of his life; matter-of-factly.)* — I killed this here whole family that wouldn't let me drive their Volkswagen bus. Shot the dog, too. Then I tried to drive. But I didn't know how to drive. So I shot the bus. They busted me — but I escaped. I been walkin' a lot. I just won't be locked up no more. Ever since I was a tiny fella, they had me locked up somewheres. Even my old granddad tied me to the clothesline, or to the tree or porch railin', so's I couldn't get run over or anything. I thought maybe I'd be lucky when he kicked off, but they didn't know what to do with me, so they put me in these here places and every time I'd get a little older, they'd stick me in another place. But I got away. Been travelin'. Climb up and down trees — it takes longer that way, and very interesting. I know a lot about bugs and bees and birds now. Been studyin' 'em, firsthand. And I found this terrific woods here. Must be some ways from yer camp here? Know something'? You're the first guy I talked to since I sprung myself from the can. (…) They fed us lots a food there. Terrible, but it was lots. I never had a mother. I was a skinny ugly mean little kid and no foster family'd take me; so here I am. Handsome and lovely at last, and too big to be adopted. I'm hungry.

The Menaechme

Titus Maccius Plautus

> **Play**
> **Seriocomic**
> **M**
> **30+**
> **Classic**

Menaechmus berates his suspicious wife for distrusting him, then proves himself completely unworthy of her trust.

If you weren't mean, if you weren't stupid, if you weren't a violent virago, what you see displeases your husband would be displeasing to you, too. Now mark my words, if you act like this toward me after today, you shall hie yourself home to your father as a divorcee. Why, whenever I want to go out, you catch hold of me, call me back, cross-question me as to where I'm going, what I'm doing, what business I have in hand, what I'm after, what I've got, what I did when I was out. I've married a custom-house officer, judging from the way everything — all I've done and am doing — must be declared. I've pampered you too much; now then, I'll state my future policy. Inasmuch as I keep you well provided with maids, food, woolen cloth, jewelry, coverlets, purple dresses, and you lack for nothing, you will look out for trouble if you're wise, and cease spying on your husband. *(In a lower tone as his wife goes back inside.)* And furthermore, that you may not watch me for nothing, I'll reward your diligence by taking a wench to dinner and inviting myself out somewhere. Hurrah! By Jove, at last my lecture has driven her away! *(Looks around.)* Where are your married gallants? Why don't they all hurry up with gifts and congratulations for my valiant fight? *(Showing a woman's mantle worn underneath his cloak.)* This mantle I just now stole from my wife inside there, and *(Gleefully.)* it's going to a wench. This is the way to do — to cheat a cunning jailer in such clever style! I have taken booty from the enemy without loss to my allies!

Money

Edward Bulwer-Lytton

Play
Seriocomic
M
40s
Classic

Graves, a curmudgeon, rails against newspapers. Incidentally, this is the author credited with, "It was a dark and stormy night..." (No extra charge for trivia.)

Ay — read the newspapers! — They'll tell you what this world is made of. Daily calendars of roguery and woe! Here, advertisements from quacks, money-lenders, cheap warehouses, and spotted boys with tow heads! So much for dupes and impostors! Turn to the other column — police reports, bankruptcies, swindling, forgery, and a biographical sketch of the snub-nosed man who murdered his own three little cherubs at Pentonville. Do you fancy these but exceptions to the general virtue and health of the nation? — turn to the leading article! And your hair will stand on end at the horrible wickedness or melancholy idiotism of that half of the population who think differently form yourself. In my day I have seen already eighteen crises, six annihilations of agriculture and commerce, four overthrows of the Church, and three last, final, awful, and irremediable destructions of the entire Constitution! And that's a newspaper — a newspaper — a newspaper!

Moonshine

Jim Nolan

Play
Seriocomic
M
40s-50s
Contemporary

In a delicious mix of the comic and macabre, McKeever, the town undertaker, prepares the body of his would-be mother-in-law.

(Singing happily on entrance.)
> E'er since by faith I saw the stream,
> Thy flowing wounds supply
> Redeeming love has been my theme
> And shall be till I die.

Enfin, le visage! Hands and face, the most important. Visible signs, d'y'see. So. No cock-ups in that department. And there won't be either — not tonight, Josephine! The embalmer, Margaret, is a creator of illusions. We banish the traces of suffering and death and present the deceased in an attitude of normal and restful sleep. We create, as Strub and Frederick so movingly put it, "a memory picture." Good old Strub and Frederick, the unsung heroes of the mortuary. Perhaps you've heard of them, Margaret. Their book, *The Principles and Practice of Embalming* is the veritable bible of our profession. Not exactly coffee-table stuff, I grant you, and I don't expect they'll surface in the best-seller lists, but old Strub and Fredrick have filled many a lonely hour for me, I can tell you. *(Pause.)* There now, clean as a new pin. *(Foreceps and cotton wool.)* Next we have the packing of the orifices. Don't worry Margaret, you won' feel a thing. *(Pause.)* You don't mind if I call you Margaret, do you, Margaret? I feel it brings us closer. And after all, I was almost one of the family one time, wasn't I? Of course, you couldn't have known that I don't suppose it matters to you now but I was yes, very much so.

(Pause. Takes remote control switch from pocket and turns off music.)
We were lovers, y'see, Lizzie and me. That shocked you, didn't it — if

you were alive today you'd die of the fright. Yes, lovers. In this very room, too. On this very trolley. Life and death. Would have told you sooner only I didn't think you'd understand. That's why she went away. Nothing to do with you or John, Margaret — it was all McKeever's fault. *(Pause.)* Don't be angry, Margaret — I meant no harm. Please. Don't get upset. It was all right. *(Pause.)* It was all right, that is, until I blew it. I couldn't cut it, Margaret. And the track record, not great. Ask the absent Mrs. McKeever if you don't believer me. Didn't want to repeat history, did we? So I rewrote it instead.

Our father who art in exile, that was me. Never around when he's wanted. *(Sings.)*

I see the moon, the moon sees me
Under the shade of the old oak tree
Please let the moon that shines on me
Shine on the one I love.

Much Ado About Nothing

William Shakespeare

Play
Seriocomic
M
30s
Classic

Benedict marvels at the change in Claudio, who has fallen in love, and takes tally of his own possibilities.

I do much wonder that one man, seeing how much another man is a fool when he dedicates his behaviours to love, will, after he hath laughed at such shallow follies in others, become the argument of his own scorn by falling in love: and such a man is Claudio. I have known when there was no music with him but the drum and fife; and now had he rather hear the tabor and the pipe: I have known when he would have walked ten mile a-foot to see a good armour; and now will he lie ten nights awake, carving the fashion of a new doublet. He was wont to speak plain and to the purpose, like an honest man and soldier; and now is he turned orthography; his words are a very fantastical banquet, just so many strange dishes. May I be so converted and see with these eyes? I cannot tell; I think not: I will not be sworn but love may transform me to an oyster; but I'll take my oath on it, till he have made an oyster of me, he shall never make me such a fool. On woman is fair, yet I am well; another is wise, yet I am well; another virtuous, yet I am well; but till all graces be in one woman, one woman shall not come in my grace. Rich she shall be, that's certain; wise, or I'll none; virtuous, or I'll never cheapen her; fair, or I'll never look on her; mild, or come not near me; noble, or not I for an angel; of good discourse, an excellent musician, and her hair shall be of what colour it please God.

The Picture of Dorian Gray

Oscar Wilde

Novel
Seriocomic
M
30s
Contemporary

Dorian experiences a production of Romeo and Juliet, which leads him to an epiphany : "...the only thing worth loving is an actress."

This play was good enough for us, Harry. It was *Romeo and Juliet*. I must admit that I was rather annoyed at the idea of seeing Shakespeare done in such a wretched hole of a place. Still, I felt interested, in a sort of way. At any rate, I determined to wait for the first act. There was a dreadful orchestra, presided over by a young Hebrew who sat at a cracked piano, that nearly drove me away, but at last the drop-scene was drawn up, and the play began. Romeo was a stout elderly gentleman, with corked eyebrows, a husky tragedy voice, and a figure like a beer-barrel. Mercutio was almost as bad. He was played by the low-comedian, who had introduced gags of his own and was on most friendly terms with the pit. They were both as grotesque as the scenery, and that looked as if it had come out of a country booth. But Juliet! Harry, imagine a girl, hardly seventeen years of age, with a little flower-like face, a small Greek head with plaited coils of dark-brown hair, eyes that were violet wells of passion, lips that were like the petals of a rose. She was the loveliest thing I had ever seen in my life. You said to me once that pathos left you unmoved, but that beauty, mere beauty, could fill your eyes with tears. I tell you, Harry, I could hardly see this girl for the mist of tears that came across me. (…) Why should I not love her? Harry, I do love her. She is everything to me in life. Night after night I go to see her play. One evening she is Rosalind, and the next evening she is Imogen. I have seen her die in the gloom of an Italian tomb, sucking the poison from her lover's lips. I have watched her wandering through the forest of Arden, disguised as a pretty boy in hose and doublet and dainty cap. She has been mad, and has come into the presence of a guilty king, and given him rue to wear, and bitter herbs to taste of. She has been innocent, and the black hands of jealousy have crushed her reed-like throat. I have seen her in every age and in every costume. Ordinary women never appeal to one's imagination. They are limited to their century. No glamour ever transfigures them. One knows their minds as easily as one knows their bonnets. One can always find them. There is no mystery in any of them. They ride in the Park in the morning, and chatter at tea-parties in the afternoon. They have their stereotyped smile, and their fashionable manner. They are quite obvious. But an actress! How different an actress is! Harry! why didn't you tell me that the only thing worth loving is an actress?

Population Growth

Aoise Stratford

Play
Seriocomic
M
30s
Contemporary

Simon, nervous in a suit and tie, waits for his Godot.

Don't mind me, I'm waiting for someone. You can just go about your business, finish your meals … I'll just wait over here. *(A beat.)* The woman I'm meeting, *(Smiling.)* and yes, it is a woman, a very lovely woman if you must know … the woman I'm meeting asked me to wait by the window. *(A beat.)* It's hard to tell isn't it? You know when a place gets a little crowded, a little noisy, lots of people rushing around calling out "Another goat's cheese ravioli over here, Sid," "Can I get the check?" "Can I get your phone number?" Well you get the idea. I'm just saying it can be a little … overwhelming. You know. All that activity. It's easy to miss a person if there's a lot of commotion around. So, being a very sensible woman, Charlotte asked me to wait here by this window. You know, kind of like a landmark. So she'd know where to look. *(A beat.)*

Do you have the time? *(A beat.)* I guess she's a little late because of the traffic. I think there was an A's game on or something. I really should have paid better attention to that. I'm not much of a sportsman. Sorry, Sportsperson. I don't much care for baseball. Very un-American of me, I know. *(Laughs.)* But you know, I'm also a very, very open person. Open in a lot of ways. Open as in honest and open as in … open to suggestions, open to new experiences. So if, for instance, Charlotte was really into baseball, in a big way, I'm sure that wouldn't be a problem. *(A beat.)* I just don't like crowds much. *(A beat.)* Not that I'm claustrophobic. I just don't like … you know what it is? I believe we are all individuals. I believe that each and every one of us has merits, you know, qualities. And we deserve individual attention and respect. (…) [W]e are all special. Even a fellow like me, huh? We can't all be good looking and confident like my brother for example. *(Awkward laugh.)* I'm sure she'll be here any minute. I'm sorry if I've been … rambling. Please, don't mind me. Go back to your coffees or whatever you have and I'll just sit here and admire the view …

Scotch and Donuts

John Longenbaugh

> **Play**
> **Seriocomic**
> **M**
> **30**
> **Contemporary**

Tom demystifies lemmings. It isn't pretty.

Actually, not a lot of people know this, but lemmings don't commit mass suicide. That's a myth. Yes, I know we've all seen that nature movie of them leaping off cliffs into the sea. But it's a fake. These nature photographers from Disney were told that migrating lemmings leap off cliffs, so they grabbed their cameras and headed off to the fjords. Trouble was, once they got there, the lemmings wouldn't cooperate. So they "assisted them." A couple of the guys stood on a cliff with a pen full of lemmings and tossed the little rodents into the sea below while their friend filmed. It was a nature snuff film.

Then, there's the irony of that narrator's voice asking, "Will we ever learn what mysterious force drives these animals to their death?" But I think, more to the point, will lemmings ever learn what mysterious force drives a bunch of filmmakers to toss their hapless little bodies over a cliff?

I used to think the lemming story taught us about the natural urge toward self-destruction. But all it really does is hold the mirror up to us.

Sleepin' at Doug's

Michael K. White

Play
Seriocomic
M
20s
Contemporary

A very serious young man enters with an acoustic guitar and a microphone with stand. He patiently sets up, sits on a stool, and stares down the audience with a violent mixture of patience and expectation.

This is my song. It's called, "Sleepin' at Doug's."

(He starts playing an aimless riff and crooning sweetly into the microphone. "Sleepin' at Doug's" is completely amelodic and meandering. The lyrics don't always follow the beat and the guitar changes are crude, to put it nicely. Still after the initial giggle, the song should start to come together. It is held together by the sweet croon of the MAN's voice. Whatever else it is, "Sleepin' At Doug's" is meaningful for him and he should sing it tenderly, from the very depths of his heart.)

(Singing.)
Well we'd go to sleep at Doug's
He lived in a garage on Poplar Street
Just off of Lake by where the bars all were

And he'd buy us beer and beat his wife
And we'd read his dirty books
And then beat off in an old aluminum shower
That barely held
Anything

Well I remember the time at Doug's
When I threw up in his closet
It got in all his shoes and socks under a picture of a helicopter
Then he woke up about three thirty

Damn he was mad.
I said it wasn't me; Mike's the one who did it.

When we'd sleep at Doug's we'd stay up late
I'd wake up first
And I'd sit there and wish that I was home
And I'd look at Doug's George Carlin album
And I'd look at a Spanky and Our Gang album
And I'd look at the demonstration record he had of a group that he
named Hollow Young
And when he played it he asked me if I'd buy it
And I lied

Sleepin' at Doug's was fun
But he never got us high
But he did buy us beer
But he should have got us high
But he bought us beer so I guess
It's OK.

Some People
Danny Hoch

Play
Seriocomic
M
20s
Contemporary

Floe runs into an old friend on the street, and tries to open up about his new relationship.

Nah! I'm serious! It's like, even just being with her, we don't even have to be doing nothing, we just be sitting there. Plus she be schooling me, 'cause you know she's in college, right? She's gonna be a sophomore at Hunter next semester. Black and Puerto Rican studies. So I'm sayin', it's like we just be chilling or whatever. And all of the sudden she'll drop the bomb of knowledge on me. Like check this out, there was this whole civilization, livin' on the islands in the Caribbean, mad hundred thousand years before the Europeans came over and fucked that whole shit up. They was called Tainos.

They had a whole civilization, architecture, medicine, culture … Tainos. … You ain't never heard of no cukin' Tainos. This nigga ain't never heard of Fritos talkin' 'bout you heard of that shit. I'm sayin' though, shit was just different with her. … That too though. It's like, even when I was fuckin' her. Ah, see I can't even say that 'cause it wasn't like fuckin'. It was like we was making love or some shit. … Shut up. Stop laughing. Your mother's so fat she jumped in the air and got stuck, shut the fuck up. … Nah, shut the fuck up, stop laughing though. I'm saying, I'm gonna tell you this 'cause it still be buggin' me out to this day. This happened like once, right? … I'm not saying I fucked her once, but listen. You know when you be gettin' busy, and like you get all into the moment and shit? Like you get all hot and sweaty and you get into the smells, like you be smelling her neck and shit. You know, you be like, "Ah, lemme smell your neck"? So, I'm saying like one time, we was all in it. And I had closed my eyes and this shit had come over me like I can't even explain it. Like in here, and I had like almost started like, cryin' and shit. I mean I'm not saying I was crying. I'm saying like, a'ight. The only thing I could compare it to is, remember last summer we went to Action Park? ... Nah, a'ight, bad example, bad example.

I'm sayin', you ever been on a airplane? ... So you know you be on a airplane and you hit turbulence and the plane drops? And your stomach goes like this, but the rest of your body goes like this? ...It's like you're separating and you feel like ... I'm saying, so they got that water slide at Action Park, and when you go down the slide you be like ... wahh. I'm not sayin' down there, I'm sayin' like in here. ... Never mind, man. ... Nah, forget it, shut up, you're stupid. Watch in like five years, she'll be some college professor, and we'll be on tour at her school. And we'll run into each other and be like, ching! ... Nah you, let me shut up, man. I be sounding all sentimental like Sally Jeffrey Rafael and shit.

The Tempest

William Shakespeare

Play
Seriocomic
M
20+
Classic

Trinculo believes he is alone on a strange island with a storm looming. While looking for shelter, he stumbles upon Caliban, whom he initially believes to be "a strange fish."

Here's neither bush nor shrub to bear off any weather at all, and another storm brewing: I hear it sing i' th' wind. Yond same black cloud, yond huge one, looks like a foul bombard that would shed his liquor. If it should thunder as it did before, I know not where to hide my head. Yond same cloud cannot choose but fall by pailfuls. What have we here? a man or a fish? dead or alive? A fish: he smells like a fish; a very ancient and fishlike smell; a kind of not of the newest poor-John. A strange fish! Were I in England now, as once I was, and had but this fish painted, not a holiday fool there but would give a piece of silver. There would this monster make a man: any strange beast there makes a man. When they will not give a doit to relieve a lame beggar, they will lay out ten to see a dead Indian. Legged like a man! and his fins like arms! Warm, o' my troth! I do now let loose my opinion, hold it no longer: this is no fish, but an islander, that hath lately suffered by a thunderbolt. *(Thunder.)* Alas, the storm is come again! My best way is to creep under his gaverdine: there is no other shelter hereabout. Misery acquaints a man with strange bedfellows. I will here shroud till the dregs of the storm be past.

Temptation

Langston Hughes

Short story
Seriocomic
M
60+
Contemporary

… I just wish we colored folks had been somewhere around at the start. I do not know where we was when Eden was a garden, but we sure didn't get in on none of the crops. If we had, we would not be so poor today. White folks started out ahead and they are still ahead. Look at me! (…) Made in the image of God … but I never did see anybody like me on a Sunday school card.

(…) [If] a snake were to come up to me and offer *me* an apple, I would say, "Varmint, be on your way! No fruit today! Bud, you got the wrong stud now, so get along somehow, be off down the road because you're lower than a toad!" Then that serpent would respect me as a wise man — and this world would not be where it is — all on account of an apple.

(…) I would have stayed in that garden making grape wine, singing like Crosby, and feeling fine! I would not be scuffling out in this rough world, neither would I be in Harlem. If I was Adam I would just stay in Eden in that garden with no rent to pay, no landladies to dodge, no time clock to punch — and *my* picture on a Sunday school card.

The Traitor

James Shirley

Play
Seriocomic
M
25+
Classic

Sciarrha counsels on how to win the eye of the Duke.

What do great ladies do at court, I pray?
Enjoy the pleasures of the world, dance, kiss
The amorous lords, and change court breath, sing loose
Belief of other heaven, tell wanton dreams,
Rehearse your sprightly bed scenes, and boast which
Hath most idolators, accuse all faces
That trust to the implicity of nature,
Talk witty blasphemy,
Discourse their gaudy wardrobes, plot new pride,
Jest upon courtiers' legs, laugh at the wagging
Of their own feathers, and a thousand more
Delights which private ladies never think of.
But above all, and wherein thou shalt make
All other beauties envy thee, the duke,
The duke himself shall call thee his, and single
From the fair troop thy person forth to exchange
Embraces with, lay siege to those soft lips,
And not remove till he hath suck'd thy heart
Which, so dissolv'd with they sweet breath, shall be
Made part of his, at the same instant he
Conveying a new soul into thy breast
With a creating kiss. Why will you
Appear so ignorant? I speak the dialect
Of Florence to you. (…)
In plain Italian,
Love him, and command him.

Two Gentlemen of Verona

William Shakespeare

Play
Seriocomic
M
30s
Classic

Launce acts out his tearful parting from his family's home.

Nay, 'twill be this hour ere I have done weeping. All the kind of the Launces have this very fault. I have received my proportion, like the prodigious son, and am going with Sir Proteus to the Imperial's court. I think Crab, my dog, be the sourest-natured dog that lives. My mother weeping, my father wailing, my sister crying, our maid howling, our cat wringing her hands, and all our house in a great perplexity, yet did not this cruel-hearted cur shed one tear. He is a stone, a very pebble stone, and has no more pity in him than a dog. A Jew would have wept to have seen our parting. Why, my grandam, having no eyes, look you, wept herself blind at my parting. Nay, I'll show you the manner of it. This shoe is my father. No, this left shoe is my father. No, no, this left shoe is my mother. Nay, that cannot be so neither. Yes, it is so, it is so — it hath the worser sole. This shoe with the hole in it is my mother, and this my father. A vengeance on't! There 'tis. Now, sir, this staff is my sister, for, look you, she is as white as a lily and as small as a wand. This hat is Nan, our maid. I am the dog. No, the dog is himself, and I am the dog — O, the dog is me, and I am myself. Ay, so, so. Now come I to my father: "Father, your blessing." Now should not the shoe speak a word for weeping. Now should I kiss my father — well, he weeps on. Now come I to my mother. O, that she could speak now like a wood woman! Well, I kiss her — why, there 'tis: here's my mother's breath up and down. Now come I to my sister; mark the moan she makes. Now the dog all this while sheds not a tear nor speaks a word!

Two Gentlemen of Verona

William Shakespeare

Play
Seriocomic
M
30s
Classic

Launce's dog proves problematic. Bad dog.

When a man's servant shall play the cur with him, look you, it goes hard: one that I brought up of a puppy, one that I saved from drowning when three or four of his blind brothers and sisters went to it. I have taught him, even as one would say precisely, "Thus I would teach a dog.' I was sent to deliver him as a present to Mistress Silvia from my master, and I came no sooner into the dining chamber but he steps me to her trencher and steals her capon's leg. O, 'tis a foul thing when a cur cannot keep himself in all companies! I would have, as one should say, one that takes upon him to be a dog indeed, to be, as it were, a dog at all things. If I had not had more wit than he, to take a fault upon me that he did, I think verily he had been hanged for't. Sure as I live, he had suffered for't. You shall judge. He thrusts me himself into the company of three or four gentleman-like dogs under the Duke's table. He had not been there — bless the mark — a pissing-while but all the chamber smelt him. "Out with the dog," says one. "What cur is that?" says another. "Whip him out," says the third. "Hang him up," says the Duke. I, having been acquainted with the smell before, knew it was Crab, and goes me to the fellow that whips the dogs. "Friend," quoth I, "you mean to whip the dog?" "Ay, marry, do I," quoth he. "You do him the more wrong," quoth I; 'twas I did the thing you wot of." He makes me no more ado, but whips me out of the chamber. How many masters would do this for his servant? Nay, I'll be sworn, I have sat in the stocks for puddings he hath stol'n, otherwise he had been executed. I have stood in the pillory for geese he hath killed, otherwise he had suffered for't. Thou think'st not of this now. Nay, I remember the trick you served me when I took my leave of Madam Silvia. Did not I bid thee still mark me and do as I do? When didst thou see me heave up my leg and make water against a gentle-woman's farthingale? Dids't thou ever see me do such a trick?

Monologues

Acme Temporary Services

Linda Eisenstein

Play
Comic
M/F
35+
Contemporary

Bridge, a personnel recruiter — "part Jewish mother, part Mafia don" — interviews a prospective employee.

This, THIS is an impressive application. Solid typing test, spelling excellent, vocabulary, whew! English major, right? I can always tell.

So the work history is, let's face it, a little spotty, a few gaps here and there, but what the hell. You look like an ideal hire. In fact, why don't we admit it? You are overqualified for almost every pissant seat-warming job we handle.

But here at Acme Temporary Services, we are looking for special clients just like you. We search high and low for one rare qualification. It's called: a sense of reality.

So, here's the sixty-four thousand dollar question.

What are you looking for in a temporary agency? Do you expect that by filing this excellent resume with us — that you are eventually going to find the job of your dreams, a permanent position on an upwardly mobile career track, that pays well and is meaningful and has good health insurance and a pension plan and contributes to the general wealth?

(A loud beep.) ANNNNH! Guess again! Of course you won't. If that's what you're looking for, take another toke on your crack-pipe, go across the street to one of our competitors: Womanpower, or the Pink Glove Girls, or some other lying scum-sucking peddler of illusions for codependent morons. You are not for Acme and Acme is not for you.

See, at Acme we deal in reality. We know what the contemporary corporate market is looking for: warm bodies, hungry bodies, desperate bodies that will chase the carrot and bend to the stick until they drop, even though anyone with one half-blind eye can see that the days of a permanent pensioned labor force has gone the way of the dodo.

In short: temporary employees are toilet paper. Toilet paper! We know that. They know that. And at Acme, we want YOU to know that. Because if you are toilet paper, fit only to wipe the ass of the system, then you might as well be GENERIC toilet paper.

It's all summed up in our Acme philosophy: Ack Me If I Care.

America (It's Gotta Be the Cheese)

Eitan Kadosh

Poem
Seriocomic
M/F
20+
Contemporary

Effective sarcastic humor is both funny and piercing ...

Everybody writes about America
And everybody paints America
Because from Jasper Johns to Allen Ginsberg
They are all looking for the same thing
Searching for the real America
The one that lies under the costumes and the war paint
      that lies under the Seinfeld and Springer
      under the bad porn and good basketball

And I am no exception
Except that one night, late last week
I actually found it, this elusive America — in the dairy case at
Andronico's market
Lurking beside the jacks and the cheddars, the goudas, swisses,
stiltons, jarlsbergs, gorgonzolas, whole parmesan, ricottas, and
myriad other imported and domestic cheeses
There — it beckoned suddenly
An immaculately wrapped unbelievably orange package of
American Pasteurized Process Cheese food glory
God bless this country

We pasteurized
We processed
We manipulated this cheese until it suited our purposes
This was engineered cheese
This was the scientific method at work — Jonas Salk Albert
Einstein Copernicus

This was smooth no lumps when melted technology at work —
the lightbulb phonograph model T radio television Internet
Nike Air rolled into one
And all for $1.99

I was so moved I broke into the Pledge of Allegiance right there
            and then
I bought Charlton Heston's autobiography
Became a Daughter of the American Revolution

Oh god how I long to be wrapped in golden singles of American
            Cheese
Drizzled with its salty goodness

Oh god put me in a sauna so that the cheese will melt and when
it does it will melt evenly over every square inch of my body (...)

America land of the free — it's gotta be the cheese
Home of the brave — it's gotta be the cheese
Land of possibility, opportunity and the certain unalienable rights of

manifest destiny — it's gotta be the cheese
who killed Emmitt Till — it's gotta be the cheese
who trained and armed Latin American torture squads — it's
            gotta be the cheese
who shot J.F.K., J.R. Ewing, J.C. Penney — it's gotta be the cheese
(...).

Mom the flag and apple pie

It's gotta be the cheese

A Midsummer Night's Dream

William Shakespeare

Play
Comic
M/F
Any age
Classic

The puckish Puck reveals his ass.

My mistress with a monster is in love.
Near to her close and consecrated bower,
While she was in her dull and sleeping hour,
A crew of patches, rude mechanicals,
That work for bread upon Athenian stalls,
Were met together to rehearse a play,
Intended for great Theseus' nuptial day.
The shallowest thickskin of that barren sort,
Who Pyramus presented in their sport,
Forsook his scene and entered in a brake.
When I did him at this advantage take,
An ass's nose I fixèd on his head.
Anon his Thisby must be answerèd,
And forth my mimic comes. When they him spy,
As wild geese that the creeping fowler eye,
Or russet-pated choughs, many in sort,
Rising and cawing at the gun's report,
Sever themselves and madly sweep the sky;
So at his sight away his fellows fly,
And at our stamp here o'er and o'er one falls;
He murder cries and help from Athens calls.
Their sense thus weak, lost with their fears thus strong,
Made senseless things begin to do them wrong,
For briers and thorns at their apparel snatch:
Some, sleeves — some, hats; from yielders all things catch.
I led them on in this distracted fear
And left sweet Pyramus translated there,
When in that moment (so it came to pass)
Titania waked, and straightway loved an ass.

My Parents

Joe McCabe

Play
Comic
M/F
20+
Contemporary

The narrator uses clichés like nobody's business.

When Mom first met him, Dad was a diamond in the rough with a gift of gab, a man of the world and a man of his word, and a barrel of laughs who never missed a trick. His big heart was in the right place, and he had an open mind on most subjects. Mom had a mind of her own and a memory like an elephant. She wasn't born yesterday, and she had a good head on her shoulders, but she was a backseat driver who made mountains out of molehills. She looked every gift horse in the mouth. Dad always had the courage of his convictions, but sometimes he seemed scared to death of her, even though her bark was worse than her bite. Money burned a hole in his pocket, but year in, year out, Mom saved all she could for the rainy days to come. Sometimes he'd put all his eggs in one basket or count his chickens before they hatched, and when he had egg on his face she expected him to eat crow. She'd cry over spilled milk, and she'd beat a dead horse till she was blue in the face. He'd bite his tongue and swallow his pride. He'd bend over backwards for her, but he rarely let her get him down. He'd go the extra mile and look for the silver lining along the way. She never quite put him in his place. Mom tried to put the best face on things, and Dad usually played along with her. "We Could Make Believe" (from Showboat) was Their Song. They knew how to make a virtue of necessity; they stuck together through thick and thin; they made the best of their hard bargain. Dad was generous; Mom was fair. If it weren't for them, I wouldn't be here at all. If it weren't for their nurturing, I wouldn't be the way I am. Between them they taught me to keep a straight face and a civil tongue, to keep my eyes open and my nose clean, to keep my shirt on and my fingers crossed. They told me to give life my best shot, to roll with the punches, to live and learn. Mom wanted to have the last word; Dad preferred to have the last laugh.

Schoolhouse Rock

Jason D. Martin

Play
Comic
M/F
20+
Contemporary

The "sweet, protective" teacher you never had; the life-preserving lesson no one ever taught you.

All right children, everyone sit down. Today I want to tell you about three things every little boy and girl should know. OK, first: Never ride with a stranger. This is very important so I want you all to repeat this rule with me. You never know, a stranger might offer you candy, then take you and put you in a box full of snakes. Never ride with a stranger. Good.

Now the second thing: Always wear your seatbelt. This is very important so I want you all to say it together with me. If you are in a car accident you might go through the windshield and get run over by an ice cream truck. *(Encouraging children to say it.)* Always wear your seatbelt.

Now this is the last and most important thing to remember. You must listen closely because I'm going to have you repeat it. The governments of the world are involved in a multinational conspiracy with an alien race from the planet Zeon; the ultimate goal of this alliance being the total domination and conversion of every man, woman, and child on this planet into hosts for a future alien race that will use all mankind like cattle for food.

Sarah? What is a multinational conspiracy? Well that's when all the governments of the world get together to keep secrets from the people. The government doesn't want you to know that you are going to be fodder for an alien race. Remember how Miss Graham, your principal, told you that little Johnny White had to move away? What really happened is that the aliens took over Johnny's Mommy and Daddy; they in turn changed into alien monsters with huge teeth and giant claws. When little Johnny went to bed, they were hiding. The Mommy monster alien was under the bed and the Daddy monster was in the closet. Little Johnny didn't even know what hit him. The monsters came out and started to tear that little boy to shreds. He screamed and screamed ... After they were done, they made a milkshake with his brain.

Oh, don't cry. Mikey? You're going to tell on me? To who? Miss Graham? She's part of the conspiracy. She's an alien dressed up to look like a principal. Go ahead and tell her. She might suck your brain out your ear.

Christopher? I'm scaring you and you're going to tell your Mommy and Daddy? Well Christopher, what if they tie you down to the table and start to do experiments on you? What if they clip your pee-pee off and put it in a bun? What if they make you eat it like a hot dog?

Now come on children, let's try this together! Ready? The governments of the world are involved in a multinational conspiracy with an alien race from the planet Zeon; the ultimate goal of this alliance being the total domination and conversion of every man, woman, and child on this planet into hosts for a future alien race that will use all mankind like cattle for food.

OK, now tomorrow we are going to talk about the letter *A,* how to wash your hands correctly, and how to make a tinfoil hat that that will keep the alien species from reading your mind. Have a good afternoon, children, and don't forget what we talked about today!

The Tempest

William Shakespeare

> **Play**
> **Seriocomic**
> **M/F**
> **20s-30s**
> **Classic**

> *Ariel has just returned from causing a tempest at sea as ordered by Prospero, and brags to Prospero of the completed task.*

All hail great master! grave sir, hail! I come
To answer thy best pleasure; be't to fly,
To swim, to dive into the fire, to ride
On the curl'd clouds, to thy strong bidding task
Ariel and all his quality.

Perform'd to point the tempest thy bade me.
I boarded the king's ship; now on the beak,
Now in the waist, the deck, in every cabin,
I flam'd amazement: sometime I'd divide,
And burn in many places; on the topmast,
The yards and boresprit, would I flame distinctly,
Then meet, and join. Jove's lightnings, the precursors
O' th' dreadful thunder-claps, more momentary
And sight-outrunning were not: the fire and cracks
Of sulphurous roaring the most mighty Neptune
Seem to besiege, and make his bold waves tremble,
Yea, his dead trident shake!!

Not a soul but felt a fever of the mad, and play'd
Some tricks of desperation. All but mariners
Plung'd in the foaming brine, and quit the vessel,
Then all afire with me: the King's son, Ferdinand,
With hair-upstaring, — then like reeds, not hair —
Was the first man that leap'd, cried, "Hell is empty,
And all the devils are here!!"

Till We Meet Again

Colin and Mary Crowther

Play
M/F
Teens
Comic
Contemporary

The trials and tribulations of puberty.

Oh no! It's happening again. I'm sweating. Do you know the first thing I'll do? When I know everything? I'll invent a cure for puberty. No more flushes and blushes and gallons of sweat and stink and ... things. I'll be able to say, "You are my body and you are under my control. You are my brain and you will think what I tell you, when I tell you, and you will never embarrass me on public transport again!" And when someone says — oh, something clever and cutting — I'll be able to come back with just the right words. Kapow! And I'll be smooth and cool and ... and not sweaty and sticky and covered in zits! Do you know my greatest fear? That one day someone will squeeze me — and I'm so oily and sweaty and sticky — I'll just go pfit and pop out of my shirt — my whole body will pop out of my clothes and up in the air and I'll be up there in full view of everyone — stark bullock naked — and they'll all laugh! Because they don't understand. No one understands ... what it's like ... to be me!

Monologues by Gender and Age

Female

Male

Classic and Contemporary Monologues by Gender

Female

Male

CLASSIC

CONTEMPORARY

Male/Female

Monologues by Voice

Permission Acknowledgments

ABSENCE OF GRAY MATTER. Copyright © 2001 by Josh Weckesser. Reprinted by permission of the author.

ACME TEMPORARY SERVICES. Copyright © 1998 by Linda Eisenstein. Reprinted by permission of the author.

ACTOR! Copyright © 2003 by Frederick Stroppel. Reprinted by permission of the author. The entire text has been published in an acting edition by Samuel French, Inc., 45 W. 25th St., New York, NY 10010, which also handles performance rights.

AFTERNOON LOVERS. Copyright © 2004 by Vanda Wark. Reprinted by permission of the author.

ALIEN IDIOTS. Copyright © 2000 by Richard Krzemien. Reprinted by permission of the author.

THE ALTRUISTS Copyright © 2001 by Nicky Silver. Reprinted by permission of William Morris Agency, Inc., on behalf of the author. The entire text has been published by Dramatists Play Service, 440 Park Ave S., New York, NY 10016, which also handles performance rights.

AMERICA (IT'S GOTTA BE THE CHEESE). Copyright © 2000 by Manic D Press. Reprinted by permission of Manic D. Press. Published in *Poetry Slam: The Competitive Art of Performance Poetry.*

ANGELS IN AMERICA: MILLENNIUM APPROACHES. Copyright © 1993 by Tony Kushner. Reprinted by permission of Theatre Communications Group, which has published the entire text in a trade edition. Performance rights are handled by Broadway Play Publishing, 56 E. 81st St., New York, NY 10028.

ANTON IN SHOW BUSINESS. Copyright © 2000 by Alexander Speer, Trustee. CAUTION: Professionals and amateurs are hereby warned that ANTON IN SHOW BUSINESS is subject to royalty. It is fully protected under the copyright laws of the United States of America, the British Commonwealth, including Canada, and all other countries of the Copyright Union. All rights, including professional, amateur, motion pictures, recitation, lecturing, public reading, radio broadcasting, television, and the rights of translation into foreign languages are strictly reserved. In its present form, the play is dedicated to the reading public only. No part of this work may be reproduced, stored in a retrieval system or transmitted in any form, by any means, now known or yet to be invented, including mechanical, electronic, photocopying, recording, videotaping or otherwise, without the prior written permission of the publisher. Particular emphasis is laid on the question of amateur or professional readings and productions, permission for which must be secured in writing from Samuel French, Inc., 45 W. 25th St., New York, NY 10010, which has published the entire text in an acting edition.

THE ARKANSAS TORNADO. Copyright © 2001 by Kathleen A. Rogers. Reprinted by permission of the author.